THE FULL-DAY KINDERGARTEN

Planning and Practicing a Dynamic Themes Curriculum

SECOND EDITION

Doris Pronin Fromberg

Teachers College, Columbia University
New York and London

This book is dedicated to
Melvin S. Fromberg

Published by Teachers College Press, 1234 Amsterdam Avenue, New York, NY 10027

Library of Congress Cataloging-in-Publication Data

Fromberg, Doris Pronin, 1937–
    The full-day kindergarten: planning and practicing a dynamic
themes curriculum / Dorris Pronin Fromberg. — 2nd ed.
      p.   cm. — (Early childhood education series)
    Includes bibliographies and index.
      ISBN 0-8077-3374-1. — ISBN 0-8077-3373-3(pbk.)
      1. Kindergarten. 2. School day—United States. 3. Kindergarten—
United States—Curricula. 4. Full-day kindergarten—United States.
I. Title. II. Series.
LB1169.F76 1994
372.21'8–dc20

                                   94-26573

ISBN 0-8077-3373-3 (paper)
ISBN 0-8077-3374-1 (cloth)
Printed on acid-free paper
Manufactured in the United States of America
01 00 99 98 97 96 95   8 7 6 5 4 3 2 1

Using the Supportive Play Model:
Individualized Intervention in Early
Childhood Practice
  MARGARET K. SHERIDAN,
  GILBERT M. FOLEY, & SARA H. RADLINSKI

The Full-Day Kindergarten:
A Dynamic Themes Curriculum, 2nd Ed.
  DORIS PRONIN FROMBERG

Experimenting with the World: John Dewey
and the Early Childhood Classroom
  HARRIET CUFFARO

New Perspectives in Early Childhood
Teacher Education: Bringing Practitioners
into the Debate
  STACIE G. GOFFIN & DAVID E. DAY, Eds.

Assessment Methods for Infants and
Toddlers: Transdisciplinary Team
Approaches
  DORIS BERGEN

The Emotional Development of Young
Children: Building an Emotion-Centered
Curriculum
  MARION C. HYSON

Young Children Continue to Reinvent
Arithmetic—3rd Grade: Implications of
Piaget's Theory
  CONSTANCE KAMII with
  SALLY JONES LIVINGSTON

Moral Classrooms, Moral Children:
Creating a Constructivist Atmosphere in
Early Education
  RHETA DeVRIES & BETTY ZAN

Leadership in Early Childhood:
The Pathway to Professionalism
  JILLIAN RODD

Understanding Assessment and Evaluation
in Early Childhood Education
  DOMINIC F. GULLO

Diversity and Developmentally
Appropriate Practices:
Challenges for Early Childhood Education
  BRUCE L. MALLORY &
  REBECCA S. NEW, Eds.

Changing Teaching, Changing Schools:
Bringing Early Childhood Practice
into Public Education—
Case Studies from the Kindergarten
  FRANCES O'CONNELL RUST

Physical Knowledge in Preschool
Education: Implications of Piaget's Theory
  CONSTANCE KAMII & RHETA DeVRIES

Caring for Other People's Children:
A Complete Guide to Family Day Care
  FRANCES KEMPER ALSTON

Family Day Care: Current Research for
Informed Public Policy
  DONALD L. PETERS &
  ALAN R. PENCE, Eds.

The Early Childhood Curriculum:
A Review of Current Research, 2nd Ed.
  CAROL SEEFELDT, Ed.

Reconceptualizing the Early Childhood
Curriculum: Beginning the Dialogue
  SHIRLEY A. KESSLER &
  BETH BLUE SWADENER, Eds.

Ways of Assessing Children and
Curriculum: Stories of Early Childhood
Practice
  CELIA GENISHI, Ed.

The Play's the Thing:
Teachers' Roles in Children's Play
  ELIZABETH JONES &
  GRETCHEN REYNOLDS

Scenes from Day Care: How Teachers
Teach and What Children Learn
  ELIZABETH BALLIETT PLATT

Raised in East Urban:
Child Care Changes in a
Working Class Community
  CAROLINE ZINSSER

United We Stand:
Collaboration for Child Care
and Early Education Services
  SHARON L. KAGAN   *(Continued)*

Contents

Preface

The half-day kindergarten was first introduced into American education in the latter part of the nineteenth century, but for many years its incorporation into the public school curriculum varied widely from locality to locality. Acceptance of public kindergarten gradually increased, and during the last 15 years in particular, such programs have been added in many regions where none had previously existed. More recently, there has also been an increase in public full-day kindergartens and extended-day variations.

The full-day kindergarten has continued to expand in the United States despite the fact that it has been a subject of controversy. It is a controversial subject because both supporters and opponents raise questions about where kindergarten children should spend their time, with whom, doing what, and how they should be doing what they do.

The issue for our discussion is not whether there should be a half-day or a full-day or an extended-day kindergarten. It is a bit late for that consideration. The public school extended day is a reality already chosen in many communities across the United States, to say nothing of what is offered in private education or in the schools of other nations.

This book deals with the reality of what already exists: Given that there is an extended kindergarten day, then what can teachers do with the additional time, and how can they work in order to promote worthwhile, humane learning experiences? Answers to these questions will evolve as we consider how teachers interact with children who come to school with a diverse range of backgrounds, abilities, and needs. A major purpose of this book is to demonstrate how different children doing different things at different times can have equivalent experiences. This presupposes that equivalent experiences often are tacit, unpredictable, and within children's range of ability.

A basic question in need of answering is how to retain the right of kindergarten children to have a distinctly human, caring, and satisfying learning experience in school while keeping open the possibility for great expectations in their lives. This question is central to our thinking about

the full-day kindergarten because there are political pressures on kindergarten teachers to use the additional time to create a workbook-oriented
program devoted mainly to teaching the three R's as separate subjects and
in a linear way. In my opinion, such a program is a sanctioned form of
child abuse.

The particular position of this book may be evident in the questions
that follow. You will come away from reading this book with specific ways
to answer the following questions:

- How can I set up, organize, and maintain a transactional, intellectual, and caring community?
- How can I plan an integrated, meaning-centered curriculum with
children from the perspective of perceptual models/dynamic
themes?
- How can I build on children's strengths and capacity for joy in learning?
- How can I encourage, keep open, and extend young children's
imaginative and creative ways of thinking?
- How can I help to strengthen children's self-concepts?
- How can I help children become focused, organized, independent,
and responsible learners?
- How can I help children to learn skills that relate to their own con-
crete and imaginative construction of conceptual knowledge in a
playful environment?
- How can I adapt activities in ways that can help children with dif-
fering backgrounds to learn successfully?
- How can I develop alternative ways to influence children's learn-
ing?
- How can I develop curriculum with children and adapt commer-
cial and generic materials?
- How can I interpret the kindergarten program to others?
- How can I involve parents?
- How can I continue my professional development?

A POINT OF VIEW ABOUT HUMAN EXPERIENCE

As implied by the preceding questions, this book presents a particular point
of view about human experience in the full-day kindergarten. I believe
that the most important issues in teaching concern power and meanings.
We need to build on the strengths that children bring to school, value
these understandings and accomplishments, and provide a stable and safe
setting in which they can express, represent, and extend their power at their

own paces. Meaning, within this context of collaboration, connotes a blending of affect and sociocognition that integrates aesthetic experience and play.

Neither the three R's alone nor socialization in a random environment constitutes an adequate human experience. Offering only the three R's devalues and undermines the children's capacity and limits the amount of time for connection-making and problem-setting and -solving activity. The unstructured socialization position denies children the joys inherent in challenge. Both the three R's and the random socialization positions put a ceiling on children's intellectual achievements. Both positions offer a facade of trivial information and isolated skills more related to trite, static, Victorian-inspired classificatory boxes than to a dynamic, collaborative, networked twenty-first century.

Children need both skills and content. Indeed, skills should support content. The three R's and other skills exist to serve and represent meanings, ideas, connection-making, and cooperative socialization; they are not ends in themselves. Thus the full-day kindergarten curriculum design in this book consists of four interconnected features:

- *Child development.* The varied current states of your children and their personal cultures, rather than a generalized stage, suggest the ways in which you can help children learn best.
- *Extradisciplinary experience.* Meanings evolve over time as you and your children interact and make connections, beyond disciplines, through experiencing perceptual models/dynamic themes.
- *Interdisciplinary conceptions.* Planning content takes into account the knowledge bases and multiple, dynamic ways of working in disciplines and includes alternative imagery systems.
- *Skills.* Concerns about meaningful ideas, feelings, and attitudes are the focus and motives for using skills.

The basic business of the full-day kindergarten is to provide involving and meaningful experiences that generate questions. In turn, such experiences help you and your children make connections and feel both satisfied and thirsting for more.

A POINT OF VIEW ABOUT TEACHING YOUNG CHILDREN

I offer all of us a challenge. It is not easy, with our backgrounds in an outcome-based, test-centered, competitive society, to set forth in predictably unpredictable directions. It is not easy, in this context, to trust that children will grow and expand their knowledge bases even if you view them as having the power to see patterns, make connections between events, and care about one another. To trust children's intellectual commitments means leaving behind a day filled with fixed activities that everybody must do. It leaves behind the notion that there are truths out there to be harvested from set lessons or particular books for everybody.

Both you and your children have active roles in this interaction; therefore, you cannot learn to teach only by reading a book. A book can offer some ways of looking at the work, some ways of approaching transactions with children, and some ideas about materials and activities that you can share with children. A book also can provide notions about how children develop, learn, and feel; how they might be likely to behave in certain situations; and alternate ways in which you can plan your work. This book will provide some such direct information, selectively filtered through my own tinted lenses.

To convey some sense of the interactive, negotiated nature of the process and the cooperative feeling of learning, however, there will be some sections that not only describe but ask that you, as a teacher, imagine yourself in different classroom settings and moments. Dialogue, examples, simulated visits, and occasional stream-of-consciousness techniques will be used to approach these experiences.

Concerns such as play, parent involvement, assessment, and professional development are integrated throughout the book. Chapters on social studies, science, mathematics, the arts, and literacy are present as such in order to offer springboards to children's integrative imagery systems within the current context of school organizations.

Beyond reading this book and others, you will need to try out these ideas, working with children in a setting in which you can have feedback about what you are doing. The feedback, through coaching by an experienced colleague or supervisor, using audiotapes or videotapes and verbatim written records, is essential. Even if you have taught older children, learning to "read" the behavior of kindergarten children requires mastery of a new behavioral language or dialect.

In order to develop your own teaching style in relationship with young children, you will need to develop the ability to select and focus teaching strategies and alternatives and to use them when you want and in ways that you intend. This book is only one step in this dynamic process. In a sense, you will finish writing it in your work with children.

I thank the staff of Teachers College Press for their support and enthusiasm. In particular, Director Carole Saltz has been a dynamic and helpful force. Lois Patton, formerly Executive Editor, persevered in stimulating the start of this project. Acquisitions Editor Susan Liddicoat has served as a wonderful conductor, editor, and guide. Professor Leslie R. Williams of Teachers College made valuable and generous suggestions.

PART I

The Interactive Context of the Full-Day Kindergarten

1

A Full Kindergarten
Day Is . . .

Let us begin with two looks at the 5-year-old, first from the child's own perspective and then from the kindergarten teacher's. We will then consider what learning in a full-day kindergarten looks and feels like, particularly as teacher and child interact. These relative views will be elaborated on throughout the book, for they provide the best means of imparting a deeper understanding of what a full-day experience in kindergarten can be.

THE 5-YEAR-OLD

The Child's View

Imagine yourself to be a 5-year-old, beginning kindergarten. You were born 63 months ago and have spent your time at home or in preschool and child care with some of the following people: your mother, father, older sister, babysitters, grandparents, teachers. You find toys and pictures in the supermarket. You have waited a very long time as your mother shopped or held her place on line in a city office.

You try to capture birds with your jacket and bring a bowl of milk to the stray cat near your house. You were hit by a swing in the park, and your teenage babysitter tried to stop you from telling your mother this when she was resting after work. New flowers in spring thrill you. Puddles are an invitation for splashing through.

You watch the older children trying to burn ants off a worm's back. You recall that, "One time my father drank so much and he was drunk and he fell asleep in the living room with all his clothes on" (Anonymous, 1978, p. 16). You believe that,

> It's a long time before you die. Everything has to die. People go around and dig and find skulls, and they say, This is the skull of a man. We saw skulls at the museum. There was a huge dinosaur skull. . . . You turn into dust when you die. (Nalim, 1978, p. 20).

When thunder or gunshots waken you at night, you feel your heart beat faster as you race to your parents' bed. Getting hugs from them is one good thing about thunder and gunshots. Jerry told you that he heard gunshots on Wednesday and his brother told him to duck.

You go to your neighbor's apartment to see if he can play ball with you, but he tells you he cannot come over because he cannot bear to part with his best friend, who is visiting. You ask your grandmother to play with you because you feel so lonely and there's nothing to do. It feels good when she tells you what a great checkers player you have become.

You feel puzzled to see your older sister's face contort with disgust when she takes the spoon you have handled. More often, she wants to take what you have long before you want to give it to her.

You will miss your friend Stanley if his family moves away. He taught you to count to 100 and shared your horror when the baby doll's paint came off in the water. You play card games together, and he taught you how to stack the deck in his favor. You talk about favorite television shows together and race to your grandmother's side because the commercial tells you to tell your mother to go right out and buy it. You can sing every commercial you hear and ride a two-wheeler. You ask your mother why your living room floor is covered with linoleum but Eileen's has a soft carpet.

You feel guilty when you eat more candy than your mother said you could have. You don't understand why your mother's not wanting to send the dentist on vacation is a reason not to eat candy. You watch the older children sneaking cigarettes in the park while their heavy schoolbooks sit on the ground. You cannot understand why they tell you not to pick up the shiny crack vials in the schoolyard.

You have been delighted by Curious George, the peddler and the monkeys, and other storybook characters; you can look repeatedly at the pictures in the monster book, *Cars*, and *The Trek*.[1] Everybody wonders why you keep collecting round red pebbles and yogurt tops. You have piles of red, green, blue, brown, and orange tops in a shoe box. The blueberry and vanilla covers are both blue, but the blueberry has more letters on it. Everybody says that you will learn to read when you go to the big school. Then you will be able to tell the difference between the cherry, the plain, and the strawberry tops, all of which are red. You wonder if your teacher will be a smiling person.

The Teacher's View

As a teacher, you have considered that each child has had many experiences, some different from others, and that each child needs a different amount of time to satisfy his or her need for repetition in order to gain mastery—whether the task is tying shoe laces, riding a bicycle, pouring liquids, writing a name, putting together a puzzle, or learning to care about friends. You have seen young children who readily repeated skills again and again and felt satisfied in doing so. They have devoted their entire attention to solving a problem. As you have walked with young children, you have seen, heard, and appreciated what might otherwise have been a lost world of novelties. You have caught a glimpse of the connections they made that sometimes felt poetic.

Your work has made you aware that young children learn most effectively when they can have physical contact with contrasted concrete materials and contrasted imagery. The kindergarten children's direct involvement is the basis for their motivation. When you have been able to provide such direct involvement, you have been able to help them build on the strengths of their experiences. The children's ways of working have been an effective vehicle for carrying out the school's intellectual and social purposes.

YOUNG CHILDREN'S WAYS of learning and the kindergarten teacher's ways of teaching are largely social, affective, aesthetic, and physical. Yet schools are the single institution charged with the major task of intellectual development. For full-day kindergarten education, the issue is not either intellect or socialization. The issue is helping young children achieve intellectual and personal success by using experiential means, through concrete and imaginative experiences that are largely physical, aesthetic, affective, and social. The bulk of this book is devoted to elaborating and representing this issue through varied ways of working with children during an extended school day.

The most caring teacher can hurt children unless she or he is skilled in translating the human fund of knowledge into activities in which children can feel competent (Dewey, 1933). Wedding what is taught with how it is taught is more important than either content or method alone. The value of kindergarten education derives much more from its ability to help the child build imagery contrasts than from isolated instances of information processing, skills building, memory cramming, or verbalization. After all is said and done, little remains of the bits of information. What remain forever are the residual feelings and attitudes that ultimately dictate how individual human beings will behave and interpret experience in life. This view concurs with Whitehead's (1929) belief that wisdom lies in the use of knowledge. Use implies action: If you think back to the most satisfying residues of your own early education, you are likely to find active participation—sometimes painful, sometimes pleasurable, sometimes actively stimulating—serving as a window back in time. The full-day kindergarten within this framework is a time that is valuable in itself, rather than only as a preparation for next year.

As teachers, we know that children enter school with many rich experiences, even if they are disturbing rather than harmonious ones. We need to harness these experiences and build upon them, because they are sources of strength for the children and the basis for building a sense of personal, intellectual competence.

SIMULATED VISIT TO A FULL-DAY KINDERGARTEN CLASSROOM

As we move together through an imaginary visit, we can see how a particular organization works. The following section attempts to share an image of what learning in a full-day kindergarten looks and feels like.

Arrangement of Space and Materials

Space is subdivided by furnishings into a series of areas similar to booths at a fair rather than desks lined up auditorium-style. Activities needing water are close to the sink. Children mostly work in small groups as the teacher circulates and visits each area in turn. A closer look at each area follows.

Sociodramatic Area. Kneeling side by side, two children take wooden blocks off the shelves in the sociodramatic area. This area also contains a hospital section and a store-front/puppet stage made of large hollow blocks. Boxes, shelves, and pegboard enclose an area containing a woodworking bench, carpentry tools, and pine lumber in a basket.

Mathematics Area. Four children take turns tossing a die onto a mat as they play a game with the Dienes multibase arithmetic blocks in base 3. The area, enclosed on three sides by shelves, houses mathematics-related materials. There is a balance scale with labeled boxes of beads, pine cones, sand, buttons, cotton balls, beans, discs, and other items. There are Cuisenaire rods, rulers, card games, and board games, some of which appear to be teacher-made. Transparent measuring cups of varying shapes sit in a tub.

Science Area. At a table that holds a pan of water, two children sort materials into two piles on the basis of whether they do or do not absorb water. Nearby, two children are changing the newspaper in a guinea pig's cage. Atop low shelves, tadpoles at various stages of development swim in an aquarium, while a salamander adds color to the terrarium.

Arts Area. Near the sink and easel, two children are weaving jersey loops at a table, while still another child writes her name with a pencil at the top of a crayon drawing. She uses a teacher-made namecard attached to her own photograph as a model. (The teacher explains later that almost all the children can write their names independently but that this child is developmentally delayed. The photograph helps the child find her own name or that of others in the class independently when she wants to write.)

Reading Area. At the opposite side of the room from the sink, arts area, and science area, there is a corner created by bookshelves and a storage cabinet. Book jackets hang on a bulletin board. A box of spaghetti and the book jacket for the book *Strega Nona* (de Paola, 1975) are hung from two lengths of blue yarn attached to the ceiling. One child is seated on a carpet square, one is seated at a small round table, and two are sitting together in a soft, slightly battered armchair. All are reading different books, while two also wear earphones. There are two mats on the floor upon which two children lie with books. One of the reclining children holds a stuffed toy. There is also a large booth-like box in which the top of a curly-haired head is visible.

Writing and Individual Manipulation Area. Children are seated at several tables that face a wall and two room dividers. Four children are writing in personal books that they have illustrated. One child is working on a puzzle, another on a card-matching game. Two children are sitting on a "gossip" chair, reading their stories to each other. There is a child-size canvas chair labeled "Author's Chair."

Teacher's Instructional Area. A child who had made his own picture book with felt-tipped colored pens dictates narrative as the teacher records his comments beside each picture. They are seated at a curved table in the corner, with the teacher's chair positioned so that she can observe the entire classroom.

The Teacher's Activities

When the picture book maker returns to the writing area, the teacher helps another child begin a two-sided sewing card in the arts area. She also obtains additional gummed paper for a collage maker, adjusts wire for a hanging mobile construction, and hangs a child's finished 12-by-18-inch painting on a bulletin board that contains an unoccupied white oaktag frame.

When she sees that everybody seems reasonably occupied and can be expected to continue their activities for a while, she sits in the mathematics area with four children, the balance scale, some standard weights, and a blindfold. The weights, while all the same size, are marked differently according to their densities. The teacher explains that she is isolating the weight from its appearance and helping the children develop seriation skills, ordering first two, then three, then five weights.

She further explains to the visitor that she plans parallel activities with other materials. These children have had prior experiences with sorting, by touch, the lengths of wooden Cuisenaire rods placed in bags. They have also used seriation pictures (Lavatelli, 1970). These pictures are on ten identical cards, with size as the only variable. The children work toward matching two series of ten pictures, one of a child wearing rain clothing and one of an umbrella, using one-to-one correspondence.

However, the teacher continues to note that the published materials are teaching conveniences. The children have many seriation experiences in their everyday lives, such as comparing sizes of berries, toys, sticks, houses, body parts, and people. This teacher has also constructed a series of cylinders using discarded paper rolls, plastic containers, lids, and buttons. She reflects that the longer day makes it possible for her to provide, in varied forms, several experiences with a concept and to plan alternatives for those children who need them.

Figure 1.1 summarizes the way in which one teacher alternated direct teaching and circulating around the room. While she circulated, she engaged in a variety of organizational and teaching functions, which are listed within each time period.

While each teacher plans ahead and prepares materials, some of the most valuable learning takes place in a teacher's spontaneous awareness of a "teachable" moment. Replanning on the spot, doing "fleeting" teaching, and matching the child's need with an appropriate activity are some of the skills that a kindergarten teacher uses. In this respect, the teacher in the full-day program has more opportunity for learning a great deal by being a sensitive observer, listener, recorder, and assessor of children's readiness for a range of experiences.

Observing the Child's Day

So far, our visit has looked at the teacher's flow of activity, but now let us replay the day by following a few children through their experience of it. As teachers, we need to pay attention to the way children have perceived their day. In this way we have a better chance of learning what activities children are asking for with their behavior as well as their overt requests.

FIGURE 1.1: Kindergarten Teacher's Flow Map

Activity	Circulation
8:50 Children arrive together Greeting (store personal effects, sit on floor facing chart paper)	8:52 Store materials Assist with materials Appreciate Question Answer questions
9:00 Whole-group planning Meeting area (record activities for day and who begins where)	9:15 Assist with materials Encourage Observe Answer questions
9:27 Science area (water activity)	9:40 Redirect social behavior Assist with materials Appreciate Question Fleeting teaching
9:45 Teacher's instructional area (writing group)	10:05 Record keeping Assessment Fleeting teaching Display child's work Plan ahead Encourage Assist at snack table
10:14 Mathematics area (balance scale: seriation)	10:30 Plan ahead Mediate; highlight a contrast Redirect social behavior Encourage questions Appreciate Do record keeping

10:32
Adds items for seriation
	10:35
	Close-down, 5 minutes' notice, be-
	  ginning with sociodramatic and
	  arts areas
	Appreciate
	Answer questions

	10:40 Redirect children to meeting area; cleanup details
10:50 Whole-group sharing	10:50 Do record keeping

(continued)

FIGURE 1.1 *Continued*

Activity	Circulation
11:05 Leave for gym class (indoors or outdoors, weather permitting)	
11:40 Whole-group story; meeting area (teacher reads story)	
12:00 Lunch in school lunchroom, then to playground	12:50 Assist with books for silent independent reading
12:52 Teacher's instructional area (reading group instruction)	(N.B.: Science and art areas are closed) 1:10 Redirect reading group Do record keeping Close-down notice for forming of puppetry group members
1:12 Sociodramatic area (puppetry group and tape recorder; play development and values discussion)	1:24 Assess Encourage Appreciate
1:28 Teacher's instructional area (reading group skill instruction)	1:42 Redirect reading group Observe Fleeting teaching Extended sociodramatic area, questioning, and encouraging
1:52 Teacher's instructional area (individual reading with three children in turn, alternating circulation)	1:56 Observe Replan Answer questions Do record keeping
1:58 Second child	2:05 Appreciate Do record keeping
2:10 Third child	2:15 Close-down, 5 minutes' notice Appreciate
2:20 Whole-group activity; meeting area (teacher reads poem) Discuss trip to seashore List on chart Sing sea songs (teacher plays guitar) 2:50 End of day	

TERRY, A HESITANT CHILD

Terry entered the classroom with a stone-like expression, put a small bag in the shopping bag hung from a name-bearing hook, and brushed past several children until he sat down near the chart paper. When the teacher made eye contact and smiled, Terry nodded grimly in return.

During the group planning, Terry stared at the chart paper, picked at a fingernail, and moved slightly away from another child. When it was time for four children to select a place in the sociodramatic area, the teacher invited Terry, who shrugged and nodded.

When everyone had dispersed, one group at a time, to their respective areas, Terry remained close to the teacher until she walked with him to the sociodramatic area on her way to the science area. As he began to remove blocks, the teacher smiled encouragingly and moved on. When another child's building grew closer, they merged their construction. The other child chatted amiably, and Terry offered brief suggestions. Half an hour later, they were cheerfully pouring and drinking juice at the snack table near the sink.

Terry's building partner went to paint at the only open easel, and Terry went to the reading corner the long way around, past the games and media area, the teacher's instructional area, and the science and mathematics areas. As he circulated, he would stop to watch what was happening, listen to a conversation, and pick up and examine various objects along the way.

Figure 1.2 shows Terry's movements for the entire day. As we analyze what he did, several patterns are present:

- Terry alternately engaged in an activity and then circulated, observed others, and touched materials.
- When not engaged in a clearly social activity, he appeared to seek time alone, for example, on a mat or a designated private space, distancing himself from close contact with others.
- Terry made eye contact with the teacher, noting and sometimes returning her smiles.
- He seemed to alternate active and sedentary activities independently.

It is important to notice that the flexible structure of this setting made it possible for Terry to choose many activities independently. In turn, the teacher could see when Terry needed the social potential of the sociodramatic area and adapted her plans by suggesting and encouraging his activity. It was comfortable for him to receive her suggestion because there were many other times when he could make independent choices.

FIGURE 1.2: Terry's Flow Map

Terry's Activity	Teacher Contact
8:50	
Arrives—stores personal effects; sits on floor facing chart paper for planning session	Makes eye contact Smile
9:00	
Listens	Makes eye contact Suggests activity Walks alongside Terry
9:20	
Sociodramatic area—blocks	Observes Smiles encouragingly
9:25	
Parallel play with other child	
9:30	
Builds with other child	Stops at blocks, appreciates, questions
9:55	
Snack table—brings snack from closet; shares raisins with other child; conversation with other child	
10:05	
Tours the room—observes others; examines and handles materials	Passes, smiles, and says, "Think about what you might do next."
10:08	
Reading area—lies on mat with a book	
10:20	
To toilet then returns to mat	
10:30	
Finishes second book and brings a puzzle to the mat	Stops to look at Terry's book; discusses briefly
10:50	
Whole-group sharing Chatting alongside block building companion as group gathers	Asks Terry and other block builder to talk about their structure; writes out large label for various parts: Terry places labels on parts
11:05	
Gym class—passes ball over head; Terry blushes as he takes lead position Laughing as participates in vigorously shaking parachute with entire group Jogs around outside of gym	Gym teacher says, "OK, Terry!" Gym teacher makes eye contact

(continued)

FIGURE 1.2 *Continued*

Terry's Activity	Teacher Contact
11:40	
Drinks water at fountain	
Listens to story	Makes eye contact
Silent during discussion	
12:00	
Lunchroom—keeps distance from others at food line; eats quickly, then slowly, looking at children across the table	
12:25	
Playground—jogs; asks aide for a ball; bounces and plays catch with another child; after balls are collected, the children roll themselves along incline and giggle	Aide provides ball
12:52	
Teacher's instructional area, with five other children	Teacher models word game, plays with children, gives feedback as they play together
1:10	
Plays word card games twice with other children	Leaves group, with writing follow-up
1:20	
Copies words from cards into personal notebook, which remains in teacher's area	Appreciates
1:28	
To toilet	
Easel—paints two pictures; hangs them on rack to dry	Observes quietly
2:00	
Washes paint from hands with lots of suds	
	Unties smock in passing (2:05)
2:05	
Games area—observes children; when they finish a game and one leaves, the other invites Terry to play a board game with a die; they play, with comments	Stops, observes, appreciates (2:15)
2:20	
Whole-group meeting	Leads discussion
Terry offers addition to list; sings along with group, taking deep breaths	Appreciates and asks Terry to tell more about undertow
2:50	
Keeps distance as group gathers to leave room	Smiles and nods

When a teacher schedules and plans most of a child's time, there is less opportunity for that child to feel capable, independent, and responsible. When a teacher changes activities frequently in other, more rigid settings, children learn not to invest their energies in school activities because the activities change too soon. There is a sense that just as they begin to get involved in something, they are interrupted.

By contrast, in this setting Terry could invest attention because his teacher had allowed for long blocks of time. When some people say that young children have short attention spans, therefore, we need to ask ourselves, "To what?" Kindergarten children can spend as long as an hour doing those things to which they feel committed. The extended and full-day scheduling provides an opportunity for this kind of active scholarship.

Pat, an Impulsive, Sociable Child

The crash of a paint can, the clatter of a long-handled brush, and calls for help from Pat punctuated the arts area. At that very moment, the teacher was helping a group of seven children in the nearby science area to organize materials for experimenting with water absorption. She made sympathetic eye contact with Pat, whose pained expression was noticed by other children in the area. One child who was coming from the water fountain brought a large sponge and handed it to Pat, who recoiled for a moment after accepting it.

By the time the teacher had disengaged herself from the science-area activities, Pat had artfully smeared paint over several square feet of linoleum floor beyond the newspapers that were spread under the easel. The teacher helped her rinse the sponge and brought more newspapers to cover the wet area. Her sympathetic, matter-of-fact, helpful attitude helped Pat to relax about the mishap. Pat eventually carried fresh paints to the easel, and the teacher returned to the science area.

Pat painted one picture and hung the painting to dry. She gave her hands a fast splash of water and a casual wipe on her jeans on the way to the snack table. She stopped off to pick up an apple from the shopping bag labeled with her name and immediately entered into a brisk discussion of a television character's pratfalls with the other children at the snack table. Figure 1.3 traces Pat's movements in this classroom.

This flexible schedule gave Pat the opportunity to bounce along, expressing her enthusiastic, chatty exuberance in many ways. Even though Pat sought out contacts with others, this option was often available. Her needs to be social, to be noticed by the teacher, and to have ready access to personal routines were met in this setting. Even sociable Pat took some time alone with the earphones. The teacher, recognizing and accepting Pat's

FIGURE 1.3: Pat's Flow Map

Pat's Activity	*Teacher's Contact*
8:50	
Arrives—playfully tackles another child, approaches the teacher with some news about home, and stores personal effects; sits next to another child and converses; turns toward chart paper for planning session after teacher begins the meeting	Engages in conversation, smiles Makes eye contact
9:00	
Listens, comments to adjacent children occasionally, and raises hand for art area	Makes eye contact Responds to Pat's comments
9:30	
Art area—drops paint materials, cleans up, and paint	Makes eye contact Assists with materials
9:50	
Snack area	Assists with materials
10:14	
Mathematics area (balance scale: seriation)	Asks children to predict, estimate, explore, and compare
10:32	
Laying out materials with partner and outlining on chart in sequence	Asks children to predict, estimate, explore, and compare
10:50	
Ambles to whole-group sharing with math partner and chart, partially completed	Asks Pat and partner to show group their chart and explain their next steps
11:05	
To toilet, then joins the last of the children on their way to gym	
Gym class—jogs around gym and joins the end of the ball-passing group, chatting to child in front; races to take a place next to math partner for the parachute, laughs hard, occasionally dropping an edge	Gym teacher redirects Pat
11:40	
Slides into space in front of teacher and tells her about the parachute	Teacher smiles, listens, questions, and comments appreciatively
Listens intently to story; comments during discussion	
12:00	
Lunchroom—chatting and jostling with other children; talks through the meal, sucking noisily at the straw in the milk container	

(continued)

FIGURE 1.3 *Continued*

Pat's Activity	*Teacher's Contact*
12:18 Playground—climbs on apparatus with several others, playing at space travel	Aide cautions holding on with both hands
12:50 Reading area—shares armchair with math partner as they look together at book, commenting quietly and pointing	Teacher nods encouragement
1:10 To toilet then puts on earphones at media center	
1:25 Looks up as teacher places hand on shoulder; listens a while longer and joins reading group	Gives notice for instructional group by speaking to one child at a time, while circulating
1:28 Teacher's instructional area, with four other children	Teacher shows children a sorting activity of pictures and captions and gives the children feedback on their sorting and sequence
1:35 Children take turns, sharing and explaining their sequence to one another; they discuss the action	Redirects reading group
1:50 Pat takes the materials to the writing area and records the sentence sequence in a notebook	
2:10 Returns notebook to the teacher's instructional area	Nods and smiles
Takes a drink of water and heads directly to another child who is playing with Tangrams; comments and makes suggestions	
2:20 Joins whole-group activity, shoving in closer to the teacher; contributes to the discussion and sings along, swaying with the children on either side	Comments, appreciates, and asks questions
2:50 End of day	Smiles and holds eye contact

social activity, provided a balance in the reading group, where individual work, manipulation of materials, and sharing were involved.

Less reflective, more confident-looking than Terry, Pat went directly to activities such as the easel and "Tangrams" (Elementary Science Study, 1976b). For both children, the full-day kindergarten offered intellectual challenges as well as exploratory, joyful activities.

REFLECTIONS

As you reflect on the experiential, full-day kindergarten, imagine hearing what is happening. There is conversing: children with other children, and the teacher with individuals and small groups of children. There is a rather steady buzz of meaningful sound. Occasionally, you hear a dramatic exclamation or the clatter of fallen materials. As a visitor, you feel welcome but not necessarily noticed. Children seem to be involved in their activities and with one another as the teacher listens responsively to children's comments. The teacher seems to be enjoying the children and the active pace.

Sometimes you see individual children or the teacher observing, perhaps while walking around. Sometimes you see a child lie on a mat, savoring a few moments of solitude, or sit alone to write, draw, read, or manipulate objects. At other times, children seek out one another or the teacher.

Teacher and children learn from one another. They live in relation to one another, the behavior of each one influencing the actions of the others. This is a shift in emphasis from the traditional setting in which children are loyally polite to the teacher as an "authority," or where children are "honest" and become "problems." Maria Montessori's (1912/1965) pioneering conception can serve us well: The children should not learn for love of the teacher or for fear of the teacher, but for the love of the learning. When children have the opportunity to learn for love of the learning, they experience a sense of power, competence, and well-being. In Chapter 4, I will describe how teachers organize classrooms so that children can feel joyful in school and learn for the sake of the learning, in fulfillment of their natural sense of curiosity and their need to make connections. First we will take up in the next chapter some significant ways in which teachers work in order to create and support this kind of worthwhile learning experience for kindergarten children who are in school for the full day.

2

Professional Roles
for the Teacher

When children spend the full school day in kindergarten, it is inevitable that the longer day will influence more aspects of their lives than would a shorter day. The greater responsibility suggests that, as the teacher, you need to be that much more aware of the impact you have on children; therefore, it makes sense to consider ways in which successful teachers function as they interact more extensively with children. These functions include the following:

Mediating social behavior
Appreciating positive behavior
Questioning
Inquiring into learning conditions
Integrating learning experiences
Disseminating accomplishments to adults (parents, teachers, administrators)
Scheduling

Let us consider each of these functions as we look at some professional roles that you can play in the full-day kindergarten in order to create and maintain a worthwhile learning experience.

MEDIATING SOCIAL BEHAVIOR

On a hot August morning before beginning kindergarten, Lee asked his father for ice cream money. Lee's father rummaged through his pockets and extricated five dimes, which he held out to his son. "No, Daddy, I need two quarters. Mr. Mack always gives me ice cream when I give him two quarters." "But Lee," his father said, "five dimes is the same as two quarters. He'll give you the ice cream. You'll see." Lee protested, "No, he won't. It's not the same." After some repetition, Lee started crying pitifully as his father, who clearly had not read about the development of the conservation of quantity, fumed and shouted at his son to stop crying about such nonsense or he would get no ice cream at all. Overflowing with tears and integrity, Lee missed an ice cream treat for his "stubbornness." Some time later, however, pained doubt about his contention nagged near the surface of his awareness.

Perhaps each of us has been Lee or met Lee and can retrieve the emotional power by which we acquired concepts. Whether or not we can recall such an instance, Lee's experience is a reminder that when children have trouble understanding, they may become anxious, aggressive, impulsive, or depressed. While early childhood educators have often cared deeply about children's feelings, we also need to be able to recognize and appreciate the interaction between feelings and thought.

Lee was learning about his self-concept when his father called him "stubborn." This child was being honest about how he understood quantity, which was based on concrete appearances rather than on any abstract concept of an invariant amount. His father's response makes us wonder if Lee will risk honesty as readily in future.

Children need help with other concepts in school that may have an impact on social interaction and feelings. As a mediator, you can help children toward building inner controls and independence by *accepting their feelings and helping them to take responsibility* for their behavior and, to a degree, control it. To do this, you need to create and support varied cooperative learning activities. Some issues and examples of mediating functions follow.

Sharing, Cooperating, and Belonging

Some kindergarten children need help in classifying "mine," "not mine," and "ours." Children share more easily when they have a sense of possession. Generosity is also a cognitive attainment, even though it seems like a purely social accomplishment.

A personal storage space and a personal writing booklet are easily provided basics that will give children an understanding of "mine" and "not mine." (Note that personal storage need not be a desk or table assignment; see Chapter 4.) Along with this sense of belonging grows the sense of "ours," which successful teachers model by sharing with a helpful and cooperative attitude. Beyond "our" toys we have "our" jobs: "When we have materials to put away, you can finish with what you used and then help a friend." If everyone has a sense of everyone's being responsible for putting materials away, children can look forward together to engaging more quickly in a forthcoming special activity. It is also helpful to choose your language carefully. For example, saying "I want you to . . ." places children in the role of satisfying the teacher's purpose. It is useful instead to say, "Now is the time for . . ." or "How would you suggest doing that?" or "Which will you put away first?" Instead of saying what you *do not* want them to do or to stop what they are doing, ask them *to do* what it is time to do. (See Figure 2.1 for some other examples of positive language choices.)

Ask children to suggest how they can help one another when you need to be occupied. Some kindergarten teachers and children have an understanding that all children in a group of two or four must help each other before they can seek help outside their group, whether from other children or from their teacher.

There are times when you can provide substitute materials to children who are struggling over possession. At other times, you can help

---

FIGURE 2.1: Examples of Positive, Appreciative Instructions

Say it with words.	Please ask.
Use your indoor voice.	Share your idea with us.
Please speak one at a time.	What do you have to tell us?
What help do you need?	Take your time.
Can you hear her?	Please sit down.
Catch him when he's done.	Now is the time to . . .
You should be at the table.	We need to wait until lunch.
Take a little at a time.	It's safer to slide off.
Try that more quietly.	Please walk.
Let's do that together.	Thank you for helping.
It's your turn.	Please hang up the . . .
Look how carefully Tom's working.	Finish in the next ten minutes.
It's his turn to speak now, and then you can tell us your idea.	Use this now; you can have a turn with that in a few minutes.
How can you solve that in a friendly way?	I notice that you work better when you're quiet.
Let's listen to what Josh has to say.	It was hard to do but you did it.
It's great when you try out new ideas.	You really seem to understand that.
"Pretend that you are a [person] who knows how to share."[1]	What other suggestions does anybody have?

1. Paley, 1984, p. 87

children negotiate waiting and taking turns. "Now" and "later" are concepts that children need to classify through repeated experiences in which their expectations are fulfilled. Sign-up sheets sometimes help with a new or popular material.

Activities that require mutual effort are useful, such as murals planned and executed together. Since children can be expected to have an egocentric notion of which side is up, a tablecloth worked from all four sides with felt-tipped pens is an ideal mural project. It could be offered for use at a parents' meeting.

In order to avoid frustration and negativity when they need cooperation, teachers try to anticipate difficulties. For example, if a teacher is planning a group discussion for the class, a child who speaks little English will do better with an activity in which there are concrete referents. This might mean planning a separate activity for that child, such as a puzzle, a painting, or earphones and a tape recorder with a story told in his native language. Some teachers have had the foresight to arrange for bilingual colleagues and parents to tape-record a translation of several classroom books.

An activity needs to make sense to a child before she can be expected to do it. If she refuses to participate or withdraws, there may be a variety of reasons. The activity may seem too difficult or too easy, and she may have trouble putting this into words. She may simply test the limits of her power by saying no. This negativity may in part be the child's way of corroborating her understanding of the situation or of asking for more information. There are other times when a child is already engrossed in an activity and nothing else seems as relevant. The teacher might then say, "You seem to prefer to do this now" (respecting her feelings). "It is important for you to have a planning meeting with me sometime today. Do you prefer to meet before lunch or right after lunch?" (offering her responsibility and a degree of control).

The way in which the teacher makes a request or offers a choice will influence a child's perception and response. You might need to explain to children who are having their first school experience that even newcomers are included when the teacher asks "all" or "everybody" to do something.

Competition is inevitable, but it does not have to be encouraged. While we may not value or seek out competitive pastimes, there are times when some people come out ahead of others. The winners have been rewarded by winning; therefore, the best that teachers can do is acknowledge accomplishment in a low-key way rather than magnify it. Instead, we might consider magnifying the efforts of everybody who played fairly, showed commitment to the larger group effort, and enjoyed the camaraderie and the effort itself. When children are worried about their standing in relation to others, competitive feelings grow. Think about the contradiction of a teacher urging helpfulness but operating a public chart with stars or points. Research indicates, moreover, that extrinsic rewards discourage already self-directed children from later engaging in extrinsically rewarded activities (Donaldson, 1978; E. Miller, 1994).

A positive force for cooperative work is created when a group shares a problem together and builds group procedures. The teacher acts as an important model by accepting children's feelings and expecting responsible behavior where it is possible.

Aggression

There is hardly a situation where human beings gather in which aggression does not occur from time to time. Besides dealing with aggression that occurs at school, we must be prepared to help children who come to school already brutalized. Much aggressive behavior at school can be traced to these roots and will manifest itself in varied forms ranging from hurting others, destructiveness, verbal aggression, and other attention-begging behavior to apathy. Whatever the roots of the behavior, each teacher needs to cope each day with aggression.

Hurting Others. When children physically hurt other children, they need to be restrained. After the hurt child has been comforted, the teacher needs to talk to the aggressor and explore and model alternatives to violence. Teachers have used some of the following statements successfully in dealing with aggression:

> "We want to be kind to our friends in school" (while hugging crying child and inviting one or two nearby children to offer comfort).
> "Come with me. We need to talk alone. We'll come back to the others when you are ready."
> "When you learn to build with this, then you may have it."
> "That hurt him. Tell him with words if you don't like what he did."
> "If you want her attention, tell her with words."
> "You need some time out." (A place and brief procedure for time out should be discussed with all children ahead of time.)
> "Let's talk when you've calmed down."

While you might physically remove a kindergarten child who is out of control, this is only a temporary measure. Teachers who find themselves physically dragging away children who do not respond to words must acquire other, more appropriate techniques and means of prevention, since the goal is to help children take responsibility for and bear the consequences of their own behavior. Certainly any teacher who hits a child is a negative model for the other children and has abandoned a professional role. Helping children to build inner controls is an important educational purpose.

As a teacher, you can prevent a lot of aggression by setting up as few restrictions as possible. When children are constantly being prohibited from activities, they may ignore an essential prohibition because it is not noticeable among all the other restrictions. The following questions can serve as guidelines for an actively positive approach (see also Figure 2.1).

- How can you give children legitimate, varied choices?
- How can you provide enough time for children to pace themselves?
- How can you assure that children have enough notice before ending an activity?
- How often are you circulating, appreciating, and planning ahead?
- In what ways are you sharing your appreciation of children's efforts when they are working in a positive way?
- How often do you set up situations in which children can make friends through working on a common task?
- When do you welcome fun and giggles?

All children, and especially those who come to school feeling powerless, need to experience success in activities that they have chosen. They need different amounts of time to engage in similar activities. They need to feel accepted and appreciated for their efforts. Daily activities would include legitimate, supervised projects that help children feel powerful. Especially relevant are activities for which there are varied interpretations, including the use of malleable materials such as clay, water/sand play, and sociodramatic play. Additional activities could include using ropes and pulleys or a pendulum. Besides being legitimate ways to socialize, many of these activities possess aesthetic potential.

Destructiveness. When a child destroys equipment or another's work, it may be accidental, a result of curiosity, or because of impulsive handling. Teachers should look at the child's intent and act accordingly. It is best to assume positive motives for children and approach each situation with an open mind. Children also need sturdy materials, and furniture should be arranged safely. Perhaps classroom traffic needs to be rerouted by relocating a table or a shelf indoors or moving it outdoors. Still other equipment might be scheduled for use at another time.

Although positive motives predominate, there are a small number of children entering kindergarten who express their extreme need for attention in destructive ways. In one situation, for example, a homeless child sought attention by pinching other children and scattering objects. Her teacher planned to (1) anticipate her need for a positive focus during transition times and (2) assign another adult to offer attention when she *was* engaged in positive activities.

Verbal Aggression. When a child calls another an insulting name or uses toilet words or sex-related words, it is usually in an angry tone. Rather than force the issue of apology by putting empty words into the child's mouth, you might have a more lasting impact if you find out what the behavior means to her. She might be copying older children, trying out new words whose meanings are unclear. She might also be testing your limits or trying to get attention. If she used to hit others but now uses words, then this is progress, an interpretation that should be shared with her. It also might mean that she needs more stimulating activity. Whatever the motives, it is reasonable to let children know that "When you call a person by that name you hurt his feelings; friends try to be kind to each other." "It upsets some people to hear those words, and we do not like to hear those words used here." You may feel confident that you will need to repeat such caring phrases because children also will repeat uncaring phrases.

Many teachers treat toilet talk as a phase or an attention-getting mechanism. They have been most effective in reducing and eliminating its presence by ignoring it in group settings, a model that the other children have followed.

Attention-Begging Behaviors. When a child takes things from others or takes home school toys as a way of feeling potent, an appropriate response is to pay special attention to him when he is working well, in terms of who he is. Notice and appreciate his positive efforts. When you personally (rather than publicly) enjoy a child's activities or just enjoy his enjoyment, you send a message of acceptance and success. It might help to show sympathy toward his desire for an object that is not his and to accept his feelings, at the same time making it clear that his behavior is not acceptable.

May (1972) suggests that human beings show at least three types of responses when they feel threatened: "fight," "flight," and a "delayed response" (pp. 183–184). Fighting is dangerous. The flight reaction may or may not directly hurt anybody, but adults do panic when a child runs away or disappears. Unlike these impulsive actions, the "delayed response" is a more mature attempt to consider alternatives. Children who fight or flee are sending a clear message that they need more positive attention and stimulating activities from parents and teachers, in the form of frequent appreciation of their work and their very childhood itself. To this end, it is useful to plan a regularly scheduled individual time to meet with each child. The longer kindergarten day permits more frequent, regularly scheduled meetings. Even in a decentralized classroom, it is possible to miss regular contact with the quieter children unless you plan it.

Apathy Versus Positive Assertiveness. When legitimate forms of assertiveness are unavailable, human beings tend to turn aggression against themselves. One historian has documented the tendency among a suppressed group to teach their children to deny or control anger (Genovese, 1974). This denial has sometimes resulted in difficulties with real self-assertion, which can lead to apathy. Sometimes obstinacy, performing a task very slowly as if bored, or "forgetting" to do something are symptoms of such feelings. Apathy harbors the threat of leading to explosive violence.

Aggression has a positive side that we need to acknowledge. When you assert yourself, you risk action. For a child, assertiveness may involve testing limits. Aggression as well as apathy may be the only ways that a child can express her growing independence and communicate that legitimate self-assertion has been blocked through overly controlled situations.

Children need to develop independence through legitimate responsibilities. When children feel secure enough to take risks, teachers have succeeded in helping them to feel competent and challenged. When children are legitimately active, they do not have the time or need to be mischievous.

APPRECIATING POSITIVE BEHAVIOR

You can influence some of the cultural priorities you value, such as independence, cooperation, empathy, perseverance, and creativity, when you appreciate children's processes as well as their products. At the same time, it is essential to become aware of children's at-home cultural values. Rather than judge the actor, therefore, you will be in a better position to focus on the action in relation to the underlying purposes of the event. It is clear that children need to see models of enthusiasm, caring, cooperation, and curiosity if they are to develop into human beings who display these traits.

Plan activities in which children can learn to appreciate each other. For example, select one youngster at a time to sit on your lap as other members of the group take turns saying something nice about the target child (Donna Barnes, personal communication, 1978). During and just after cleanup time are good opportunities to highlight children's efforts and achievements. Plan activities in which children can see their own progress and the cooperative products of others. Examples include cumulative individual art or science products, cooperative class books, and a list of books read by all.

Teachers have successfully used these ways of working with kindergarten children who have varied learning needs. Their sense of challenge, which should include a perceivable chance for success, will motivate their attention to activities.

QUESTIONING

When one new kindergarten teacher asked how many children had had hot cereal for breakfast, three-quarters raised their hands. When she asked how many had had dry cereal for breakfast, three-quarters raised their hands. It dawned on her that children might respond to a question because they want to be right or agreeable, regardless of what might be accurate.

Types of Questions

She began to notice how the ways in which she phrased questions influenced the quality of children's thinking and responses. She noticed that children came up with different responses when she asked questions *conditionally* (e.g., "What might, could, or would you or somebody else do . . . ?") than when she phrased her questions more *emphatically* (e.g., "What is . . . ?"or "Who can . . . ?" or "Why do . . . ?").

Next she tape-recorded group discussions and individual conferences— and noticed how many yes-or-no questions she asked unintentionally. With practice, she built up a stock of alternative ways of phrasing questions. Instead of asking *yes-or-no* questions, such as "Did you ever get picked for something?" or "Did you ever feel sad because . . . ?" or "Was it . . . ?" or "Will you . . . ?" she began using *descriptive* questions, such as "What happened when you got picked . . . ?" "Tell us about a time when . . ." and "What might you want to do next time?" Instead of asking "Would you like to . . . ?" when she really needed them to say "Yes," she became more honest and said, "Please take this."

If children needed information in order to engage in a discussion, she would offer the information instead of asking for "correct" information. When she asked for information, such as what results children found in an activity, she continued accepting ideas after the "correct" contribution. She would ask children how they decided on that idea.

She realized that when the focus of activities and discussions called upon children's observations, attitudes, opinions, personal reactions, and evaluations, they had plenty to say because they were committed to the content. Children also had expansive comments about inter- and intra-personal experiences to which they felt committed. Instead of a cycle of teacher-child interaction, there was much more interaction among the children, who listened to each other and elaborated upon one other's statements.

Honest questions concerning children's experiences can help to expand their oral and written language as well as focus their reading comprehension and critical thinking. In order to extend their thinking possibilities, it is useful to *reduce* reliance on yes-or-no and informational questions whose answers the teacher already knows, focusing instead on questions that are descriptive, comparative, evaluative, predictive, and explanatory. Look at questions as opportunities for children to contribute, share, and find out what others are thinking and how they connect ideas, rather than as times for children to "answer" questions. The following are examples of such questions:

- What else might you add? change? What might you think/plan/wish [rather than "feel," which often leads to a one-word, static comment]? (*descriptive*)
- How is it like that? not like . . . ? (*comparative*)
- What do you prefer? What is more important to you? When might you not . . . ? (*evaluative*)
- What might happen if . . . ? How would things be different when . . . ? Suppose that . . . . Pretend . . . (*predictive*)
- What does it mean when . . . ? Why might . . . ? How did you do that? Why might he do that? (*explanatory*)

These examples illustrate that the act of questioning alone will not achieve the aims of a caring education, but that careful attention to the content of questions is important. From a moral standpoint, we need to ask "real" questions for which we need an answer because we do not already know it.

Discussion Techniques

Children often become enthusiastic during committed discussions. In order to provide opportunities for more children to be heard, you can use various group-discussion techniques. For example, you may need to refocus the group's attention on individual contributions as often as every second or third time they speak:

> Let's listen to Mary.
> Van, can you hear Jamie?
> I wonder what Phil is going to tell us.
> Let's see if Dan agrees with you.
> Imagine how far that game piece could move.
> Let's all listen/look to see what will happen when . . .
> What do you think about what Ali said?
> It's great to see how interested you are. Now try to remember what you want to say, and you'll have a turn to say it after Jerry finishes. Let's listen to Jerry finish his idea first.

You might find it effective to seat overly enthusiastic children next to you, where they can be reminded with a gentle hand motion to wait their turn. Occasionally you might summarize what the group has agreed upon, in order to bring together different viewpoints. This is different from repeating each statement that a child makes, which might encourage children to listen only to your repetition.

As pointed out in the previous section, the best questions to ask are those for which there may be more than one response. You can emphasize that different people may have different ways of thinking about an issue. Encourage children to reflect upon their responses before speaking: "First think about this question before you let us know what you think"; "Fold your idea into your hand/close your eyes/sit on your answer before we share." "Thinking first" also permits individual children to formulate their own responses before they are influenced by hearing somebody else's views. This is also a way of building some early self-awareness (metacognition).

Techniques for Aiding Comprehension and Critical Thinking

It can be exciting to share ideas during a discussion about hearing a story, seeing a film, taking a trip, or engaging in any stimulating activity. These kinds of discussions can be self-contained or lead to prewriting activities, experience charts, role playing, future planning, values discussions, or problem-setting and -solving sessions.

Preparation. Before the children participate in an activity, it makes sense to prepare by helping them to predict what might happen. Questions could include

- What do you suppose you/we might find? Why do you think so? Where might the people be coming from/going? Why would they need to . . . ?
- What are some other things that we might find?

Finally, instead of the usual practice of a teacher asking questions, consider inviting children to ask questions: "What do you need to find out/know?" "What questions do you have about this picture?" (J. D. McNeil, 1984, p. 30).

Follow-Up. When children have shared an experience, you can help to sharpen their critical-thinking skills by highlighting their reactions:

- What part of the story/film/trip did you like the best? Why? Other views? Why?
- What part did you like the least? Why? Other views?
- Which part did you find the most exciting/ interesting/funniest? Why? Other views?
- Which character did you like the best/least? Why? Other views? Why do you dislike/like the character?
- Why do you agree/disagree with [name of classmate]?
- When did something like that happen to you/somebody you know?
- Think about this: What else might this character have done?
- What might have happened before the story began?
- What might have happened if he had not . . . ?
- What might this character wish? When was a time when you felt the way he did? What might have made him feel this way?
- If you had been this character, what might you have done when . . . ? How might you have changed what happened?
- If you could ask the characters questions, what would you want to know?
- How would you continue this story?

Role playing after children have had experiences helps them to express their understanding and to make connections with other feelings and experiences that they have had. You can begin this activity with some questions that help children to place themselves inside a character:

- Let's imagine that you could become that person. What would you want to do? Say? Ask? Know? Have happen? Why?
- What might be happening in this picture? Other views? Why do you think so?

- What do you think about what Robin said? What else might be happening? Why?

You can then ask the group to agree on one problem and try to act it out. Later the children can take turns trying out other problems and solutions. (For other role-playing ideas, see McCaslin, 1980; Shaftel & Shaftel, 1983.)

Values questions often arise. Questions such as the following tend to encourage children to consider alternative viewpoints:

- Why do you suppose that was important/worthwhile to them? When might they have begun to see it that way?
- What would happen if you were there?
- How might you help them to find a peaceful/friendly/ honest solution?
- Why is that important to you?
- What are some things she bought that you wouldn't buy? Why? What would be more important for you to buy?
- What might happen if you/they felt differently?
- How might they do it differently the next time?
- If that happened to you, what might you think/do/plan?
- Why do you think that some people tell lies?
- What might make him more friendly toward you?
- When might you choose to do it that way?

In the expanded interaction that is likely to result from such questions, you may find that, after planning half a dozen questions, only one or two are used in a particular session because children have raised other relevant issues.

Networking. The networking, webbing, or mapping of ideas and feelings after a discussion is one way of representing content and comprehension. Usually networking takes the form of a structured experience chart, a constellation of pictures or of pictures with labels. It is possible to explore and represent an issue by making a kind of inventory. For example, using a "feely box" of textured items, you can ask children to feel an unseen object—always an attention-getting and suspenseful activity. Then they are to imagine "becoming" that texture (or fragrance or appearance) and share, as you record, (1) what they might be, (2) what they might think, (3) what they might do, and (4) what might be the advantages and disadvantages of being that.

Problem Setting and Solving. Setting and solving problems involves recognizing patterns and making connections, and hence seeing things in new ways. Analogies are among the devices that help us to see things in new ways. In looking at the other side of Dewey's (1933) notion that teaching is "making the strange familiar," Gordon and Poze (1980) make the point that creativity and problem solving "make the familiar strange." The conscious use of analogy is a tool that helps learning, creating, and problem setting and solving because analogies help us find some familiar elements upon which to build solutions.

You can work at solving problems with direct analogies, in which children draw on parallels to increase their understanding (e.g., for a behavior problem, "What animal acts like that?") or with personal analogies, in which children imagine that they have "become" the animal or object and indicate how they think or what they can do in their analogous role. It is useful for you to explore with the children how the analogue is like and not like its referent, in order to suggest new possibilities.

In trying to solve a social problem, young children may focus on a surface variable rather than addressing the essential factors. However, when their teacher helps them build rules together and explore analogies, children tend to become more independent as they come to see other points of view (DeVries & Zan, 1994). Piaget's (1947/1950) concept of decentration reflects this interaction of affect and cognition and supports the notion that "logical thought is necessarily social" (p. 164). Both he and Vygotsky (1962, 1978), from their distinct perspectives, recognize that, through social interaction, thinking becomes more flexible. The teacher's role as a questioner who welcomes children's questions and curiosity is pivotal.

INQUIRING INTO LEARNING CONDITIONS: IN-SERVICE DEVELOPMENT

Let us think back for a moment to the questioning teacher, mentioned earlier, who tape-recorded group discussions and individual conferences. She noticed her pattern of asking yes-or-no questions, decided that she did not want to use these, and then refined and expanded her questioning techniques. By wondering about the impact of her questions, finding a way to collect information, and then trying out alternative, preferred types of questions, she became an inquirer, a researcher into her own teaching. There are a variety of ways in which you can study your own teaching, some of which you may take for granted without labeling them as "inquiry" or "research." These ways include observation, record keeping, looking at children's work, and being reflective about your own work while sharing ideas with colleagues.

Observation. Observation begins as you greet each child in the morning and intuitively experience his or her mood, energy level, or state of health. Observation continues as you circulate and teach throughout the day, assessing what children have accomplished, where they need help, and what they need to learn next. More systematic observation may take place after identifying, for example, one child's need, whenever he is nearly finished with an activity, for help in planning a transition to the next activity.

Record Keeping. When you find a child who has problems with other children or with work, and you are not sure what to do, it may be helpful to keep brief anecdotal records about problem moments for a week or two, in order to gather information. If you need to know more about what a child is doing, you may want to jot down what he is doing at regular intervals for a day or two. When you review these notes after some time has elapsed, a pattern of behavior and a possible alternate way of working may emerge. Sharing such records with other teachers may provide fresh ideas for handling a problem.

Product Samples. When looking at children's behavior and the products that they create, you can gain additional insight into how to work with them. For example, several months into the school year, one teacher found that a particular child had never painted. Others have found that the drawings and play of children who have been sexually abused may reveal their victimization (Koblinsky & Behana, 1984). The writing attempts and artwork of kindergarten children also show you their coordination, perseverance, and representational accomplishments, and reviewing this material may also suggest ways to plan new experiences. In a similar way, sociodramatic play serves as a window through which to see a child's perspective. Anecdotal records of such play and occasional audiotaping provide another kind of "product" sample.

The point of keeping records and samples of children's products is to have data upon which to base your plans. Such items also serve as documentation in creating "portfolio assessment" formats instead of summative kinds of report cards.

Portfolios consist of selected products that develop in the context of daily life. They contain "a systematic and organized collection of children's work" (Gullo, 1994, p. 82). You, together with the children, can decide on which samples of art, writing, constructions, photographs of projects, dictated stories, and audiotapes of retold stories to include. You might also decide to include anecdotal records as well as interviews with children concerning their reactions to events, their preferences, and other observations. Such material is useful for sharing with other professionals or parents.

Reflective Inquiry. The more reflective we are as professional teachers, the more able we will be to restructure our ongoing work. The process of such reflective inquiry involves the following steps:

1. Defining a problem, whether it is child behavior, the teacher's procedures, or the context
2. Collecting information about what is happening
3. Trying alternative procedures or materials
4. Collecting information over time and comparing old findings with new ones

There are limits to each teacher's personal, informal observations or even more systematic "action research." The use of autobiography and keeping of a reflective journal that is shared with others has also helped to transform practice. Reflecting upon autobiography can help us to become aware of practices that are based on what we experienced as students but that may no longer be consistent with the values we now hold. Some teachers have found that collaborating on such inquiry with others, such as colleagues and school support or local college personnel, provides for stimulating work conditions and an intellectual challenge (Elliott, 1993; Genishi, 1992; Stenhouse, 1980). Ultimately, as institutions redefine the roles of teachers and college personnel and provide support for expanding the teacher's inquiry role with such things as time and personnel, we can create a stronger professional teaching practice and improved working conditions for all (Fox, Anglin, Fromberg, & Grady, 1986). Each teacher can take an advocacy role in encouraging collegiality that may influence change in practice.

INTEGRATING LEARNING EXPERIENCES

It is not enough only to mediate effectively, appreciate appropriately, question relevantly, and inquire meaningfully. All these various functions must be integrated in a balanced way. Examples of these functions are present throughout this book. Computers and trips are additional examples of other provisions for learning that cut across program perspectives and are more available in a longer kindergarten day. Although they can easily become isolated events, they also can be integral to the task of including rich experiences for children. For example, computers, with or without voice synthesizers, have been used in kindergarten for word-processing programs as well as for graphic constructions that affect artistic, mathematical, and scientific understandings. Trips have taken place in order to study the community as well as scientific understandings, and been followed up with graphic, mathematical, and literacy activities.

Computers and Other Technical Resources

Computers, with or without voice synthesizers, are resources in many full-day kindergartens. When they are well integrated, they conform to a number of consistent criteria, represented by the questions in Figure 2.2. Working with computers in an interactive way, there are times when you might stimulate children's critical-thinking skills and perhaps tickle a sense of self-awareness—for example, by using the question pair: How did you do that? What might you want to do next time?

Since it is apparent that computers and television are realities in the lives of children, teachers must be prepared to use them in ways that support significant learning. There are relevant publications on the use of microcomputers with young children (Burg, 1984; Clements & Nastasi, 1993; J. I. Davidson, 1989; Hill, 1985; Hoot & Silvern, 1988; Kreinberg, Alper, & Joseph, 1985; Swett, 1984). There are also relevant materials that deal with the use and impact of television and film culture on young children (Forman, 1992a, 1992b; Honig, 1983; Singer & Singer, 1992; Winn, 1977). It is apparent from researchers and commentators that computers can provide an opportunity for children to engage voluntarily in social activity, problem setting and solving, and extensions of graphic representations through design and literacy explorations. It is also apparent that computers can serve as an electronic version of the workbooks, drill, competition, and exclusionary practices in which children are pressured to participate. Each teacher's purposes and attitudes toward early learning will influence the degree to which the medium facilitates the children's taking positive control or becomes a noxious imposition that they must suffer.

As we look at the influence of television subject matter, we need to consider the ongoing direct changes in children's play themes, such as forms of violence and fantasy. Despite the strides that have been made to include people of color, alternative lifestyles, women, and people with disabilities in recent years, the mass media continue to project stereotypical imagery and expectations. Therefore we need consciously to create inclusionary curricula, integrating underrepresented groups and taking intentional steps to develop an egalitarian curriculum.

There is also persuasive evidence that parents need help in integrating computers and television into children's lives. Perhaps it is most important to influence parents to help their children become selective, critical users of these resources while they maintain time for children to be alone quietly, to be with other children of different ages, and to be with the family at meals and other extended opportunities for conversation.

FIGURE 2.2: Guidelines for Using Computers in an Integrated Kindergarten Curriculum

---

- How can children set their own problems and explore alternative ways of solving them?
- When children find problems to solve, what are the opportunities for alternative ways of solving them?
- How can children use the technology independently, alone and with other children? A cadre model often develops when some children become resources for a particular procedure. Consider introducing procedures to small groups and monitoring them periodically. Does excessive adult monitoring time take away from other priorities?
- How does the material add to the children's concrete knowledge base?
- Does it minimize the time available for a more worthwhile, concrete, manipulative activity for which it is a less effective substitute?
- How does it introduce, demonstrate, or help children learn something worthwhile?
- What provisions have you made so that children can feel comfortable with the medium?
- Do girls as well as boys have equal access, so both may gain a sense of comfort in using the computer? With kindergarten children, perhaps comfort with the medium is a reasonable goal.
- What are the opportunities for cooperative work among children? A computer may invite use by dyads or small groups who are working together on a problem or game, quite as much as it may be used by individuals.
- What meaningful learning can be represented by these resources? For example, the perceptual model of *indirect progress* where a player might sacrifice a turn in order to gain some other advantage, might be experienced in a computer game just as it might in a game of checkers. However, the graphics in a LOGO format might more flexibly represent *indirect progress* than would numerous variations on paper.
- Is the expenditure justifiable in relation to other budget needs and priorities? Parental and community pressure is sometimes a persuasive consideration regardless of how you answer this question.

Trips

Somehow trips seem to abound in the springtime in northern climates; however, learning is supposed to take place throughout the year. Are trips less valuable at other times? There are certainly plentiful ideas for brief educational trips within and directly around the school, if only for environmental studies and even if the school has a hard-surface playground

(Russell, 1990). Teachers should consider looking further at what places are worth visiting in their region, so they can extend and tie together school experiences with such visits. Some criteria for taking trips are represented by the questions in Figure 2.3.

Teachers find that the longer kindergarten day provides for more meaningful trips. All on the same day, they can accomplish what otherwise would be separated into several days, possibly diluting the educational impact (Sheila Terens, personal communication, 1984). There is time for the following steps to take place:

1. Planning together with the children
   • Considering what they might find and predicting the possibilities
   • Planning for data collection, which might include tallying, drawing, copying signs, or making lists
2. Taking the trip
3. Classroom follow-up
   • Discussing and comparing their experiences and findings
   • Creating a variety of graphic and symbolic representations of their experiences

Children can retain more connections this way than by waiting until the following day or after a weekend has passed to participate in follow-up activities.

A BASIC CONSIDERATION in integrating any resource is that it be consistent with your expressed values about worthwhile education for human beings. A real pressure upon you may be the needs of the community as they are expressed directly and as they are interpreted by school administrators.

DISSEMINATING ACCOMPLISHMENTS TO ADULTS: PARENTS, TEACHERS, AND ADMINISTRATORS

It is reasonable to state that parents want their children to achieve well in school without much suffering. While this may seem to be a fairly negative statement, it contains a degree of accuracy on the face of it. That is, parents generally perceive that it is worthwhile for children to "work hard" at school, but they complain when they perceive that a teacher is harsh or does not appreciate their child. This interface between teachers and other adults has another aspect to it as well. Children who are active and learning generally are using concrete materials and engaging in cooperative work

FIGURE 2.3: Guidelines for Using Trips in an Integrated Kindergarten Curriculum

- What can children see on the trip that is otherwise not available directly?
- How have you planned and prepared together with the children? What questions have children planned?
- What are the reasons for believing that this particular trip is relevant and that the children are likely to be receptive to this particular exposure? Can all the children focus, even with different degrees of commitment and understanding?
- How can your mediation during the trip help the children to see familiar things in new ways? For example, while all of the children might have been to a supermarket with a parent, they may or may not have focused systematically on the setting of buying priorities, the monetary transactions, or the various roles of employees. You might arrange for a visit when the class could observe deliveries as part of a study of the food cycle. A study of the economic cycle might take the class on a visit to farms and processing factories. It might also touch on issues of the homelessness visible to children in everyday experience.
- How can the trip serve as a reason to use representational skills and make comparisons and connections?
- How can you plan sufficient time for some follow-up, preferably on the same day?

with other children. To some parents, active children look as if they are enjoying themselves too much. Unless you take time to explain this look of learning in kindergarten, some administrators, next year's teacher, and many parents may dismiss what they see as "just playing."

There are several points at which you might communicate with other adults about how significant learning is taking place, including through children's sociodramatic play. One way is labeling important areas in the classroom, such as "mathematics area," "cyclical change," "science area," and so forth. Another is preparing educational bulletin boards and displays of children's work that explain their work and learning. Just before children leave at the end of the day, you could discuss briefly what they did that day and remind them of one or two highlights. In this way, they may acquire the necessary language with which to retain something, other than a puzzled expression or shrug, to share with adults who meet them after school.

You can report on individual and group learning activities by arranging for parent conferences and parents' group meetings. You also can send one-line notes home each day to the parents of four or five children about whom you have collected anecdotal notes. There could be a periodic— perhaps quarterly—one-page kindergarten newsletter for parents, other teachers, and administrators.

You should be sure to tell what you are doing to help children learn the skills that parents, other teachers, and administrators understand and care about, while de-emphasizing those methods that you do not value. For example, Chapter 9 suggests a four-part approach to literacy and language instruction. There are materials that children use and products that they create which are concrete and visible. Chapter 7 suggests a seven-part approach to acquainting other adults with mathematics education in the kindergarten. Chapter 5 offers activities that reflect how children move toward more mature understanding of their social lives and the social sciences. These approaches focus on active, cooperative experiences that are meaningful and reflective of how young children learn.

SCHEDULING

How activities are scheduled each day reflects your priorities. There are important ways in which scheduling can contribute to a positive learning atmosphere in the full-day kindergarten. Research findings have shown that full-day kindergarten programs have helped children to achieve more academic skills and have helped to reduce the necessity of repeating grades in later school years,[1] and that parents and children have shared a positive view of the kindergarten experience (Adcock et al., 1980; Cryan, Sheehan, Wiechel, & Bandy-Hedden, 1992; Humphreys, 1983; Nieman & Gastright, 1975; Winter & Klein, 1970). Unfortunately, the researchers provide less clarity about what curriculum models were used in their studies. Many half-day kindergarten teachers say that they need more time with the children. How they would use additional time reflects a broad range of philosophies for kindergarten curriculum development.

This book supports a dynamic, experiential full-day curriculum, the intellectual and social purposes of which function in a caring, egalitarian context. This curriculum develops through ongoing transactions rather than as a body of plans fixed on the calendar. This book proposes that representational skills need to be learned not as ends in themselves but by being integrated with substantive activities. The real work of education is to extend children's knowledge bases and their capacities to think critically and make new connections in ways that build their self-esteem and satisfaction in learning. This experiential position exists in full-day kindergartens that have flexible, varied schedules.

If you see children as curious, active builders of knowledge, you will be likely to follow their pacing needs, encourage options, support their questioning and imagery, and organize longer blocks of time. If you see the full-day kindergarten as providing additional time for transactions involving the teacher, the children, and the nature of meaningful experience, then it will make sense to you that different children doing different things at different times can have equivalent experiences.

The possibilities for scheduling daily and longer-term curricula are determined by the following four broad categories of kindergarten structure:

1. The full-day kindergarten with a single teacher responsible for the class (and varied assistance by another adult)
2. The full-day kindergarten with different morning and afternoon teachers
3. An extended day each day, with or without alternate day extension for part of the group
4. The half-day kindergarten with a single teacher, providing alternate full days for part of the class

The school districts that are most enlightened, in my opinion, subscribe to the first of these alternatives. They expect the full-day kindergarten teacher to provide an integrated learning experience and use the additional time to deepen and extend significant kindergarten pursuits. An experiential, intellectual curriculum based heavily on direct activities is possible in this format. Figure 2.4 represents a possible schedule.

Some districts, as in the second model, have tried to economize by using two teachers for each half of the children's full day. Usually one half-day teacher is paid at the contracted scale and the other teacher is paid at a lower, hourly rate. The scale-paid teacher is expected to provide more academic work and the hourly teacher, more exploratory and recreational activity. The meaning of "academic" depends on the school: In one, it may mean intellectual, experiential curriculum, while in another it may mean an alienated, rote approach. In either case, teachers have expressed a sense of "not having enough time." In practice, when some teachers have agreed that the two emphases, knowledge and socialization, should be integrated, they have planned together and felt less pressed for time.

In the third and fourth types of schedules, the teacher works with the entire kindergarten group each morning or extended morning, and half or a quarter of the class each afternoon. The rationale for extended-day scheduling is to provide more individual attention. Some settings focus on building skills with individual children while others focus on social

FIGURE 2.4: Experiential Full-Day Schedule

8:50 Arrival.
      Whole-group planning.
9:20 Activity period. Teacher circulates and works in turn with three small
      instructional groups and individuals in reading, writing, mathematics, or
      science. Variety of self-paced activities in all subject areas, including
      reading, mathematics, sociodrama, cyclical change, science, media, arts
      and crafts, and games. Depending upon teacher philosophy, snacks are
      either integrated or offered at a separate time. Integrated snacks mean
      that children can have a snack at their own pace, alone, with another
      child, or with a small group. A separate time means a setting in which
      everybody takes their snack at the same time. Ideally, in either
      arrangement, the teacher would join the children in snack time and
      extend conversation and collegiality.
10:50 Whole-group sharing.
11:05 Gym. Music, movement, dance, group games, or calisthenics; indoors or
      outdoors.
11:40 Whole-group story time and discussion.
12:00 Lunch/playground; activity period or planning.
12:50 Quiet time, reading, or listening with headphones. The time directly after
      lunch/playground is often designated a rest time, a quiet time, or a
      diminished activity time. Sometimes music is played.
1:10 Moderate activity period. Teacher circulates and works in turn with three
      small instructional groups in either reading, writing, mathematics,
      science, or social science. Variety of self-paced activities, excluding
      woodworking. In general, a less active time; fewer large-muscle
      activities are available.
2:20 Whole-group sharing. Social studies discussion/planning, experience
      chart, creative dramatics, or special event. A special event may include a
      birthday time each month, other celebrations, the visit of a resource
      person, planning a trip, recounting and recording a trip, taking a short
      trip in or around the school, learning to use new equipment, cooking, or
      viewing a film.
      Day ends with singing, clapping, riddles, poetry . . .
2:50 End of day.

and collaborative pastimes, still others use a combination of approaches,
and others offer an extended experiential curriculum. Often the extended-
day formats are the result of district precedent, politics, and economic
priorities. Figure 2.5 depicts a sample schedule for what schools have done
with this setup.

FIGURE 2.5: Schedule for Half- or Extended-Day Kindergarten with Alternate Afternoon Programs

 8:50 Arrival.
      Group planning, discussion and sharing.
 9:25 Activity period. Teacher circulates, alternately working with small
      instructional groups. Children self-pace activities in reading, mathemat-
      ics, cyclical change, science, sociodrama, media, arts and crafts, and
      games. May or may not include snack.
10:45 Whole-group sharing.
10:55 Gym. Music, dance, group games, calisthenics; indoors or outdoors.
11:30 Creative dramatics, science subgroups, special event.
12:10 Whole-group story time and discussion.
12:30 End of day [1] for some children. Lunch for all or small remaining group.
      Size of small group can be six to twelve, depending on whether children
      return one or two afternoons each week.
 1:00 Quiet time, reading, or listening with headphones.
      Individual instruction in concepts, reading, or writing.
 1:20 Language arts, mathematics, or science lesson, using concrete materials.
      May include drawing, graphing, or writing follow-up. (One or two
      groups of six children or three groups of four children with teacher
      circulating.)
 2:00 Creative dramatics; experience chart; games.
 2:30 Story time, music, or language games.
 2:50 End of day.

1. The morning may end at 12:00, in which case kindergarten children join the whole school's supervised lunch program. If the morning ends at 12:30 or 1:00, there might be a separate kindergarten lunch; a teacher aide begins the afternoon with the children, in order to give the teacher a contracted lunch period.

REFLECTIONS

In various ways, the longer kindergarten day provides an opportunity for teachers to plan for extended, significant development of meaningful content and integrated skills in ways that coincide with children's natural pacing and development. It must be remembered, however, that these opportunities and present practices exist in a community climate where there is often pressure for teachers to do more than is natural, sooner than it is possible. Some of these concerns are discussed in the next chapter, which looks at the larger societal and developmental contexts in which the full-day kindergarten takes place.

3

Influences on
Human Learning

The full-day kindergarten is like a partly empty house that needs furnishing. Now that there is more time, we need to consider why and how to fill it so that the inhabitants experience a sense of harmony. We face the challenge of using the additional time for experiences from which children can construct meaning, skill building that is integrated with content, and learning activities so that they can perceive the patterns and connections in their experiences.

This house does not stand alone. The kindergarten is influenced by society, by our understanding of what knowledge is worthwhile, and by how young children learn. This chapter will deal with each influence in turn and then consider the implications of these influences for the organization of full-day kindergarten.

THE INFLUENCE OF SOCIETY ON KINDERGARTEN EDUCATION

Human beings need to learn how to survive in society, to be able to make sense of their experiences, and to be able to have certain expectations met. Presumably, society supports an educational system that will make possible the survival and improvement of its community. The increasing numbers of full- and extended-day kindergartens, and talk about whether or not to extend half-day programs, reflect some societal influences.

When we look at the great diversity of political systems around the world and throughout history, we are confronted with the reality that there are many ways to organize human society, some better than others in serving different purposes. We therefore need to be aware of how our society, or our culture, influences our assumptions about education for young children. With increased awareness, each of us may be in a better position to decide what is worthwhile education for human beings of kindergarten age and to respond to the following questions:

What sort of human being do we want in this society?
What knowledge is worthwhile?
What can and should children learn?
How can learning take place in humane ways?

Cultural Orientations to Time and Priorities

As an example of cultural diversity and its impact on our lives, let us consider how different political and family cultures value time. Those cultures that tend to value a future-time orientation rate more highly scientific knowledge, abstract thought, and indirect, vicarious experience. Those cultures that emphasize a present-time orientation favor intuitive knowing, particular results, concrete examples, and direct, immediate experience. In a parallel vein, those who have political power experience time differently from those who have less control over time (Morgan, 1982). People who feel powerless are less likely to make long-range plans because they have a sense that time is not in their control.

This is not to say that either perspective excludes aspects that the other values, but merely that there is a difference in the emphasis and degree of significance given to certain activities and aspects of human personality and interaction. While it is clear that all human beings are capable of developing the capacity for the full range of human experiencing, cultural differences mean that people who grow up in different societies will interpret their experiences with somewhat different emphases.

Similarly, some theorists perceive a hierarchy of developmental stages as representing a more technical, male orientation and an affiliative, situation-specific, transactional view as representing a more personal, female orientation (Cherryholmes, 1988; Donaldson, 1978; Gilligan, 1982; Lather, 1991). As we consider such cultural dimensions, it becomes apparent that basing curriculum on a particular developmental stage theory might make it difficult to see young children as functioning within distinct personal cultures. Young children might *focus* on those things that adults take for granted as *subsidiary*. The psychological study of child development, therefore, while an important resource, is insufficient as the center of early childhood education. The center of early childhood education is meaning, those experiences to which children can feel committed; and children's personal cultures and event knowledge generate their commitments.

Different cultural outlooks mean that schools will have different priorities. As awareness of the richness to be found in cultural diversity has increased, some educators have become concerned that our schools offer too narrow a view of the world. They have recommended that schools need to offer a better balance among the varied ways of knowing (Eisner, 1985). For example, our schools traditionally have held that informational and scientific studies are more prestigious and take precedence over such "frills" as the arts. Budget allocations reflect these values quite dramatically.

Our schools also value rapid learning of print conventions while often overlooking the oral strengths that children from diverse cultures bring to school. Children's oral language reflects significant, valuable ways of knowing and representing the world. Oral language development within sociodramatic play is part of the continuum of literacy and writing development. The issue of work first, play later (if there is time), therefore, is damaging to early learning and reflects the devaluing of the locus of children's power, play, which is part of the oral culture. The loss of oral heuristics also reduces human potential for related perceptions and imagination (Egan, 1988). From a cultural standpoint, it is immoral to devalue the competence in oral language that young children learn from their families. From an ethical perspective, the children's own spoken language is the power base that they bring to school.

Young children also bring to school diverse social and cultural perspectives that have served as strengths in coping with daily life. Heath (1983) has documented the distinctive stances with which black and white, middle-class and working-class children approach their early schooling. Although she found many similarities in the outlooks of the black and white middle-class children, she found differences in the black and white working-class children. The white working-class children learned the "correct" way to use each toy and the single space in which to store things, which might help them to prosper in a workbook-oriented program but not serve them well in a program that expected creative and flexible interpretations and plans. The black working-class children learned to interpret events in a more flexible way and to use narrative and metaphor creatively.

Although broad economic and ethnic influences point to ways in which we might adapt to children, it is helpful to consider each family as its own cultural creation. Another cultural consideration as teachers interact with children is the relative need for privacy. Some families, and some cultures (Erickson & Mohatt, 1982), employ a cultural "etiquette" of "private" social interaction, rather than "spotlighting" a child by addressing him or instructing him in the presence of others. Teachers who are sensitive to such cultural etiquette would place themselves near a child when talking to him, rather than publicly appreciating or redirecting him. When organizing classrooms, such teachers circulate as they reduce whole-group and offer mainly small-group work.

In order to help all children to extend their learning, therefore, teachers need to try to be sensitive to children and to adapt activities to children's multiple ways of knowing and feeling. Inasmuch as young children's intellectual learning occurs best through physical, aesthetic, and socioemotional activity, their schooling looks as if it is more concrete, sensorial, and playful—and therefore less "serious"—to the untrained eye. Often for this reason, budgets for early childhood education have been cut during strained economic times, despite research that documents the cost benefits of early education (Lazar, Darlington, Murray, Royce, & Snipper, 1982; Schweinhart, Weikart, & Larner, 1986).

Impact of Technology and Economics

Technological factors and economic priorities also reflect cultural perspectives and contexts and, in turn, influence what children experience in school and how they perceive it. Children have spent hours each week watching television and have seen movies. Many have played computer games, traveled on airplanes, and been to the fantasy worlds of Disney. They have been entertained by content that changes focus every few seconds, exploiting their excitement levels and pumping their adrenaline. They have been manipulated by sophisticated advertising techniques that grab their attention, influence their perception by creating particular "figures" out of "backgrounds," use multimedia approaches, and command attention with sensory volume. With increasingly complex technology, it is difficult for children to understand how things work in direct, concrete ways. Their schooling experience can be confusing by sheer contrast. It is often programmed by textbooks in which variables frequently are not carefully controlled. Time seems to flow more slowly, and teachers often control physical movement and verbal initiatives. Even when teachers attempt to "entertain," by offering frequent changes of activities, they cannot duplicate film culture. The only way in which today's schools, therefore, can engage children in productive ways is to offer them opportunities to pace themselves and the power to make choices among challenging individual and social activities.

Technology also has had a profound impact on the economy by changing the nature of employment and the way families function. Jobs have become increasingly informational rather than industrial (Naisbitt, 1982); but "knowledge is inside people and information is external to them" (Purves, 1990, p. 3). This means that more people than ever before are spending more time studying in preparation for employment, depending upon specialists who are literate in information technology rather than learning on the job. Many are having children at an older age than did preceding generations. Teenage pregnancies, however, are rising (Frost,

1986). Many mothers who work outside the home are either in one-parent households or in families that depend upon the mother's wages. The majority of mothers (59.9%) with children younger than age 6 work outside the home (Children's Defense Fund, 1992). Thus there are increasing numbers of "latchkey" kindergarten children who return to an empty home after school.

With public schools increasingly extending the kindergarten day despite budget cuts in some locales, however, a closer match is developing between the needs of the community and the offerings of the schools. Even when school districts have debated whether or not to have full-day programs and have given parents the option of sending their children part time, only a handful of families have used that option. With a highly mobile society, a high divorce rate, the frequency of serial marriages, and uncertain child-care arrangements, the school may be one of the most secure places for young children.

Implications for Kindergarten Education

Societal influences—philosophical, technological, economic, cultural, and sociopolitical—relate in significant ways to what happens in schools. In U.S. society, there is a tendency to emphasize abstract, cognitive accomplishments, even though this is not in the best interests of young children. At the same time, the kindergarten curriculum has been based on the traditional folklore reflecting the "here-and-now" experiences of kindergarten children (Mitchell, 1921). And the here-and-now approach often has been trivialized without crediting children's imaginative and creative potential (Roldão & Egan, n.d.).

What we are finding is that society provides children with here-and-now data very different from those their parents received. Even where both parents are present, families are often isolated from other generations and children have fewer siblings than in earlier generations, sisters and brothers who could serve as role models and caretakers. Children are closer to adult imagery, to adult violence, and to adult technology (Paley, 1984). The crux of this issue is that the content of their play symbols may be changing, but their capacities to understand remain those of kindergarten children.

Kindergarten teachers find that they need to consider what children bring to school and help them classify their information, compare and contrast their data, make new connections, and deal with their feelings. Indeed, school is the single agency in society that is designated to help children develop their minds. We need to remember that thinking processes are supported or blocked by feelings and social contacts. If we do not pay attention to feelings and social concerns, we are setting the stage for academic failure.

The most well-intentioned, benevolent teachers cannot shield children from failure and a devastated self-concept unless they adapt to children's ways of learning and developing. Plainly speaking, children's sense of success affects their self-esteem, which, if damaged, leaves them vulnerable to compensation through expressions of violence as well as teenage pregnancies. Those children who feel good about themselves are more likely to be able to resist peer pressures to take drugs and engage in group vandalism.

It is more difficult for children to behave independently if their sole reason for doing things is the appeal of an authority figure. It is crucial, therefore, to identify what knowledge may be worth knowing, and how young children may learn about the world while retaining their sense of competence and caring for themselves and others as human beings.

THE INFLUENCE OF HUMAN KNOWLEDGE: TOWARD PERCEPTUAL MODELS/DYNAMIC THEMES

While society has helped schools to define what knowledge is valued, we are finding that knowledge is no longer as absolute as we once believed. Even in physics, pioneering research indicates that understanding of and knowledge about subatomic particles and space are relative, not absolute (Capra, 1982; Hawking, 1988; Waldrop, 1992; Zukav, 1980).

As this relativistic view has grown, there has been an increased development of interdisciplinary teaching. Antibias and multicultural education reflect interdisciplinary studies that include sociology, anthropology, geography, political science, and the arts. Global education ties political socialization and multicultural education with history, geography, and science as concerns develop about human rights, national conflicts, and the environment. These approaches suggest egalitarian ways of viewing other human beings, regardless of gender, ethnicity, age, ability, race, or beliefs.

Classifying and Connecting Knowledge

In the context of the full-day kindergarten movement, school people and community members are searching for relevant knowledge bases upon which to "furnish the rest of the kindergarten house." This period is a time for reforming kindergarten education to take into account both the *depth* offered by each discipline and the *breadth* that is possible through the interdisciplinary approach, while considering the extradisciplinary creativity with which children perceive events and construct meanings. "Extradisciplinary" refers to the observation that children's powerful imagery systems may represent neither disciplinary nor cross-disciplinary structures. An outlook must be created to help teachers plan with children for both depth and breadth that is meaningful. From an extradisciplinary stance, the central work of early childhood education is meaning, those experiences to which children can feel commitment.

As we consider how to make plans for a full kindergarten day, we need to account for the processes by which children both classify and connect experience to create meanings. For purposes of communication, this book is organized to reflect established bodies of school knowledge in such areas as the physical sciences, the social sciences, mathematics, the arts, and language and literacy. However, because kindergarten children naturally organize their experiences in continuous ways that cut across these politically sanctioned and artificially disconnected areas, plans for perceptual models/dynamic themes are integrated within chapters in order to suggest the continuous ways in which children connect their conceptual understandings through networks of activities. In this planning context, *perceptual models* are the recurring patterns of related elements, the similar underlying isomorphic images that we can perceive in various surface forms.

Although units and topics are approaches to planning that attempt to help children connect ideas across disciplines, teachers plan differently than when planning with perceptual models/dynamic themes. Using perceptual models for planning purposes also differs from the structure-of-disciplines approach. These approaches to planning curriculum are discussed further in the following sections.

Structure of Disciplines Contrasted with Perceptual Models

The structure-of-disciplines movement of the past few decades has been an attempt to deal with understanding rather than only with information. Educators and subject-matter specialists have tried to define the uniqueness of each area of knowledge in terms of its idealized domain, distinctive "key" concepts, unique methods of inquiry, and language (Bruner, 1961; Phenix, 1964). Thus organized knowledge has served as a source of kindergarten activities.

As a separate-subjects view of knowledge, the structure-of-disciplines approach does not fully reflect the continuity of human experience. It presents children with a preconceived view of knowledge. Children are expected to act upon, process, and order events within the scope of existing disciplines. Although the advocates of separate disciplines would not spoon-feed it, they propose that the school provide children with a precut pie, with each discipline existing as a piece of that pie. One may detect occasional juices dripping into adjacent pieces, but the cuts have, after all, already been made, and the relative sizes are culturally determined. The political question of whose cultural perspectives predominate is a contemporary issue of concern to educators and philosophers (Foucault, 1982).

This concept of knowledge stands outside of children, and this is a problem. While reality may or may not exist "out there," knowledge is an inside experience, the child's transaction, the result of the child's receptivity and responsiveness in particular social settings.

As disciplines reflect ways in which a particular culture classifies knowledge, perceptual models reflect ways in which children connect and blend meanings. Experiencing a perceptual model, even while using the ways of knowing that have developed within one discipline, helps children to make new connections with a similar model external to this discipline. This encourages new learning, whereby the "strange" becomes "familiar" (Dewey, 1933) at the same time that it reflects the creative potential "to make the familiar strange" (Egan, 1986, p. 47).

The perceptual-models framework and the structure-of-disciplines approach, which includes the various ways-of-knowing, are both compatible with Dewey's vision of the teacher as helping children move toward humanity's "fund of knowledge" (1933, p. 137) in ways that are consistent with children's total capacities. Each approach uses a different way of looking at humanity's "fund," but both conceive of learning as being active. They value a setting in which children engage in inquiry that matches their capacities and is consistent with a view of knowledge as constructed by children (Piaget & Inhelder, 1964) in a transactional (Rosenblatt, 1978), social (Vygotsky, 1978) setting.

Comparing Units, Topics, and Perceptual Models/Dynamic Themes

This section compares the curriculum-planning approaches that are based on units, topics, or perceptual models/dynamic themes as inhabitants of regions on an idealized continuum. A focus on winter, for example, might appear as a unit or topic, but might only appear as a part of the perceptual model of *cyclical change* or *dialectical process* (conflict/contrast). Figure 3.1 offers contrasts along several dimensions.

Units

The unit focuses on information and separate subjects connected on a surface, static level for a brief period, such as a self-contained week or two. Teachers often label the unit as "social studies" and plan an activity repre-

Figure 3.1: Units, Topics, and Perceptual Models/Dynamic Themes

	Units	*Topics*	*Perceptual Models*
Philosophy	Behaviorist	Constructivist	Social construction
Process	Academic	Cognitive	Intellectual
Product	Information	Concepts	Isomorphic imagery
Communication	Linear	Interactive	Transactional[1]
Teacher	Major planner	Joint planner	Negotiated, flexible
Child	Information gleaner; Respondent	Concept constructor; Problem solver	Connection maker; Problem setter and solver
Representation	Uniform products	Child-structured, varied	
Content	Separate subjects	Cross-disciplinary	Extradisciplinary
Play	Release, Peripheral to work	Valuable Parallel, Representational	Integrated Recursive, spiral Representational
Time	Mostly short blocks	Short and long blocks	
Grouping	Mostly whole groups, individual tasks	Mostly smaller groupings, cooperative and individual	

1. Louise Rosenblatt (1969) sees meaning as a "transaction" between past experiences, present motives, and a particular text.

senting each of the subject areas of arts/crafts, music, science, and language. Holidays, ritually observed in trivial ways, often form the unit focus. Besides holidays or the season, the subject might be zoo animals, pets, community helpers, families, farms, popcorn, hats, or vehicles. Children would spend the week hearing stories, playing with related props, singing songs, drawing pictures with a representative color, practicing writing an isolated letter, using uniform crafts materials, cooking, having a science or mathematics activity, and dancing in relation to the unit's subject matter. Art products often are uniform. Bulletin boards herald the unit. A culminating activity might take place that celebrates the week's focus, such as a parade, trip, party, mural, food sampling, or film. Teachers can repeat the format next year because children are not involved in planning and the information teachers offer children basically remains the same.

TOPICS

Teachers who use topics might engage particular children in planning and adapt the time frame to children with or without representing each subject. Examples of topics are tools, homes, underwater life, dinosaurs, insects, working women, hospitals, shadows, seeds, or great art classics. Topics differ from units in that activities have a greater depth of content and might recur throughout the year. The teacher's focus is on children's making discoveries and their own connections, with information as a by-product rather than the center of learning. In contrast with units, the teacher might structure art activities by providing particular children colors or textures for them to organize in their own ways. Similar topics in different years might consume more or less time, involve more or fewer children, and include more or fewer activities, depending upon the ways that the teacher adapts to different groups.

PERCEPTUAL MODELS/DYNAMIC THEMES

Perceptual models/dynamic themes weave throughout the year as teachers see opportunities for children to make connections between experiences. "The activities that potentially represent possible connections and similar perceptions might vary for children who have had different experiences and come from diverse multicultural backgrounds" (Fromberg, 1993, p. 72). Activities build on the child's potential for constructing and integrating similar models of perception, the images that underlie different forms of experience—physical, social, personal, aesthetic, and representational. The discussion that follows provides my perspective as a child and then a description and explanation of perceptual models as a framework for planning early curriculum.

A Child's Point of View. When I was 5 years old, I wondered about how small was small in terms of rough and smooth. If I looked through a very strong magnifying glass, would there ever be a point at which I could see nothing smaller, so that there would be a perfect smoothness?

I would look at water on the stove and watch for the moment when it would begin to make waves and bubble. I would blow bubbles in my bubble pipe and try to catch bubbles with other bubbles and wondered why some bubbles were hot and some were cool.

I wondered, if I were to spit into a stream, what would happen to the saliva. Would it ever meet parts of itself again?

My cousin and I would lie on a blanket looking at the clouds. We would watch the edges change as they moved, while we imagined that they formed the shapes of people, animals, and things.

At school, I remember being taught the single correct answers to questions that did not measure rough/smooth, the nature of turbulence in boiling water or clouds, or the phase transitions of matter, that is, the behavior of matter near the point where it changes from one state to another—from liquid to gas, from unmagnetized to magnetized.

My cousin, my friends, and I, in an explicit way, never connected the clouds, the stream, and the boiling water as parts of the same process. Physicists, biologists, other scientists, economists, and artists at the frontiers of their fields today are doing just that (Gleick, 1987). They are studying *turbulence*, the moments when states of matter change, and the outlines of rough and smooth things that can be measured. They are finding patterns in nonlinear events that appear to be chaotic. They are finding ways to measure the rough edges of the world, like broccoli and jagged shorelines, by thinking about *fractals* (McDermott, 1983) and the patterns in *scroll waves* (Briscoe, 1984; Sullivan, 1985). What these scientists are discovering is that these apparently chaotic, nonlinear events follow a deeper, underlying structure that they can express in nonlinear ways. Young children experience these underlying structures as perceptual models.

Young children, through their isomorphic imagery, are able to apprehend many such perceptual models. They also are able to perceive other, less exotic perceptual models, such as *cyclical change, synergy* (the whole is more than the sum of its parts), *double bind* (incongruous appearance and reality), *dialectical processes* (conflict/contrast), and *indirect progress* (nonlinear movement) (Fromberg, 1977).

As we consider these personal, valuable, often tacit, sometimes aesthetic or physical experiences that children have as they look at the sky, play at the beach, poke and splash in puddles, and watch older children form teams and strategies for group sports, it is apparent that their event knowledge is potent. Intellectual challenges in kindergarten, therefore, need to take forms other than an academic, textbook-driven, or trivial linear curriculum that can create conditions for developing behavioral problems and rob children of time for committed learning.

Some teachers expect children to harvest the same predetermined crop of information and isolated skills at a common season. They expose children to the same stimuli, at the same time, and expect them to achieve the same learnings. There is a fallacy in this approach because different children process experiences differently and are likely to learn more when we employ varied approaches. In any case, variability rather than uniformity is the result when children are taught all together.

Perceptual Models Connecting Meanings. Teachers can use perceptual models as a way of sequencing activities that support children's tendency to make connections between their experiences. Thus we may construe the teacher's role as one of creating potential opportunities for children to experience "echoing patterns" (Gardner, 1983, p. 169). Children experience the "echoing" isomorphic imagery as they make their own connections in the form of multiple mental models. Such mental models typically are "incomplete and approximate" and transferable by analogy (Halford, 1993, p. 23).

Thus the significance of content resides within the learner. "Meaning emerges from and only from isomorphism" (Hofstadter, 1985, p. 445). Meaningful activity within this view, then, begins when children employ multiple ways of knowing that they can connect across time with other activities. Figure 3.2 charts the intersection of four perceptual models with each of ten disciplines that have been taught in school. At each intersection are some activities and ways of working that children can use to build connected meanings. A teacher using Figure 3.2 may begin to plan within any cell of the grid and consider moving horizontally or vertically in an attempt to sequence activities. Teachers set priorities on the basis of those activities that appear to offer more potential for children to make connections. It should be clear, though, that the point of departure is to be negotiated between children and a teacher in a particular situation. In this way, we can see knowledge as a social transaction. Examples of how to integrate some of these perceptual models in planning content for the full-day kindergarten are discussed in Chapters 5 though 9. The major purpose of such fluid planning is to help children make new connections that transcend separate subjects.

The perceptual model is part of the human potential for pattern recognition and dynamic imagery development. It has greater generalizability than its representations, just as the finite structures of language relationships or genetic molecules or myths can generate infinite possibilities from a finite set of symbols. Other transformational theories parallel perceptual models.[1] As a kind of grammar of experience, perceptual models represent young children's capacity to distill the imagery that crosses disciplinary domains. This "transformational grammar of experience" encompasses a holistic integration of socioemotional, psychomotor, cognitive, and aesthetic experience.

THE INFLUENCE OF KINDERGARTEN CHILDREN:
CONDITIONS FOR LEARNING

In addition to considering a contemporary societal context and the nature of relevant knowledge, a modern curriculum for the full-day kindergarten—whether we call it an experiential, extradisciplinary, transactional, social construction, transformational, dynamic themes, or perceptual-models curriculum—needs to adapt to the ways in which kindergarten

FIGURE 3.2: Sample Activities for Use with Perceptual Models

Disciplines	Cyclical Change	Dialectical Activity	Indirect Progress	Synergy
History	Hear oral history. Compare past customs and artifacts. Create a personal timeline.	Narrate and compare conflicting events.	Compare experiences of being lost and other incongruent events.	Compare surprises and explosive events.
Geography	Map city:country population shifts. Trace garbage recycling.	Map wind action and erosion.	Create and use obstacle courses.	Map immigration and change in children's families. Run relay races.
Economics & Sociology	Survey food cycle, group memberships, and changing groups.	Survey action vs. reaction, scarcity, & group conflict.	Play with short-term sacrifice. Role-play social leverage and values differences.	Experience sociodramatic activity. Make cooperative products.
Political Science	Narrate political shifts and rule changes in school and current events.	Narrate human conflicts and values. Humorously invert reality during discussions.	Attempt to influence school administrators or elected officials.	Role-play voting and outcomes. Vote.
Physics	Observe and record seasons. Map shadows outdoors.	Observe gravitation, interactions of forces, and aerodynamics, by varying shapes of materials.	Explore levers. Experience centrifugal force with objects and other people.	Explore physical actions and reactions. Assemble simple machines.

Chemistry	Observe evaporation and condensation. Create electrical circuits.	Observe and change solubility of materials. Mix oil, water, and color.	Identify substances by using household materials.	Cook representative food products, e.g., popcorn, yeast dough, make butter.
Biology	Make seasonal returns to sites of outdoor educational trips. Raise plants and animals. Classify dinosaurs. Survey human growth.	Observe interaction of environment and life forms. Control variables and compare.	Study nutrition of plants. Control variables.	Study growth and reproduction of plants and animals.
Mathematics	Classify varied objects. Measure time and change.	Classify object differences. Measure polarities.	Measure physical progress. Estimate quantities. Play games that include strategies of sacrificing pieces.	Measure transformed changes. Combine shapes and sizes.
Arts	Create present-time aesthetic experiences, e.g., bark rubbings of younger and older trees.	Play with counterpoint in music, dance, and visual arts.	Experience movement education exemplars, e.g., partners, group contradance.	Contrast melodies with choral and ensemble work. Collaborate in movement education, visual arts, and dance. Mix colors. Create murals.
Language	Listen to literature about the past, mythic monsters, and poetic cycles. Record past and present.	Select poetic forms and literature about oppositions. Do related composing. Compare different descriptions of the same event.	Select poetic forms and literature about indirect progress. Compose.	Select poetic forms and literature about collaborative elements. Co-author.

children learn best. It is the position of this book that young children have the right to learn in exploratory and playful ways that help them to see patterns and make connections and that teaching in the context of how children learn best is worthwhile and ethical.

The conditions that influence children's learning function in a meaningful social, emotional, physical, intellectual, and aesthetic context. Children's feelings of competence and their social experiences are as critical to their learning as are the availability of manipulable materials and opportunities to participate in imaginative activities. Therefore, we need to attempt to assure success for children by respecting their ways of learning. Seven *integrated* ways in which kindergarten children learn the best are highlighted in this section. Examples of activities that use these ways of learning appear throughout subsequent chapters.

Inductive Experiences

One of the ways kindergarten children learn best is through direct, inductive experiences. They have the opportunity to perceive a new "figure" emerging from the *contrast* with a known "background" when you provide active contrasts through multiple physical or linguistic experiences. Therefore, as teachers, our job is to provide contrasting experiences as we control variables. Children then have the chance to perceive the change and to extend their learning. It is simply easier to perceive something that is moving in this controlled way than something that is still and camouflaged. The isolated instance, difficult to perceive without a meaningful framework, however, relies on rote memory.

Research into memory has shown that once we perceive something as a "figure" highlighted against a "background," we never forget it (Luria, 1968; Piaget & Inhelder, 1973). In fact, as we grow, our perceptions become part of the networks of other perceptions and thoughts and become more accurately retrievable. Accounts of memory and connection making by Einstein (Sullivan, 1972) suggest that much of the imagery of the young child is an initial form of creativity.

Cognitive Dissonance

Another way kindergarten children learn is through cognitive dissonance (Festinger, 1957).[2] When children expect something to happen and something else happens, there is an opportunity for cognitive dissonance to take place. Cognitive dissonance involves a three-part process: (1) predicting, (2) transforming events through experiencing, and (3) comparing. This is an essential learning process and the way in which critical thinking develops. Children restructure their expectations as a result of this ongoing analysis of the contrast between what they expect and what they find. They become better at differentiating what they may perceive and what is real.

Theories of logical development suggest that young children are much more centered than adults on concrete comparisons and on what they can see, touch, and hear (Bruner, 1966; Piaget, 1965). They are much less able than adults to stand outside of themselves (decenter) and see their behavior as others see it or to appreciate somebody else's ways of viewing a situation. They perceive the logical world in unique ways, based also upon the perspective of their personal culture. As they classify their experiences, the decentering process is an occasion for growing self-awareness. The birth of a sibling is an example of growing self-awareness as a child perceives that he is no longer the youngest child (Merleau-Ponty, 1964).

It is important to note that the development of *metacognition*, an awareness of one's own thinking, is a gradual, dynamic process that includes intuitive functioning without self-awareness or with incomplete awareness (Piaget, 1976). Research based upon Vygotskian theory, however, suggests that social context influences insightful development and decentration (Lee, 1989). Sometimes young children who appear to function and act adequately in a familiar setting will contradict what they have done when asked to describe or explain their own actions or to direct others to do as they have done in an unfamiliar setting.

Metacognition progresses as we get feedback from our environments and experience cognitive dissonance. In early childhood, multiple mental models serve as part of the development toward metarepresentation that we can observe in children's pretend play (Perner, 1991). There has also been conjecture that improved metacognition can strengthen and develop the functions of the brain's left hemisphere, which deals with logical ways of knowing the world.

Imagery, by way of contrast, is the creative aspect of experience and the capacity of human beings to make connections. For young children, it is an early form of symbolic representation in such activities as sociodramatic play and personal analogy. There has been conjecture that the right hemisphere of the brain, dealing with metaphoric and aesthetic ways of knowing the world, can be developed and strengthened by experiences that are rich in imagery. The child's metacognitive processes interact with imagery processes, working together to solve problems, which is central to creative and critical thinking. They become coordinated through direct social experiences.

To attempt to "teach" young children these integrative skills separate from direct, concrete experiences is akin to trying to learn to ride a bicycle on a stationary exercycle. To use workbooks for these functions that develop naturally with healthy play is to be irrelevant.

As children begin to classify experience, it is possible that they will connect properties and variables in special ways that may be closed to adults as a result of acculturation. Where adults see a scientific phenomenon, a child might surrender to an aesthetic experience. During the ascendancy of this perceptual processing, young children are probably at the zenith of their absorbency, creativity, and flexibility in ordering the world. Losing this imagery diminishes an individual's humanness and range of action. A lost fact or abstraction can be found, but lost flexibility is probably beyond recuperation. Kindergarten teachers have a responsibility to help children maintain this flexibility of thought in a world marked by explosive change.

Social Interaction

A third way that kindergarten children learn well is through social interaction with other children. As they interact, children have the chance to observe the different ways that other children solve problems. They can also disagree and exchange conflicting points of view. These contrasts between the way they behave and how other children behave, and between what they want and what other children want, are important ways in which they experience cognitive dissonance.

While young children may have difficulty "conserving" quantity in mathematics, they learn about the perceptual model of *double bind* emotionally. They learn, for example, that others may mask hostility with a friendly exterior and deliver words of love through clenched teeth. They are socially "bound" to respond to the exterior expression, while experiencing the discrepant emotion. Children learn to "conserve" feelings in this sense before they learn to conserve quantity, as Vygotsky might predict.

Children also explore different ways of satisfying their wants and needs and have the chance to develop ethical alternatives, a uniquely human trait. The teacher's ability to plan activities and use unanticipated moments to explore ethical issues through skillful discussion techniques is pivotal.

Physical Experiences

Kindergarten children also learn well through physical experiences. When children move and manipulate the physical world, they begin to understand relationships between themselves and objects and between different objects. Concepts of space, time, change, causality, quantity, and, ultimately, quality develop first on a physical level. This is why physical knowledge has been a foundation for early science and mathematical study (Kamii & DeClark, 1984; Kamii & DeVries, 1978/1993), and it is certainly a central way of knowing and using the arts.

As children engage in large-muscle activities, they perceive in kinesthetic and aesthetic ways many images and concepts for which they will later develop language, other symbols, and logic. Moreover, by exploring space physically, children come to appreciate and be aware of their own bodies in new ways. Space is another medium in which they can feel successful and strengthen their self-concepts.

It is apparent that young children need to move, observe directly and closely, and manipulate materials most of the time. Teachers facilitate their learning by arranging for small groups to work together with sufficient opportunities for physical involvement.

Play

A fifth way that kindergarten children learn best is through play. When children play, they use their imaginations to try out perceptions and represent experiences. They can feel competent, powerful, and in control. If exploration is their attempt to see how things function, play is their way to find out what they can do (Hutt, 1976). When children play, their experience is "optimal" (Csikszentmihalyi & Csikszentmihalyi, 1988) in that their present-time satisfaction and focus transcends the moment.

It is through imaginative play that young children extend development and behave in advance of their years by subordinating themselves to rules, even flexible ones, thereby acting less impulsively (Vygotsky, 1978). During their sociodramatic play—leaving, planning, negotiating, and reentering the play frame—children demonstrate metacommunicative behavior and problem setting and solving that might be less accessible in a less social setting.

Through play, children integrate the rational and intuitive aspects of experience. It is a process by which young children achieve cognitive development by reconciling the aesthetic, physical, linguistic, and socioemotional means of learning. Thus play, a kind of lymphatic system of kaleidoscopic nourishment, is the ultimate integrator of experience.

Revisiting

The sixth way in which young children learn is by revisiting phenomena, because learning is not linear but recursive. While it is not possible to "go home again" in an identical way, young children reencounter situations a few days, weeks, or months later with fresh, sometimes new, enthusiasm. Their intervening experiences offer opportunities to develop new imagery networks.

Young children do not always share adult needs for closure. Their exploration, play, and learning tend to be episodic. There is evidence that their conceptual development and artwork can develop in fruitful ways by such revisiting (Edwards, Gandini, & Forman, 1993). At the same time, they are quite willing to repeat an activity that satisfies their sense of mastery. Self-motivated construction projects, writing activities, and solving puzzles attest to such practice.

Competence

The final way that kindergarten children learn best is through a sense of competency. Children feel able to risk themselves and to try new things when they can anticipate the possibility of success. They are willing to maintain or create tension both because they are curious and because they need to feel effective (White, 1959). They can feel satisfied by the process of being active, with or without a clear product.

When children create—and the teacher provides—activity ideas that they can do legitimately in divergent ways rather than only one way, there is a greater opportunity for children to feel competent. When there is only one possible way to do things or only one "correct" response, there is more likely to be competition, a sense of powerlessness, and added discord. When children perceive that others appreciate their efforts and views, they feel better about themselves and their school experience, conditions likely to support their capacity to behave in caring, cooperative, and civilized ways. They are more likely to become independent thinkers and to risk new learnings that have meaning.

Children who practice skills can feel more powerful if they can use concrete materials that have built-in self-correcting devices. When skills are integrated with meaningful activities, children have motives for practicing them in order to pursue their curiosity about meanings and a sense of competence. Skills are not ends in themselves. Skills are merely tools that serve the human needs to understand, create, and make friends.

REFLECTIONS

In order to provide an education in kindergarten that helps to develop caring, intelligent, cooperative, independent, curious, competent, responsible, ethical, and concerned human beings, successful kindergarten teachers have been taking into account these seven ways in which kindergarten children learn. They have considered the integration of knowledge, remained open to the ways that children construe their worlds, and helped children integrate skills with meaningful content in active, concrete, imaginative, and careful ways. Exemplary teachers have done so with sensitivity, warmth, intelligence, and good humor.

The full-day kindergarten, an outgrowth of societal changes, is an opportunity to reform kindergarten education and to continue the work begun by enlightened half-day kindergarten program developers. It challenges us to use the time in a coherent, distinctive way that reflects our contemporary understanding of knowledge as a social and contextual phenomenon that kindergarten children construct out of significant, direct experiences. In the next chapter we will discuss how to organize and manage a full-day kindergarten classroom that reflects the influences that have been considered in this chapter.

4

Organizing a Full-Day Kindergarten

This chapter focuses on how the exemplary classrooms referred to in Chapter 1 came to be organized, in light of the influences previously discussed. In order to understand these "decentralized" settings, it is useful to look at how teachers and children decide on their

Choices—what they will be doing
Space—where they will be engaged
Pacing—when they will be participating
Social activity—how and with whom they will interact

As we consider decisions about how to organize a coherent kindergarten year, it is important to keep in mind that classroom organization reflects what you value about individual children's commitments to meaning during the day.

CHOICES

Kindergarten children are quite capable of making relevant choices from among activities at home and school. Indeed, when any human being chooses to do something, her level of attention and commitment is likely to be much higher than if a choice were not available.

This is not to say that "anything goes." Clearly, the materials and activities that exist in a classroom have been largely preselected by you, the teacher, beforehand. You also have filtered the activities or materials that children have brought from home for use in school, after sharing criteria with families ahead of time.

There are also degrees of choice that children understand because they have become conventions in your classroom. A real choice is an informed choice, an activity to which children are receptive and that they can pursue at a level of challenge or possible success. For example, you might say, "These are the activities with which we can begin the work period":

- *What.* What would you like to do to start your day?
- *How many.* We can have four people at the science area water table. Who else would like to join Deb?
- *Now or later.* Alec, you had some writing to finish today. Would you like to begin with it now or do it later this morning?
- *Either/or.* Eden, you haven't been in the art center or in the socio-dramatic center for a while now. Please choose either one or the other.
- *Now.* Mel, we will be starting the day with a base-3 block game. You are ready for it now after doing so many games with base 2. (Even at the level of "now is the time," it is possible that if Mel had a pressing need to work in a different area, you could respect his plan and feelings and include him in a base-3 block game with another group at another specific time.)

Beginning with the first day of school, children have repeated practice in asking themselves the questions "What will I do when I finish this?" and "What will I do next?"

Where space in an area is limited, teachers use various signals to limit participation. They hang up a limited number of hooks on which children can place their photograph or nametags. Sometimes they post a number card with a specific number of marks so that a child who wants to enter an area can match the marks, one to one, against the number of children already there. Some teachers attempt to keep track of use of an area by having children place a mark next to their own name in the area or on a personal record sheet of areas.

As a rule, kindergarten children can carry on without continuous teacher supervision, but their responsible behavior earns them access to certain independent activities. For example, if you were unable to monitor the ongoing work, you would not send a child who has trouble sharing to the carpentry bench. When children are more self-directed and independent, then you have more opportunities to teach small groups and individuals. The most important support for this system takes place when you take the time to *circulate* before and after each brief instructional time in order to keep in touch with the entire class as individuals and small groups working together.

SPACE, INDEPENDENCE, AND RESPONSIBILITY

How you organize the space in your classroom communicates how independent and responsible you really want children to be. It also communicates what kinds of activities you value and how children will spend their time.

For example, if the chairs and tables are lined up in one direction facing a chalkboard, it would seem that children are expected to focus on the teacher at the chalkboard or the materials on their individual desks rather than on cooperative work with others. This placement also signals that a major activity will be to sit at assigned seats and work with paper and pencil for much of the day. Because this setup means that materials are placed in areas other than where they will be used, either traffic will be created when children need to acquire materials independently of the teacher or a monitor will have to be appointed to distribute materials to passive recipients.

Exemplary programs arrange space differently, so that materials are stored in the places where they will be used. This way, books are in a reading area, writing materials and children's individual writing notebooks are in a writing area, and art supplies are in an art area. Old newspapers are stored where potential messes are likely. Children work in the area where materials are stored. From time to time during the year, you could change the focus or size of one area or another in order to highlight new concepts/experiences or underutilized materials. Active work areas should be located at a distance from those parts of the room in which the children are expected to concentrate and reflect.

Keeping materials in the areas in which they are used means that the children can get them independently. The only time they would need to ask you for help might be when materials run low unexpectedly or when unanticipated events suggest the need for things that are not present. When everybody needs to get a jacket from the wardrobe at the end of the day, you might invite children "whose names begin with the same sound as Sam's" or those "who are wearing red" to get their clothing together. This practice cuts down on stampedes and traffic jams, as well as providing a gender-neutral way to address people (other than "boys and girls").

There would be no designated "front" to the classroom, just as there would be no assigned seats or tables. Children would store their personal materials in a number of ways other than in desks, such as in:

Cubbies
Clothing closets
Shopping bags hung from clothes hooks
Storage drawer cabinets

Shelves marked with children's names
Teacher-created "mailboxes" made of empty ice cream cylinders or
    large cans nailed together
Shirt boxes
Empty commercial tea containers

You can use a variety of furniture to create spatial divisions, nooks, and areas defined by functions. Low bookshelves, screens, and your desk placed perpendicular to the wall immediately create areas in which children can feel part of a smaller group, focus on a particular activity, or even find a place to be alone. Consider the design of a classroom as a variation on L-shaped arrangements or configurations resembling perpendicular E's (i.e., set base to back).

Creating areas for limited uses helps children to be more independent because it helps them answer the self-directing questions, "What will I do next?" and "Where will I put this when I finish?" A limited-use area should be labeled for everyone to see, such as "Art Studio" or "Cyclical Change Area" or "Science Lab" or "Writing." This also helps parents and other adults who enter the room to understand what is happening.

When you are establishing an area for limited purposes, it is useful to ask yourself what you would need to use if you were a child in that area. Writing materials, for example, should be available in more than one "writing" area. As we will discuss later, in addition to content, the needs for privacy, participation, and social activity are things to consider when placing furnishings and materials in your classroom.

One early childhood educator, Sheehy (1954), suggested that a good environment held "invitations to learning." Building from this image, you can be a legitimate merchandiser of significant activities. Some advertising techniques that you can use include:

- Creating an aesthetically attractive setting with such things as lighting, dried flowers, mirrors, draped fabric, or funny hats
- Contrasting a focal figure against an uncluttered ground
- Using redundancy of product image and name, including such means as different colors, print sizes, negative space, and the attaching of meaningful objects to a stuffed toy or driftwood
- Changing the packaging, name, or location of a product or a service, for example, from chemicals to "mystery powders," from a coffee can to a gift-wrapped box, from along the wall to a central location

Space should be comfortable as well as inviting. Since young children feel comfortable on the floor, you need to legitimize it for them. Arrange for the school, parents, or local businesses to provide mats or carpet remnants. Also consider having commercial carpet in the block-building area, in order to cut down on clatter. Other ways of making space inviting include providing a variety of seating arrangements beyond but including institutional chairs. Some classrooms include one or more soft armchairs or a couch that has been donated. Occasionally a small set of stairs for sprawling, a window seat, cushions, or a five-sided packing crate are present.

PACING AND ROUTINES

When children are engaged in different activities, or even when they are doing the same thing, you can expect that different children will need different amounts of time to finish their tasks. As you circulate throughout the classroom, you will notice who is nearly finished and who may need more materials, a more varied activity, or additional tasks. When you anticipate children's attention spans, you can help individuals or groups to replan for their next activity or for a new phase of the current activity. In this way, by modeling the need to replan or to break down a task into subparts, you also reinforce the children's independent involvement. For children who have problems with focus or who have special learning needs, you simply do this more frequently. For such children, initial planning might also include locating a space in which they can focus without distractions, such as a study carrel arrangement. When working near other children, these children need sufficient space in order to avoid unintended destruction and spills. Some children who have been labeled as having an "attention-deficit hyperactivity disorder" can benefit from such planning and monitoring. If you notice a few children who appear to be distracted or are distracting to others during group meetings, you might ponder whether the group meeting is too long or the content less than relevant. You can also plan separately for an alternative activity with an individual child before a large-group meeting.

During a full kindergarten day, there might be whole-group planning times at the beginning of the morning and afternoon, and perhaps a shorter gathering around 11:00. Then again, you will do frequent miniplanning with individuals and small groups throughout the day, as you circulate.

Successful full-day kindergarten teachers have found that it is critical to plan at least two long blocks of activity time each day during which children can engage in different degrees of choice and self-pacing. This encourages children to make longer-range plans and increases their relative sense of personal control. Some teachers begin such a time block with more sedentary activities and establish a signal, such as hoisting a flag or matching two pairs of clock hands, to show when larger-muscle areas, such as the sociodramatic area, are open.

Everyday Routines

Some of the activities in the full-day kindergarten classroom can be scheduled to occur at the same time each day, but others depend on the pace of groups or the needs of individual children. Successful teachers have found it best to anticipate these routine occurrences and develop strategies for handling them that are easily communicated to the children and minimize the demands on the teacher's attention.

Cleanup Time. From the first day of school, children can learn how to be responsible for replacing equipment or materials so that they can find them again and other people can use them. You can help build responsibility by suggesting that children repeatedly ask themselves the question, "Where will I put this when I finish with it?" One teacher modeled replacing materials during the first days and would permit only "very capable" helpers to assist, explaining the need for keeping the materials and equipment in place for the next users. Replacing materials became a prestigious activity. You might outline the places on shelves where blocks can fit and the places on pegboards for woodworking tools or musical instruments. Then cleanup time also becomes a matching activity. One teacher, noting a child's hesitancy at cleanup, focused on the positive and asked whether she planned to begin by replacing the larger or smaller blocks.

You can show consideration and respect for the children's need to concentrate by circulating with the reminder, "Finish what you are doing because it will be cleanup time in a few minutes," then following this with, "Now is the time to put away the materials." Remind those children first who have the biggest cleanup job and last of all those who have little more to do than finish reading a sentence. This way you are less likely to have children with little to clean up wandering aimlessly and getting into mischief.

This is also a good time to appreciate children's work and assess what help or instruction they may need. After most children have finished their work and before it is cleaned up, you can take a few moments for the whole group to focus on the different accomplishments of small groups and individuals, appreciating efforts and progress as well as results. You can encourage children who are less inclined to take risks to try new kinds of materials by having them see work in progress and projects in varying stages of completion.

Snack. Just as many teachers respect children's need to pace themselves differently when they engage in scholarly tasks, they respect different needs for food, privacy, rest, and toileting.

When it comes to snack, more and more full-day kindergarten teachers are setting out a snack table around midmorning. Often a few children prepare and set out the snack with the teacher, and they can take their snack when they need it, much as they would do at home. This practice eliminates the time spent in transition from an activity period and permits children to move at their own pace in finishing activities as well as in taking a snack. Since children learn this routine very quickly, there is not usually a problem of mass attack at the snack table. Children learn that it will be there for them as others vacate the chairs.

In those places where children bring a snack from home, consider listing for parents those foods that you recommend for their nutritional value, such as fruits, vegetables, cereals, and baked goods that are free of sugar and of artificial color and flavoring. Some teachers have asked parents to contribute a rotating set of specified raw materials from which some children can prepare their own nutritional snacks for the group.

Toileting. Toileting also should be self-directed rather than scheduled. At most, before beginning a story, the teacher might suggest that anybody needing to use the toilet do so before the story, in order not to miss a part or interrupt the attention of the group. Similarly, 5-year-olds should be encouraged to use the toilet before leaving on a trip outdoors.

Emergency Signal. There are times when you need the immediate attention of the entire group, especially when there is an emergency. When you have a shared signal, and use it only rarely, children are likely to respond right away.

In one setting, on the first day of school, the teacher shared an emergency signal with her children. This signal was used only rarely for such occasions as fire drills or special scheduling reminders. She said, "When you see my arms up or anybody else's arms up (as in the 'halt' position), then look to see where I am and raise your arms for others to see. I will use this signal only when we have to do something very important right away or when there is an emergency."

Raising both arms has the effect of stopping activity and producing a quieter atmosphere, and using a body signal eliminates the problem of trying to find a piano, bell, or light switch that may not always be at hand, such as when you are outdoors.

Schedule

The hours as well as the length of the full-day kindergarten need to be considered. In one school district, for example, the bus company dictated that the kindergarten should begin at 9:30 A.M. The teachers and principal protested because so many of the kindergarten children tend to wake up very early and already have been active for two or three hours before school begins. Then, by afternoon, they seem to need more time to be alone (Sheila Terens, personal communication, 1984). Although the bus company prevailed in this case, the school staff continued to appeal for the school day to start at 8:30 A.M. It makes sense to start the school day when children are most active and social and to send them home earlier.

It is also advisable to pace the day so that, after the initial activity period, more active choices are alternated with more sedentary ones. Teachers have observed that children are able to concentrate better after active play than after quiet activity. It is not wise to string several whole-group listening activities together any more than it is to overstimulate children with whole-group large-muscle activities one after another.

When you schedule long time blocks in which children can choose among varied activities, they will naturally develop the stimulation sequence that they need, just as Pat, one of our case examples in Chapter 1, did. Such scheduling can relieve the pressure you may have felt in the half-day kindergarten to "fit in" the varied program components while helping with boots and sweaters for two classes. The longer kindergarten day makes more relaxed scheduling practical, outdoors as well as indoors. Lunch, recreation, and rest and relaxation also need to be planned in consistent ways that sustain the wholesome pacing of activity throughout the day.

Lunch. Your school may either have food available for children at lunchtime or simply offer milk or juice for sale. It is important for someone to escort the children to lunch. During the first week of a full-day schedule, you might be the one to do this in order to provide a smooth transition. At the same time it is helpful if the regular lunchroom aide can come to the classroom ten minutes before the children leave for lunch in order to escort them. This should be sufficiently important to the principal and teachers in a school for them to find a way to make it happen, even though flexible scheduling and minor budget adjustments may seem daunting at first.

Consider also that, if your school was not built to accommodate kindergarten children in the lunchroom, you may need to check the height of the cafeteria counters to make sure that young children can see what food is available and to manage their trays (Joyce McGinn, personal communication, 1984). Also, cafeteria lunch service normally will take a bit longer for kindergarten children than for the general population.

An alternative to the cafeteria arrangement in any school is to have children take turns bringing and serving food family-style at their tables when lunch is available in the school. If children bring lunch from home, they might take turns serving milk or juice and setting the table, even if only with napkins. It is preferable for children to sit at smaller tables rather than at tables for 20 or so. This encourages conversation and a sense of belonging.

Recreation. Following lunch, and before rest, many schools have a recreational period in the schoolyard or gymnasium, depending on the weather. As each of the kindergarten children finishes lunch, it makes sense for them to have access to an area containing equipment that fits their size and is suited to their capacities.

Some schools have tricycles, climbing apparatus, and large hollow blocks available, both indoors and outdoors. A sandbox, a garden, balls, hoops, ropes, and other equipment for large-muscle use are also often provided. At one school, music for free-form dancing was played during indoor lunchtimes. Some interesting choreography resulted among a group of kindergarten boys and girls. In still another setting, from time to time the gym teacher or an aide would lead group games, ball-and-rope games, or "new games" (Fleuegelman, 1976).

When there is enough constructive activity available and several adults who can circulate, converse with children, and appreciate their efforts, children are likely to be constructive and civilized. It is worthwhile to teach lunchroom aides to use positively worded suggestions and instructions and to speak to nearby children rather than to those at a distance. If constructive activities are not present, children will seek stimulation with one another, sometimes in asocial ways.

It is worth asking yourself whether the children perceive that what they are doing during lunchtime is relevant and stimulating. If you find yourself in a school with a tradition of requiring children to stand in line for any length of time, consider finding another teacher ally who can help you plan and implement more appropriate alternatives. Then children can return to class ready to concentrate and focus their energies constructively. It is this sort of activity—wondering about what is happening and acting on your values—that makes you a professional.

Rest and Relaxation. Even though teachers and children find ways to pace themselves with ongoing active and sedentary pastimes during the full day, teachers find that it is important to plan ahead and pause for rest, relaxation, and quiet recreation. Let us look for a moment at 5-year-olds at home. After lunch, what do they usually do? It is unusual to find a 5-year-old taking a regular afternoon nap at home. With rare exceptions, most toddlers give up a regular afternoon nap between 2 and 4 years of age.

Consider also how a family deals with interage planning when there may be a baby, toddler, kindergarten child, and older children at home. Clearly, whoever needs a nap takes a nap. Whoever does not need a nap is either involved in independent activity, playing near an adult in the home, or doing things with an adult or another child. If somebody is taking a nap, the others at home would either move to another area or keep down the sound level or sudden noises in order to avoid waking the sleeper.

These observations may seem quite ordinary; nonetheless, teachers sometimes find themselves engaged in lengthy debates about rest time, naps, and discipline problems that arise during this time after lunch. In schools where caring people have thought about these matters, there is usually a flexible rest time. You, the teacher, also need time to yourself. In some settings, there is an area of the classroom where mats are placed for the occasional children who may have fallen asleep after the others have put away their mats. Often the rest time for full-day kindergarten children is about 20 minutes in duration.

In the Lawrence (New York) Early Childhood Center, children lie on their mats in a dimmed room and listen to recorded music. One week might be Mr. Mozart's week, and the next might be Mr. Beethoven's. You can see children lying down, sometimes with a stuffed toy, listening and keeping time to the music. In other schools, children might sit or lie reading a book, playing quiet board or card games with one other child, or working on a puzzle.

Different individuals have different needs for quiet and privacy, so provisions should be made for meeting these needs throughout much of the day.

PRIVACY, PARTICIPATION, AND SOCIAL ACTIVITY

The school setting is, at best, contrived. Because of this, it is especially important that you carefully consider providing for private experiences as well as for social participation in the full-day kindergarten.

Human beings' need for privacy some of the time and social participation at other times is a personal one. A child at home with one or two siblings often has a favorite place to be alone. Whether this is in an armchair, in a space behind a couch, underneath a table, or in a bathroom, it is important that it is there.

Kindergarten children have created privacy spaces under a table or by building walls with "big books." In your kindergarten, too, consider how to create places where a child can feel alone when he or she feels the need. Montessori encouraged children to retire to a mat, taking with them something to learn from, a signal to others that they were working alone. Other teachers have used

Crannies in the reading area
Carrels (sometimes created by cartons) facing a wall
A listening center with earphones, facing a divider
A pup tent or tepee in the classroom
A carpet square under a table
A cushion in a corner
A blanket-lined packing crate

Teachers discuss with the group the courtesies of privacy for individuals who are using these or similar facilities.

In quite as conscious a way, you will need to plan for social interaction that is constructive and for activities that lend themselves naturally to cooperative work. Learning, after all, is strengthened by social interaction (Piaget, 1965, 1976).

Spontaneous social interaction creates opportunities for repetition of ideas and techniques that children need to learn. Indeed, the oral repetition for children that takes place in cooperative learning situations increases information storage and extends memory (Johnson, Johnson, Holubec, & Roy, 1984; Slavin, 1992). Teachers in exemplary full-day kindergartens plan for significant, independent, small-group learning opportunities.

There are also a number of occasions during the school day when participation in whole-group activity is reasonable. Periodic planning periods for the whole group already have been mentioned. Among other occasions for the whole group to be together are:

Story time, at least once each day
Celebrations
Specal resources (e.g., a film) or visitors
Discussions of group-process issues
Plays and performances
Music and movement education
Sports
Sharing work
Lunch
Rest time

In some classrooms, snack time is a whole-group activity, with the teacher participating in conversations. In other classrooms, as noted above, snack is a flexible time for small groups and the teacher to meet and help themselves at a natural break time.

You will find additional ways of providing for privacy, participation, and cooperative work throughout this book.

REFLECTIONS

A professional teacher in the full-day kindergarten spends the majority of time instructing small groups and individuals and circulating among groups. In well-organized, effective classrooms, teachers spend more time on instruction and less time on procedural distractions (S. Barnes & Edwards, 1984).

If you are working with an aide, you should explain your organizational purposes, plan together, and review events, sharing observations of children. In order to foster complementary work between adults, it helps to decide on territory to cover and responsibilities to perform. During an activity period, you might ask the other adult to work in a single area in particular ways or circulate so that you can focus on one area. During a whole-group story, you might ask him or her to sit beside specific children who need help in focusing.

Looking at your current program, consider reducing the number of transitions between shorter time blocks and increasing the duration of fewer, longer time blocks. If the first hour of the day is a whole-group activity, then analyze how you might increase the time for integrated small-group and individual activities, while reducing the whole-group time at the day's start. In general, how might you reduce whole-group and increase small-group and individual pastimes? At the same time, reduce the number of single-subject occasions, while increasing the integrated use of time blocks. Also, consider what new learning-area focus you might add. What area might you enlarge? reduce? furlough? retire? revisit?

Organization and content blend to create the quality of learning experiences that children have in school. Creating a focus on learning areas/centers begins on the first day of school with a few areas, to which you gradually add in the succeeding days and weeks. Such provisions can help your children to become more independent and responsible within the classroom organization. In these ways, you provide a forum in which to create a caring and secure community. As you circulate—essential to establishing independent child activity—among these areas during the first month or two of the school year, you will have numerous contacts with each child. You can assess what they can do, how they interact, and what help they need. You then will be in a good position to plan systematically for activities in which you can work more intensively with small groups for up to 10 or 15 minutes at a time before circulating again. In the chapters that follow, there are numerous activities that you can use in the full-day kindergarten organization that has been presented here.

PART II

The Interactive Content of the Full-Day Kindergarten

5

The Social Study
of Social Sciences

This chapter looks at how children can learn about their social world in ways that promote understanding, cooperation, and caring. The chapter opens with a discussion of the significance of sociodramatic activity as a major social learning medium and tool in the kindergarten. The remainder of the chapter is devoted to an analysis of three other approaches to learning about social life: interdisciplinary perspectives on the ways of knowing in several social science disciplines, the interdisciplinary approach of multicultural education, and the extradisciplinary approach of the perceptual model, cyclical change.

The multiple ways of knowing about history, geography, economics, sociology, and political socialization occur as a transaction within the context of each young child's extradisciplinary potentials for perceiving unpredictable connections. Activities are highlighted that reflect these processes and the interdisciplinary connections they suggest.

Next we examine two other approaches that include learning about the social studies. The first takes a look at the unique area of multicultural education. The second discusses another perspective, the perceptual model of *cyclical change*. We will see how it can be used to integrate knowledge and activities across and outside of disciplines, thereby bringing great breadth to the social study of social science.

Before we begin, it is worthwhile to note that there is considerable controversy concerning schools' engagement in social study. There are neoconservative political constituencies who oppose the study of diverse lifestyles and the consideration of viewpoints other than their own. There are others who suggest that the study of fact-based history and geography would be sufficient. (This is based on the assumption that scholars can agree on the social "facts" of these interpretive domains.) At the same time, it is apparent that neither education for citizenship nor education for community concern and justice is served by the trivialization inherent in ritual activities and empty forms in the name of social studies curriculum. Still another viewpoint suggests that neither young children's imaginative and passionate commitments to learning, nor the purposes of multicultural education, are served by the "expanding horizons" curriculum currently institutionalized in early education classes: "By putting the self, the family, the neighborhood, the country at the beginning, we assert these as the norms and the paradigms by which other places, times, experiences are to be considered meaningful or valuable" (Roldão & Egan, n.d., p. 12). As you read in this chapter about the perspectives offered, you will have an opportunity to consider your own options against the background of these broader debates about social studies.

THE SOCIODRAMATIC AREA

Sociodramatic activity is a valuable, legitimate medium that helps kindergarten children develop in a variety of ways. By engaging in imaginative play with others, children come to appreciate that other human beings have feelings and ideas that may be the same as or different from their own. When they represent themselves, however incompletely, in other roles, children are mapping relationships and working out personal moves and alternatives for which mathematical sociologists might produce complex matrices. Children are experiencing through social, emotional, aesthetic, linguistic, and physical dimensions what eventually will become cognitive awarenesses, as they continue to weave new connections.

As in all human interaction, "reversible thinking" begins to grow as children come to recognize the legitimacy and possible relevance of other persons' views and feelings. Children, originally centering their perceptions on their own views, strengthen their perceptions of others as they continue the process of decentering through negotiating sociodramatic activity.

In this respect, fantasy and imagination play important parts in extending cognitive development. Fantasy and imagery are early forms of symbolic representation that begin children's progress in interpreting and using humanity's full range of symbolic forms, such as written language, mathematics, and the arts. There is plenty of research that confirms the importance of sociodramatic play in the development of social competence, language, associative fluency, and cognitive development (Fromberg, 1992). Beyond these expectations concerning development, however, play itself is worthwhile activity for young children. Through playing, children can build the self-esteem that comes from a sense of power, learn more about being part of a caring community, and encounter the aesthetic impact of a transcendent experience. (See also Chapters 2 and 3.)

Setting Up an Egalitarian Sociodramatic Area

Children come to school with a "background" of experiences, the event knowledge on which they can build imaginative social plays. You as a teacher bring to the children provisions for extending these experiences by introducing tangential activities, new "figures" that children might perceive and use. You can focus attention on social studies by creating a defined space for sociodramatic activities. It is worthwhile to ask why you might choose to provide certain equipment and materials and then consider how they could be used.

The equipment and materials in a sociodramatic area can serve various functions for children in today's world. Sociodramatic play has traditionally been invested with the major task of supporting the incidental learning of young children. Some adults have narrowly defined this learning in terms of bits of factual accretions and conversational skills; however, there are further-reaching implications for such experiences.

When teachers talk about starting to provide instruction for children at their developmental levels, there is a tendency to refer unquestioningly to the here-and-now experience of children. This appears on the surface to be a reasonable principle; however, as we discussed in Chapter 3, the here-and-now of today's young child has changed dramatically since Lucy Sprague Mitchell (1921) coined the term, and it continues to change. Judging from the material provisions given in many schools, we might conclude that there has been only the barest recognition given to these changes. For example, while not all kindergartens today provide for a sociodramatic area, the housekeeping corner and the block corner, when they are present, are relatively stable and predictable as unquestioned assumptions. Yet a closer look will tell us that children's play in the housekeeping corner tends to reflect their relatively specific base of experience in some specific sort of home. By contrast, their experience base in construction activities, which is reflected in block-corner play, is relatively unspecific. It is axiomatic that that which is specific provides clearly convergent guidelines for its use, whereas that which is unspecific suggests more divergent interpretation.

With the changing roles of women and men in our society, especially in relation to each other and their work, the traditional housekeeping corner and block corner appear to be at best contradictions and at worst repressive tutors. When we look at children's play in these areas, it is apparent that sex-role stereotyping often is present. It is mainly boys who play with the blocks and girls who play at housekeeping. Although there is visiting between areas from time to time as part of the play, and an occasional girl will venture into building or an occasional boy into parenting, the larger picture remains segregated.

Research shows that children's language in the housekeeping area is severely restricted (Cazden, 1971). It may be that the rituals and routines are sufficiently repetitious and limit expanded possibilities, especially when the same children repeatedly meet one another. The very furnishings, being highly specific, appear to sustain traditional images and close off one of the major purposes of early education—the maintenance of openness to new connections and alternative possibilities. In contrast, block play, building with nonspecific materials, promotes symbolic representation, divergent imagery, and comfort with spatial relationships. Girls are willing to play with blocks, particularly when the teacher is present. Boys are more likely to reject typical housekeeping tasks. Researchers corroborate that traditionally female roles already have been categorized as less desirable in the early years (Maccoby & Jacklin, 1974).

This is not a surprising finding when you review the popular cultural images of women and men, strongly communicated by television, books, and adults who are the repository of generations of shaping. Women are usually presented as people who have passive, convergent, and trivial pastimes, while men have active, divergent, and creatively adventurous pastimes. Indeed, observers have found that teachers tend to perpetuate these images by complimenting girls on their appearance and boys on their achievement (Leipzig, 1992). Very early, therefore, teachers need actively to avoid the subtle ceilings that are placed on the aspirations of girls as well as on members of other groups who have been culturally mistreated or underrepresented. When school experience affects aspiration levels, it also touches the very marrow of an individual's self-concept and general feelings of success.

There is a growing redefinition of the role of women in the family and in the larger community. This reflects an increasing commitment to preventing the establishment of a caste system within a society that intends to be democratic. With this in mind, consider the possibility that a large investment in a separate housekeeping center, filled with specific equipment, is unjustified. Particularly now, when school districts are doubling the numbers of classrooms as they move from half-days to full days in the kindergarten, there are reasons for spending limited funds in ways that reflect modern values.

The sociodramatic area provides an excellent alternative to the housekeeping or doll corner. In it, there would be a place for a variety of dolls, nonspecific at-home symbols, and blocks, alongside puppets, props representing retail shops, hospitals, other community experiences, and travel opportunities that empower children to include and move beyond a limited piece of here-and-now experience. By including and extending dramatic play beyond housekeeping, all children may comfortably participate.

Activities in the Sociodramatic Area

At different times in different classrooms, kindergarten children engage in a range of sociodramatic play other than housekeeping. A look at these varied activities suggests several sorts of provisions for socialization. Children play at varied forms of traveling and moving materials; visiting community and imaginary sites; engaging in different occupations; becoming other persons, animals, or objects; expressing feelings; and resolving moral issues.

Children play not only at going and coming, but also at arriving at, participating in, and maintaining the environments that they have created. As they do so, they plan, negotiate, disagree, set and solve problems, celebrate, nurture, reward, and punish one another. These encounters provide a lens through which you can observe and assess their language, concerns, cultural gestures, and perspectives. The children also display power in humorous ways as they act out television commercials and substitute their own frequently uncomplimentary words and phrases. In addition to playing with the sounds of words themselves, children are displaying skepticism about propaganda and advertisements that seems to grow more readily when they have had contacts with older role models. Therefore, consider planning for inter-age projects, keeping in mind that for kindergarten children, activity is often episodic in that there may or may not be a clearly defined beginning or ending.

Props. The following things serve children as props in their sociodramatic play:

- Puppet frame, purchased or made out of a cardboard carton; puppets
- Wooden screen
- Two-dimensional facade of a wheeled vehicle
- Floor blocks and other blocks used as dishes, foods, nonstandard measures, microphones, tickets, weapons, splints, gems, and furnishings for different interior and outdoor settings
- Cut-out board "television" screen
- Wooden or cardboard cartons of varying sizes used as a lake, vehicle, hospital bed, coffin, suitcase, or tray
- Ropes and strings

- Real and toy telephones
- Variety of caps, hats, belts, badges, buttons, ribbons, vests, boots, shoes, scarves, and other articles of clothing for costumes, including possibilities for representing international clothing
- Sticks, twigs, broom handles, and rubber or plastic piping, used as a magic wand, stethoscope, fire hose, fishing pole, sword, saw, axe, sceptre, or orchestra conductor's baton
- Disembodied wheel taken from a broken toy or shopping cart, made from a circle of cardboard, or commercially purchased
- Pulley system with ropes and boxes or baskets that extend across a section of the room

In addition to these imaginative uses of everyday objects, children can use commercial toys such as miniature trucks, cars, airplanes, animals, dolls, and wooden people. Be aware if you include wooden people that there are those that suggest careers. Ideally, these should represent both men and women of different ages and different ethnicities in an equitable way. Literacy materials also have a place in sociodramatic play. A hairdresser's shop, for example, can use pencils, a price chart, an appointment book, appointment cards, business cards, receipts, books and magazines to read while waiting, and a telephone. An airport needs signs, posters, tickets and boarding passes to write, brochures, and advertisements. A hospital needs signs for visiting hours, patient charts, medical insurance forms, prescriptions, menus, appointment cards, and so forth. (See Christie, 1991, for additional ideas.)

Be careful about overstocking to the point of inhibiting activity or movement. Sometimes less material can lead to more imagination. One kind of screen or frame can serve as a retail store, a ticket booth, and a cashier's counter. You may find puppetry and a supermarket too much to handle in the same space, or you may find a way to fit in both activities. How many options and when you make them available are important administrative decisions that you can discuss with the children.

Puppet Play. Provision for puppet play is an important element in a sociodramatic area. Hidden behind the puppet character, more reticent individuals can enter the stream of social interaction. Kindergarten children can use puppets (or masks) that they have made alongside or instead of commercial puppets. They have made puppets from some of the following materials:

Paper bags
Oaktag or paper plates stapled to sticks

Styrofoam balls with buttons held on by pins
Stuffed toys with capes draped over them
Stuffed stockings
Balloon "heads"
Woodwork constructions
Papier-mâché

As children experience the security of hiding behind the puppet, they can save face when the puppet is reprimanded. An entire commercial "self-concept" kit (Dinkmeyer & Dinkmeyer, 1982) uses puppets as a major vehicle for discussing socialization issues. When children use puppets, their voices change. Stutterers will occasionally speak more fluently. Children often identify comfortably with the puppet character.

Puppets alone do not create dialogue; they are only a vehicle for dialogue. Children need ideas and a positive focus in order to use puppets in a constructive way. While ideas will come from their experiences, they will need your help from time to time if puppetry is to develop beyond a punching show or peek-a-boo humor. You can help by addressing the puppet directly.

Flannel Board. A flannel board with felt forms to manipulate is a variant of puppet play. Children can act out their fantasies, reproduce parts of stories that they have heard, or alter sequences of stories. *The Very Hungry Caterpillar* (Carle, 1970), embodying *cyclical change*, and other simple cumulative tales are easily adapted and seem perfect for this medium. You might provide some uncut felt from which children could construct their own characters or props. Inasmuch as a certain amount of cutting, sewing, and possibly gluing could be part of these activities, the flannel board should be near a crafts shelf.

Blocks. Large floor blocks are stored in the sociodramatic area as an integral part of that area and its activities. When this is done, various props and costumes, which may increase verbal interaction, can be integrated with the block play, and boys and girls are more likely to work together. In this way, all the children can build skills in spatial relationships. (The uses of blocks are discussed also in Chapter 7.)

Other Playthings. Such materials as Lego, Tinkertoys, and Erector Sets should be nearby. It is easier to manage and retrieve the many pieces of these toys when children use a cloth mat on which they can play with each of the sets. Most kindergarten children prefer to use these materials on the floor. Each set can be stored with its own mat.

These toys can be used by two or three children at a time, or by an individual, together with floor blocks, miniature animals, or other figures. The toys can also be used to make representations of figures and miniature furniture. As long as their purposes have a constructive focus, the children's new associations should be encouraged and appreciated.

From time to time, children may want to include the class guinea pig in the sociodramatic area. As they create mazes with blocks, they set and solve a variety of problems. The mazes then become an opportunity to observe the directions the guinea pig takes as well as to measure how long it takes to travel (Althouse, 1988). They can also construct and use their own electric circuitry to light the puppetry area and other projects. When science materials are nearby, children may come to see new relationships and divergent ways of using materials.

Symbolic Representations. Children's writing and other expressive forms often grow out of sociodramatic projects. Children welcome labels and picture symbols on their constructions and projects. They have created shopping lists, receipts, and tickets.

Sometimes children feel impelled to repeat their episodic play, at which times it becomes ritualized. The play then lends itself to written records, audiotaping, and photographed records. Teachers and children can "save" cooperative constructions by photographing and drawing them. Saving children's work in these ways signals to them and their parents that you appreciate and value their cooperative ventures.

Outdoors and Indoors. In the full-day kindergarten, teachers schedule a balance between classroom activity and the large-muscle activities that are possible outdoors or in a gymnasium. These latter areas are outfitted with such things as large hollow blocks, a climbing apparatus, and tricycles. Sometimes there are tunnels, huge parachutes, inflated trampolines, ropes, pulleys, balls, large wagons, and hoops, all of which are useful and enjoyable equipment.

The outdoors and the gymnasium are important socialization resources. When packing crates, real discarded boats, automobile tires, hollow blocks, and wagons are available, the sociodramatic activities continue. Most important, outdoors or in the gymnasium, activities can be much louder and larger in scope. While facilities vary, it is particularly helpful when there is an easy flow between indoors and outdoors.

The Teacher's Role in the Sociodramatic Area

Researchers have shown that teachers can intervene successfully in children's sociodramatic play without unduly influencing its content (Smilansky, 1968; Smilansky & Shefatya, 1990). A combination of the teacher's help in learning play techniques and the children's direct, school-enriched experiences is demonstrably more effective than one or the other alone. Smilansky observed that the early childhood teachers she studied initially resisted intervening in children's sociodramatic play. Although the same teachers felt comfortable in stimulating their own offsprings' play at home, their philosophical preparation for teaching inhibited such activity with the children in their schools. The contention that "creative imagination" improves with stimulation and experience (Piaget, 1951/1962, p. 289) is in harmony with Smilansky's findings. Modeling and supporting cooperative and problem-solving social interaction are far better than a laissez-faire atmosphere or training children to say the "right" thing.

Experienced teachers circulate in the sociodramatic area in unobtrusive ways to help children extend the imaginative possibilities of their play. As they do so, they assure that children retain the power to choose their own paths. Among other things, they:

Engage in episodic role playing with children
Raise questions about alternative social solutions
Stimulate questions and contrasts that grow from aesthetic, mathematical, or scientific perspectives
Introduce vocabulary
Bring together children who need one another
Appreciate cooperative efforts
Provide "verbal harmony," describing and narrating children's engagement as it occurs

In these ways, teachers provide social, cognitive, and material support, as detailed further in the discussion below.

Add a Material. When an activity has been well developed, perhaps repeated, it may be useful for the teacher to add a material to help extend the activity. Teachers also can add signs such as "stop," "no parking," or "gas station," or they can supply play money, bags, boxes, string, a box marked "cash register," and even writing and drawing materials.

Remove a Material. Occasionally it makes sense to remove a material from the activity, such as when children ignore the presence of a thermometer or have had access to the cardboard television screen for more than a month. If it is relevant to bring back a material after a few weeks or months, the children often perceive it in a fresh light and create new adventures. Sometimes the removal of a particular doll, truck, or wagon can be synonymous with the removal of a conflict. It may help an individual who is fixated to move on and try other materials.

When you remove or move one or more items, you may create needed space into which children can expand other activities or in which they may see other equipment in fresh ways. When you change the number of children permitted in an area, the activity may improve because there are more opportunities available.

Redirect or Add an Idea. You might redirect or add an idea by a direct suggestion, such as, "Try to find out what happens if you add more beans to the bag" or "How can you make a train of people on the slide?" Children might find a new direction through a well-timed question: "What other way could you go?" "How could they solve their problem without hitting?" "What things about a person make you want to be her friend?" Distressed by violent "superhero" play, one kindergarten teacher (Paley, 1984) struggled with ways to redirect it and found that one way was to take the highly aggressive fantasy and accept it by postponing it, with the children's cooperation, to a later group role-playing time. Then she could supervise the activity, first by inviting children's oral dictation as she wrote on an experience chart, and then with role playing. This combination of composing and role playing with teacher involvement generated fluidity and elaboration.

Step into a Role. You can also elect to step into a role during sociodramatic activity in order to extend the action or expand language. You can suggest a problem to be resolved by adding comments such as the following:

"Uh-oh, I see a truck coming."
"Look out, the hose is about to break."
"How many centimeters is that?"
"That dog looks so ill, he might need hospitalization."
"I just lost my watch, and it's floating all over our space vehicle. How might we retrieve it?"

In addition, you can take a role in order to avert stereotypical actions.

Bring Children Together. Another significant way in which you can intervene in children's social activity is to bring children together. You can encourage a child to join an activity by focusing on a task to be done: "They need your help in order to attach the hook." You can suggest that a group invite another player: "This store seems to need a cashier as well as salespersons and stock clerks. George looks as if he's just finished painting. Perhaps he would want to make change." If you notice that three children are ready for more stimulation after some individual, sedentary activity, you could suggest directly that they work together at the flannel board or with the puppets they have made.

While you may be anxious to enrich children's experiences through social activity, it is also important to respect children's right to privacy as well as to recognize individual styles of working. In addition, the intrinsic structure of some activities suggests that they are pursued best in a solitary area.

Experienced teachers respect the developmental significance of parallel play, when children may use materials side by side with other children. Children have a chance not only to concentrate, focus their energies, pace themselves, and extend their scholarly skills but also to observe others as alternate models. It is only when the same child persists in an exclusive pattern that you need to intervene. You might bring other children to sit near him and share the materials or develop activities that require cooperative effort. Rocking boats, extra-long clay rollers that need more than one person to operate them, and various games and surveys lend themselves to joint efforts. With predictably bendable rules, kindergarten children can play checkers and some chess. They can take turns jumping rope.

In short, you can find many ways to bring children together in the sociodramatic center, to give them a balance of experiences. The sections that follow discuss additional active ways of working with children to enrich their social knowledge.

INTERDISCIPLINARY CONCEPTIONS AND WAYS OF KNOWING SOCIAL SCIENCES

From whichever avenue you enter the social studies, it is essential that meaningful social experiences remain the destination. One direction that you can take is to approach social studies through the ways of knowing in several social science disciplines.

It is the contention throughout this book that children construct a strong base of information, knowledge, attitudes, skills, and social wisdom when they are directly and actively involved in an interactive environment. Teachers observe children, plan with them, bring activities to them, and expose them to new phenomena. Both children and teachers are active participants who can influence what takes place.

When teachers maintain the social dimension in children's studies of their world, they help children to approach new situations with an appropriately tentative attitude. Our approach to the five social sciences discussed in this section focuses on the multiple ways of working that can help kindergarten children increase their understanding of the social sciences in both active and imaginative ways that encourage connection making.

Understanding History Through the Interpretation of Events

Historians agree that a tentative attitude is basic to their interpretation of past and current events (Genovese, 1974; Meyerhoff, 1959). It is important for students to approach history with the understanding that alternative interpretations are valuable. As kindergarten children grow in their ability to decenter themselves, it is easier for them to appreciate shifting perspectives.

Whenever possible, it is important that children use original sources on which to build their own interpretations. Original sources include photographs, artwork and artifacts, oral histories, and diaries that can be read to them. Other independent views can be contrasted through discussions. Activities such as those in Figure 5.1 encourage diverse interpretations of as well as critical thinking about history.

There are many ways in which individuals can order and interpret human experience. These personal constructions are as concrete in their way as are block buildings that children construct, and they ultimately influence children's social interaction. When children hear or see how others have handled situations, they may follow these models. By focusing upon the process of interpreting events and practicing the ways of working used by historians, young children have the opportunity to be active in ways that are compatible with their development.

Understanding Geography Through Mapping

If the interpretation of events is a tool for studying history, mapping is a tool for studying geography. Just as the use of tools that are physical instruments suggests active uses, so do various ways of working in a discipline suggest active ways of learning more about it. In this section we will focus on the human aspects of geography, and we will see how mapping and other activities lead toward an understanding of the interdependence of human beings and their environments. (Additional related activities are found in the later section on multicultural education.)

For those tools that require skill in symbolizing, kindergarten children need different kinds of practice from that used for tools that are extensions of the hand. Maps are such symbolic representations that can extend the understanding of young children, but they need systematic help

FIGURE 5.1: Activities to Promote Critical Thinking

- Read to the children different biographies about the same person, such as books about Mary McLeod Bethune by Anderson (1976) and by M. M. Greenfield (1977).
- Have children dictate or tape record their own biographies and compare them.
- Read stories written by different authors on the same topics, such as new babies or friends.
- Present more than one edition of a particular story or tell a story from the point of view of a different character (Cullinan, Karrer, & Pillar, 1981/1993).
- Listen to different singers render the same song, for example, "City of New Orleans," by Steve Goodman, sung by Judy Collins, Arlo Guthrie, and Willie Nelson. Discuss why different children vote for or rank the selections differently.
- Poll children about a presidential election or other controversial event.
- Use pictures, puppets, or flannel-board figures that interact in ways suggesting varied interpretations.
- Role play different interpretations of values-based pictures (Shaftel & Shaftel, 1967/1983).
- View several brief motion pictures that show varied human patterns of life.
- Use a diorama with figures that move in relation to it (Lavatelli, 1970). These materials involve changing perspectives and promote the beginnings of reversible thinking.
- View different photographs of the same subject, then draw about, write about, tape record, or personally photograph similar subjects and discuss their different renderings.
- Elicit analogies and compare the different outcomes. (See discussions later in this chapter and in Chapter 2 for other uses of analogy.)
- Highlight the multiple interpretations of driftwood, artforms, mystery boxes, and incomplete data.

in learning to use these tools and inquiry skills. We will use as an example a discussion that was observed in a kindergarten classroom[1] as children greeted a visitor from India:

> TEACHER: Do you know where this visitor comes from?
> CHILDREN: Yes! India!
> TEACHER: How did you know?
> CHILD 1: My grandmother lived in India for a long time. (To visitor) Did you know her?

DR. D: I don't think so.

TEACHER: Let's find the place where she came from. (Brings globe to the group; Dr. D shows children the place in India from which she came.)

TEACHER: (Pointing) What does the blue mean?

CHILDREN: Water.

TEACHER: What does the green mean?

CHILDREN: Land.

TEACHER: How do you suppose Dr. D came all the way here? What might she have used?

CHILD 1: Maybe she came by boat.

TEACHER: You think that's possible? Let's see. (They trace some alternate routes.)

CHILD 2: Maybe she came by car.

TEACHER: Let's see if she could really come by car. (Children note water part of the globe.) Let's ask her how she came.

DR. D: By airplane.

CHILDREN: I was on an airplane. . . . Me too. . . . I went. . . . (Sharing experiences.)

TEACHER: She could have come around this way, moving east, or the other way, moving west. Let's find out which way she came. (Dr. D points out the route.)

CHILDREN: How long did it take you?

It is clear that these children have acquired some beginning understanding of and skills in using the globe. First let us imagine the steps they may have taken in acquiring the knowledge they do have. Then let us use the gaps in the children's thinking to suggest the next steps they might take.

PREPARATORY ACTIVITIES

Beginning geography activities can include the following:

Sorting by Color, Size, and Shape. At first, children can try sorting objects of two contrasting colors into two separate boxes; then they can sort by shape or size. Each single variable becomes a new "figure" that is contrasted against a known "background." This prepares children to understand how color, size, and shape are used symbolically in maps.

Imagery Building. Objects can be placed in boxes and bags so the children can feel but not see them. One property at a time can be added gradually as the children get better at projecting their imaginations toward the unseen. In addition to building toward mapping landforms, this sensory play is a step in building toward future conceptions of unseen phenomena such as atoms.

Creating Physical Representations. Children enjoy bringing home a map of their own hand, outlined with crayon on paper or impressed into plaster of Paris attached to a paper plate. They are fascinated by watching their friends' silhouettes become larger and smaller shadows as the teacher moves a light nearer and farther away. They can be asked to decide whether they want a tiny silhouette, a real-sized image, or a giant-sized image of themselves.

These activities build a foundation for the concept of scale in architecture and mapmaking. Children's play with pegs and peg-city accessories, miniature animals, dolls of varying sizes, play houses, wooden puzzles, Playskool Village, Lego, Lincoln Logs, Tinkertoys, and large building blocks also contributes toward this development of the concept of scale. The teacher can take photographs of children, or they can bring their own from home. When they use a series of pictures in various sizes, they also are strengthening their concept of relative scale.

An especially enjoyable representational activity is to offer each child the opportunity to lie down on the back of a large sheet of discarded wallpaper and have her or his body outlined by another child and the teacher. Then, according to ability, each child can "map" the terrain within her or his own boundaries, using large felt-tipped pens, yarn, and other textured materials. For some children, this may be one of the first times that they have started an activity on one day and completed it over the next few days.

Children can be shown a "rough-smooth" globe that differentiates land and water, such as the Nystrom "Readiness Globe" (1991, #33-47). When they then compare it to a colored globe, they translate tactile experience to the visual sense.

Matching Objects and Patterns. The teacher can set out a box of colored cubes and cards with square patterns that are the same colors. The cards progress from simple patterns using a few colored squares to complex patterns using many colored squares. The children place each cube on the corresponding square on the card. After some practice, children can construct the patterns of cubes directly on a cloth and use the cards as a reference. A similar activity sequence can take place with pattern blocks. (Using a ring binder helps to keep the cards in sequence.)

Exploring Spatial Relations Through Body Movement. Children can explore different spaces and directions with their bodies as the teacher accompanies them on a drum. The children can use hoops, boxes, furniture, ropes, and a wire-and-cloth tunnel as accessories to the exploration.

Obstacle courses that use these kinds of props, in addition to interspersed low balance beams in a circular pattern, also support the development of visual-spatial concepts for children in general as well as for those who have special learning needs (Kranowitz, 1992). A cooperative game that adds to this growing sense of space is "Turtle," in which a blanket serves as the shell that covers several children who need to move together collaboratively in order to keep everyone covered (Ramsey, 1987; Orlick, 1978; see also Chapter 8).

Learning About Landforms. In one class, some of the children traveled with their teacher to collect possible collage materials outdoors in the autumn, and they had a long discussion about reaching some seed pods across a small stream. After discussing alternate ways of crossing and ruling out a log that looked too brittle, they walked to a small wooden bridge. They talked about its construction and other bridges they had seen. One child mentioned a tunnel he had been through that had a toll like some bridges. The next day the teacher set out in the library corner mounted pictures of bridges and various views of tunnels, from her own collection, and related picture books.

Telling Stories. This interest in bridges and tunnels was not pure happenstance. The teacher had planned in advance to stimulate the stream-crossing discussion as part of a collage the class was making about outdoor activity in the fall. She was delighted with the various connections children made as well as with their large and small block representations and dramatizations.

Other books that the teacher read to the children that year included McCloskey's *Blueberries for Sal* (1948/1968) and *One Morning in Maine* (1952). These stories are about the hilly terrain and style of life on an island, as well as about wholesome family relationships. *Rosie's Walk* (Hutchins, 1968), Jonas's (1983) Escher-like illustrations in *Round Trip, Bayberry Bluff* (Lent, 1987), about an island's growth from tents to a town, and Burton's (1942/1988) representation of *cyclical change* as *The Little House* becomes transformed from a rural into an urban setting and then back again, provided alternative perspectives of spatial relationships. She also read them MacDonald's (1971) *The Little Island,* a story of a cat's aloneness experienced as a purely existential moment.

NEXT STEPS

Once children have engaged in preparatory mapping activities, they can go on to more complex matters. Ongoing activities for the kindergarten children in our example would include the following:

Classifying. Each child in a small group places a sheet of paper on the ground in areas such as a construction site, beach, business street, and grassy plot. They can note what was under their pieces of paper and collect samples in separate bags. When they return to school, they compare notes, and the teacher can record their findings on a large pad of paper. Throughout the several weeks during which these data are collected in different locales, the teacher can read the children such books as Clark's (1962) *The Desert People,* Credle's (1934) *Down Down the Mountain,* Lipkind and Mordvinoff's (1962) *Russet and the Two Reds,* and Tresselt's (1968) *I Saw the Sea Come In.* Later on, children may enjoy matching objects to photographs of locales in which they might have been found.

Mapping Family Trees. Many of the children can "map" their family trees during the latter part of the year, using invented spelling or copying the labels for such family members as mother, brother, stepfather, and uncle. Teachers need to be sensitive to, and appreciative of, the diverse family constellations that children represent. Books such as *All Kinds of Families* (Simon, 1976), depicting various family constellations, and *Living in Two Worlds* (Rosenberg, 1986), dealing with biracial children and ethnic diversity, are among a growing list of relevant books.

Seriating. The children can continue to play out increasingly numerous seriations with pictures and generic objects, as well as with such toys as nested eggs or dolls. Children who have sorted two objects by size then go on to order three and more. Chapter 7 provides examples.

Creating Physical Representations and Exploring Spatial Relations. Children continue their use of blocks and woodworking materials in increasingly complex ways. Some teachers report 5-year-olds using blocks and other materials to represent and dramatize their firsthand study of harbors (Imhoff, 1959; Mitchell, 1934; Spodek, 1962). Other related concrete activities include dioramas, sandbox play, and work with clay.

The Elementary Science Study's (1974a) Color Cubes are used with colored loops to extend children's concepts of spatial relations. They learn to develop and plan towns as they use these materials, and some have experienced great pleasure when they have set their own rules for building and then asked other children and adults to guess their rules. (For example, one rule was that only houses of a different color from the loop may be built within the area of the loop.)

Our sample class was fortunate to have a mobile three-dimensional model of the planets available for observation and manipulation. While the concept of ordinary earth-bound space grows slowly, this kind of concrete exposure merely adds a referent for the children. Problem solving in space can be extended by the use of three-dimensional wood puzzles and mazes.

Imagery Building. The teacher can help children to project their thinking by using picture matrices, such as those suggested by Lavatelli (1970), and block matrices, such as those suggested by Elementary Science Study (1974a), by using Color Cubes. Through the year, children can progress to the use of six-by-six matrices. For example, the teacher can set out alternating color, size, or shape patterns, or their combinations. Small groups of children or individuals can play various games with the matrices. "What's Missing?" is one such game; another involves reversing two elements and finding which ones have been reversed.

In still another variation of matrices, children set problems for each other and the teacher. It is intellectually and personally valuable for children to set problems for adults to solve. Using task cards that have stick-figure/picture directions made by their teacher, children can create designs on geoboards. (Geoboards, made in various shapes, are boards with pegs in varied patterns.) They may also work in pairs, back to back, and take turns describing actions and comparing the patterns that result. These comparisons can become moments of cognitive dissonance. When children have repeated experiences with concrete and pictorial systems, they strengthen their ability to deal with varied symbolic systems.

Using Maps. As skills grow, the children can build approximate outline maps of their room and set simple problems for others to solve. The children's tasks will vary in complexity as different pairs of children set out to find a missing item or a hidden object, using pictorial "treasure map" instructions.

Exploring Directionality and Relative Thinking. During the kindergarten year, children can refine their own left and right orientation skills in functional ways, including body movement games. The classroom walls can be labeled "north," "south," "east," and "west," and the teacher can use these terms regularly.

When children practice setting the table for special occasions such as an "international harvest dinner of foods from A to Z," they can discuss the spatial relations among the utensils. Consider also taking account of cultural differences in placing utensils.

Learning About Landforms. In the class above, during the week that the visitor from India came, the teacher hung some strikingly colorful aerial photographs of varied terrains, islands, and locales. She also set out some maps near the globe.

These activities represent integrated ways of planning possible sequences that offer increasingly complex pastimes. They embody the contention in this book that we need to plan in ways that encourage individual children to make their own connections and to value the increased diversity among children that is likely to result.

Understanding Economics and Sociology
Through the Concept of Interdependence

By viewing economics as the study of scarcity, the disparity between what we want and the resources available to fulfill these wants, we can see that people are placed into relationships with one another and their environments. Sociology as the study of human groups focuses on the relationships involved in group behavior.

Scarcity enters into sociology in terms of personal needs, just as scarcity exists in economics in terms of material needs. Since the concept of interdependence is common to both disciplines, they are treated together here. Some relevant activities for the kindergarten are presented in the following sections. They have in common some ways of working in economics and sociology—among them the use of contrasts and descriptions that sometimes lend themselves to surveys.

Going on a Field Trip. "Engineered" visits to local construction sites touch on many issues relating to interdependence. Teachers can ask the construction workers of different cultural backgrounds and different gender to bring family photographs and possibly pictures of trips, athletic events, or other outings with friends. In this way, children can see the varied group memberships of the construction workers.

Children also can observe the workers' dependence upon one another for hoisting, dumping, building, signaling, and measuring. With repeated visits, children are able to see the progress (*cyclical change*) of the building and hear about such problems as plumbers finishing in time for the painters to begin. The contributions of each worker to the whole project also embody the process of *synergy*.

Telling Stories. In one classroom, kindergarten children heard the story *Benjie on His Own* by Lexau (1970). They wondered about how their lives would be different if they were a member of a different family in which their nurturant grandmother had become hospitalized.

The issue of scarcity emerges from the book *A Chair for My Mother* (V. B. Williams, 1982), in which a hardworking single urban parent saves for a chair, symbolizing renewal, after help from neighbors. In *Grandma's Joy* (E. Greenfield, 1980), scarcity of funds stands in contrast to the plenitude of nurturance.

Contrasting Data. The interdependence of people and their environments and the influence of locale on employment, social opportunities, and group interactions may be understood best when children can perceive a contrast with their own experience. You can help invert children's sense of reality by asking how their lives might be different if they lived in a house rather than an apartment, or on a farm rather than in the city. You can help them to find answers to these questions and to raise their own questions by gathering lots of contrasting data. Visiting community sites, meeting people, seeing films, contrasting books, listening to recordings, and building their own models and representations are among relevant experiences for kindergarten children. Kindergarten children, for example, have planned questions and interviewed each school employee and school board member, then categorized their functions. The answers they found by contrasting these experiences, rather than by memorizing bodies of verbal information, are likely to remain more closely connected with their lives.

Learning about economic concepts includes learning certain conventions about money, exchange of goods and services, and the nature of producers, distributors, and consumers. These learnings take place as children have repeated opportunities to observe contrasts, compare events, validate, and revise their thinking. Researchers have noted that young children believe that receiving change and going to the bank are ways to acquire money, without connecting the systems of employment and compensation or sales and profit (Berti & Bombi, 1988). The implication for teaching young children, for example, is not to focus on technical description of the "facts" about "community helpers," but to see their employment from social (economic and sociological) perspectives, in terms of their meaning to users of their services—for example, "What would happen if their services were not available? How might our lives be different? How might we have education, medical care, transportation, protection, merchandise, and so forth?"—and in terms of where payments go and how they are used. Teaching situations and questions are most effective when they create cognitive dissonance, which can help children to question perceptions. Being in the presence of older children also helps to generate cognitive dissonance. It is also worth noting that different sociocultural settings offer more transparency or opacity to these learnings. Consider, for example, the street children of India or urban children in the United States, whose exposure to economic exchanges makes the transactions more transparent and easier to observe.

In a similar manner, children learn language inductively (see Chapter 9) and build understandings about living communities. They can compare a series of aquarium or terrarium containers that are influenced by different conditions. Although such comparison studies typically fit into "science," it is apparent that designing a meaningful curriculum with children builds on their capacity to make connections that are based on shared, underlying imagery, beyond traditional subject-matter boundaries.

Using Induction. Inductive learning can take place when you carefully provide clear contrasts. Children have a chance to perceive a new "figure" because it appears in contrast with a known "background." Such figures wear different "costumes" in relation to the different questions and purposes of the activities.

For example, when a group observes the supermarket receiving a delivery of produce from a truck, they also acquire background information for comparing marketing patterns in a book or film of an Asian community that uses water transportation. Their observations may lead to a study of the food chain, economic comparisons, or the interactions between people and their environments.

As long as children have many samples of direct data, they can extend their thinking inductively. These connections take place over time. Children need time and the opportunity to leave and return to data so that the bits of experience can be fully absorbed. Kindergarten children build toward an understanding of economics and sociology as they engage in a variety of activities that reflect the concept of interdependence. Some of these activities also represent the particular perceptual models of *indirect progress, dialectical activity, cyclical change,* and *synergy* (see Figure 3.2), as they intersect with economic and sociological concerns. Sample activities are presented in the next two sections.

Appreciating Indirect Progress. Economic policy decisions frequently reflect short-range sacrifices in favor of longer-range progress, much as do playing strategies in checkers or chess. Children learn to sacrifice a playing piece in order to gain a better position. In addition, they become increasingly proficient in considering alternate moves.

Many other games that children play provide practice in indirect progress, a perceptual model. The extended exposure to indirect progress in varied forms provides children with a stronger network of associations and ways of knowing than if they had only a single way to view economic sacrifices. For example, "Tangrams," detailed in Chapter 7, is a classic game that entails the breaking of set expectations. "Knock Hockey" is a large-muscle game that uses triangulated action as children knock a disc of wood against the sides of the board in order to bypass obstructions. Three-dimensional wood puzzles also require planning several steps ahead. Many 5-year-olds are able to play these games.

When children save together for a common purpose, rather than immediately consuming their property, they are collaborating to exchange short-term for long-term benefits. Sales of baked goods, potholders, needlework, and wood crafts are some activities that can encourage longer-range planning.

Cooperation Among the Parts. Cooperation among the parts underlies a good deal of economic and social life. In economics, effective mass production requires cooperation among people. One group of kindergartners compared their assembly line of Easter baskets to individual production and were able to see how the joint effort was more productive (Robison & Spodek, 1965). The books *Chicken Sunday* (Polacco, 1992) and *Jamaica-Tag-Along* (Havill, 1989) tacitly integrate cooperation among children of different ethnicities.

The study of family life illuminates cooperation, and kindergarten children have engaged in the following studies of families, among others:

Different roles and functions within each child's own family
Different kinds of families
Families in different cultures
Different climatic conditions and terrains and how they support family life and survival in different ways

Films, stories, pictures, trips, and visitors add data with which children can build contrasting views of alternative ways in which human groups live and work with each other. Through these resources, families at a distance in time and space become a kind of here-and-now experience.

Dramatic play and more focused simulations occur when children role play with props. This is another way to expose children to synergy from a social standpoint. As children identify with their roles and the problems that their characters face, their sensitivities to other people can deepen. In these ways, children also can deal with feelings and values.

Understanding Political Socialization as the Result of Imagination

Political action is an outgrowth of values. There is agreement among educators, psychologists, and political scientists that political awareness grows with self-awareness, which in turn grows through socialization processes and cognitive development (Hess, 1968; Hess & Torney, 1967; Lasswell, 1958; May, 1972; Peters, 1967; Sorauf, 1965). While conceptual awareness of political phenomena does not become measurable until after the early childhood years, it has its roots in these years.

The child's family, peer group, school, and community relations provide initial exposures to the core of politics, which is power and its use. Laws and rules, authority figures, political leaders, and government institutions are among the forms through which children may perceive the uses of power.

Social forms precede cognitive forms in learning about power relationships. Children directly experience rules and limitations as "given" and behavior as "good" or "bad," depending on whether or not it conforms to the rules. We would expect kindergarten children to have difficulty separating an individual authority figure from that person's institutional role (Hess & Torney, 1967). As children mature, the idealization of adult political figures gives way to the notion of fallibility. It is this very distinction between appearance and reality that teachers can help children to perceive in the kindergarten.

The "double bind," which is part of the *dialectical* perceptual model (see Figure 3.2) in which appearance and reality contravene one another, includes politics and also takes many forms outside politics. Through many concrete experiences and their accompanying verbal exchanges, children participate in the long process of distinguishing between intent and action, between the officeholder and the office. This understanding, and critical thinking in general, grows when one engages in discussions that welcome different views and when one has experiences in which first appearances prove to be inadequate, including activities that promote cognitive dissonance.

Children need to work in an atmosphere where varied suggestions are aired and attempted; where they are encouraged to predict, guess, set problems, and try alternative routes to solving problems. Teachers add to this learning when they comment on children's intentions and express appreciation for their motives.

The main focus of political education in the kindergarten is action rather than knowledge, emotional attachments, or attitudes for their own sake. Kindergarten children can engage in a variety of activities that help build their political skills, as described below.

Sense of Power. One school that houses all the K–4 children in the community has successfully used inter-age student advisory councils that include kindergarten children (Raywid & Shaheen, 1983). The governance is based upon Kohlberg's "just community" concept and focuses on "civic ethics" and "fairness." Leaders or class officers need to have responsibilities, which the group and the teacher work out together and respect. In your classroom, voting for the kinds of games or materials to order, the place to visit first on a trip, whether to go outdoors or to continue an exciting indoor activity, or what theme will dominate a party may be a way for children to develop a further sense of what "majority rule" means. The dialectical model of power also is present in books for children such as *Borreguita and the Coyote* (Aardema, 1991), in which children can identify with the power of intellect over threat.

Sense of Reality. You can ask, "What might happen if there were no police (governor, judge) in a particular situation?" "What might happen if we selected a president in a different way?" This sort of dialectical questioning can provide contrasts that sharpen children's understanding of conditions as they actually exist. Looking at pictures of candidates during the presidential election, young children have had discussions concerning such questions as the following: "If you could talk to the president, what might you tell him? If you were president, what might you do to make the country a better place to live? What do you think might be some good/bad things about being president? In what ways might you help the president make our town a cleaner, healthier place? What do you think a woman president might do differently?" (Glenn Perigaut, personal communication, 1992).

When children see scenes of war and violence on television, they need help in relation to their own experiences with aggression. Urban children, for example, sometimes have heard gunshots or had neighbors shot, and they need a safe environment in which to discuss their concerns and fears. Children can consider ways to resolve ordinary disagreements with alternative means, such as collaborative rule setting, restitution, talking, grab bags, and contests. Such discussions become a dynamic, meaningful part of children's lives, quite different from a static show-and-tell format for "current events."

Sense of Efficacy. Children need to build a sense of efficacy in relation to government. If they see things that concern them, such as graffiti, they can dictate a letter to the mayor and offer advice concerning ways of coping with it. When such a letter draws an answer from an elected official, children have a chance to feel effective. Sending petitions to the principal or school lunch director are other possible activities.

Critical Thinking. Kindergarten children often put together images from adult concerns that come to them on the level of mythology, and in this way they pick up a good deal about political matters. They notice major adult elections as they look at television and hear adults repeating the same names and issues. Parents add to this mass of imagery when they bring their children to polling places each year and arrange for them to watch the voting process. Teachers add to these experiences when they talk with children about the names of candidates, political parties, and the kinds of issues that are present. Children certainly have asked about war, nuclear bombs, and pollution.

Some activities that help children to perceive varied points of view and forms in which human beings organize their experiences include the critical-thinking activities in Figure 5.1 above. Children can also discuss practices in their community that reflect career aspirations, sex-role stereotypes, and minority-group roles. To do holidays justice from a political and critical perspective, consider asking children to consider the viewpoints of the Native Americans whose homesites and belongings were appropriated by Europeans. Young children understand about having, holding, and wanting. Begin such study with the children's direct social experiences. Planning to use the perceptual model of *dialectical activity* as apprehended through varied activities, such as those suggested here and in subsequent chapters, can assist in the growth of critical thinking.

MULTICULTURAL EDUCATION AS SOCIAL RECONSTRUCTION: A UNIQUE INTERDISCIPLINARY APPROACH

Each of us prefers to believe that we are egalitarian and fair. Because of the society and times in which we grew up, however, various attitudes, values, and expectations have come to control us without our having as much awareness of them as we might like. As teachers, we need to make a particular effort to become conscious of our values and to move beyond consciousness to action. If we were to ignore differences, in the light of predominating human similarities, then we might silence the development of a proactive program while tacitly accepting the status quo (Aiken, Anderson, Dinnerstein, Lensink, & MacCorquodale, 1988). Multicultural education provides us with a perfect opportunity for nudging along the process of social reconstruction.

As we consider in this section the possibilities for multicultural education as an interdisciplinary approach to social studies, we must do so with the understanding that this is a relatively new area in education. This means that the knowledge base for multicultural studies is still very much in its infancy and that teachers may be learning almost as much as the children they are teaching, not simply in the area of factual information but also in the understanding of the meaning and working of culture in human lives. It is simultaneously a body of knowledge, attitudes, and behavioral strategies. As a body of knowledge, it resembles a synoptic discipline; as a combination of applied attitudes and behavioral strategies, it cuts across disciplines.

Under the umbrella of multicultural education are many areas for concern, drawn from history, geography, sociology, economics, anthropology, and the arts. We need to keep in mind that these disciplines already reflect existing cultural biases and our reference to them needs to remain tentative and critical. Some programs include attitudes, values, and skills in living with other people. Specific concerns involve cultural pluralism, global education, career education, and preventing or undoing stereotypes about culture, ethnicity, gender, age, and disability. A central purpose of multicultural education is to foster understanding of the diversity of human groups and to cultivate appreciation for the uniqueness of each person as well as the needs that all human beings share. Moving beyond such understandings and appreciations, beyond verbalisms or empty forms, some advocates call for education that includes "social reconstruction" and positive action to eradicate divisive and discriminatory systemic practices such as tracking and standardized testing (Banks, 1993; Sleeter & Grant, 1987). Seen in this way, another central purpose of multicultural education is to bring about inclusionary practices while helping children adapt to a variety of social situations and settings.

When teachers plan activities, it is worthwhile to distinguish between the surface and the deeper structures of a culture. Educators suggest that we differentiate among the three levels: "what" things are visible in a culture, "how" members of the culture behave, and "why" their values direct their behavior (Williams, De Gaetano, Harrington, & Sutherland, 1985). Too often, schools have offered activities primarily in the "what" area, with attention paid occasionally to "how"; "why" is frequently neglected altogether. While kindergarten children inferentially understand the values level of "why," it is important for teachers to consider that the variety of human behavior within a given culture is a function of the values that people display when they choose to respond to, ignore, praise, or sanction a given action. Teachers who provide activities that display contrasts and look at issues and events from different ethnic, cultural, or gender perspectives may help children to appreciate deeper values.

It is important to expose young children to the variety among cultures only after they have taken part in activities that reveal some of the human commonalities among cultures. When teachers use relative rather than absolute language, such exposure takes on more profound meaning. For example, instead of suggesting that all people from Hispanic cultures share an extended kinship structure that includes godparents, or that all elderly people retire from useful work, Morris (1983) suggests that it makes sense to use terms such as *some* or *many*.

In order to help kindergarten children sort the similarities and differences between other cultures and categories of people, we need to provide activities that begin with a data base that they can relate to their own experiences. This is why many kindergartens engage in a study called "Myself." Some components of self-study that children can engage in are presented in Figure 5.2.

FIGURE 5.2: Activities for Self-Study

Self-portraits. Children can create framed self-portraits early and late in the
school year. Other children dictate narratives of nice things about each child.

Map. Children collaborate by outlining each other's bodies on paper and then
each one fills in his or her map with paint and/or collage materials.

Timeline. Children can choose to use drawings/photographs to create a timeline
of major events in their lives.

Birth Weight. Children compare a bag filled with sand equal to their birth weight
with one equal to their present weight (Seefeldt, 1993).

Surveys. Children, using nonstandard measures and then standard measures,
survey body parts such as height, arm length, hand span, and so forth. They
can use a sticker to chart each lost tooth. They can survey family sizes,
defined as people who live in the child's house, or survey different generations.

Board Game. Children can play a teacher-made board game that includes
photographs relating to one child or several children in the classroom (adapted from Williams, De Gaetano, Harrington, & Sutherland, 1985).

Personal Book. Children can create a book about themselves, sometimes with
one or more photographs or drawings of themselves and their family.

Idea Books. Children can create a book of their favorite things, things they hate,
and funny or frightening dreams, using illustrations and/or collages. (When
using magazines and catalogs, include those that represent diverse ethnicities,
cultures, and physical challenges.)

Future Collages. Children can create collages representing "What I want to be"
or "wishes." Expect that children with different cultural roots may have
different orientations to the future.

Family Tree. Children can draw an individual family tree.

Immigration Map. Help children to decorate an immigration map of the world,
with personal markers indicating the locations from which families came.
This map is nice to have at a family breakfast for which children participate
in preparations. Parents and other relatives can attend. A related activity can
be an immigration museum consisting of family keepsakes from other times
and places, such as a foreign passport, citizenship papers, old photographs, a
special spoon, a pair of chopsticks or bowl, and even a braid of hair. Native
American children, whose sociopolitical history includes enforced migration,
have much to offer.

Immigration Quilt. Children can contribute drawings on squares of muslin or
oaktag to the formation of an immigration quilt.

When children have considered the roles and functions of members of their own families, such as their family customs and the ways in which their families celebrate holidays, they can compare other families and cultures. Photographs of families in different parts of the world—including physically challenged family members—and of children in other environments who are engaged in activities of daily life can form the basis for contrasts and commonalities that generate discussion questions. Here are some examples:

- How does a new baby change the culture of the home?
- Where do people sleep? On what do they sleep? When do they sleep? For how long do they sleep? (Adapted from Muessig & Rogers, 1965, p. 87.)
- What are some things that all people need besides sleep?
- What might be the same in your life if you were to need crutches/ were hard of hearing/were legally blind, and so forth?
- What are the different ways that people find shelter? serve food? celebrate holidays? dress?
- What are some different head coverings? (See Williams et al., 1985, pp. 77–78, and Grant, 1977, p. 160, for head-wrapping ideas.) (Making hats, as well as using hats that represent different cultures and occupations in sociodramatic play, is a popular kindergarten activity. Wonder together about the variety of forms.)
- What titles can we create for these photographs? (Arrange for pairs of children to create titles and then share them. Cognitive dissonance can take place as children compare the different results.)

Many kindergartens provide for a variety of music, songs, dances, and games that originate in different cultures and in different languages. Children can be encouraged to taste and categorize foods from different regions. They can celebrate a variety of holidays, taking into account the context and traditions of holiday practices as well as the surface symbols. Looking at the social significance of such events helps to avoid what some have called a "tourist" curriculum (Derman-Sparks & the ABC Task Force, 1989).

Patricia Ramsey (1987) offers a five-strand planning framework for multicultural education that teachers have found to be helpful in analyzing their current practices and adapting them to provide multicultural experiences. The framework includes consideration for

- *The physical setting*—providing representative books, illustrations, photographs, toys with authentic features, egalitarian work roles, features of culturally diverse dwellings and household utensils, and inclusive of dark colors as aesthetically valuable

- *Holidays without the "holiday syndrome"*—focusing on the underlying connections in celebrations that are cross-culturally seasonal or significant commemorations of human events
- *Construction of physical knowledge*—demonstrating relationships between people and their different natural environments, including activities that all share, such as systems for eating, heating, washing, sheltering, and engaging in artistic pursuits
- *Understanding of self and others*—building self-esteem, cooperation, autonomy in moral decisions, social responsibility, and concern for others through challenging stereotypes and perspective taking in games and other activities
- *Multilingual issues*—encouraging families to use the at-home language to build concepts, while teachers learn the families' key phrases and amenities for sharing at school, thus valuing diversity while extending English-language learning at school.

These kinds of multicultural provisions come into play constantly throughout the school year because young children often acquire multicultural information, attitudes, values, and skills that reappear in their daily lives. You can support critical thinking by highlighting aspects of children's exposures, by contrasting and comparing, and by helping children to classify data without the pressure to produce a single "correct" answer.

Countering Sex-Role Stereotypes

Critical thinking about gender equity can be encouraged as teachers ask children to compare characters in books who are having adventures, helping or being helped, rescuing or being rescued. Books such as *Mommies at Work* (Merriam, 1961/1989) offer alternatives to stereotypical activities, as does *William's Doll* (Zolotow, 1972), in which a boy engages in sports activities but also wants to nurture a doll, justified as a preparation for "fatherhood." There are numerous biographies of scientist Marie Curie and Underground Railroad conductor Harriet Tubman that also provide opportunities for children to compare how different authors present their subjects.

In addition to identifying and compensating for the "missing pages" in books, teachers also need to be conscious of the more subtle presence of their own reactions to children's expressions of aggression. Women teachers, in particular, are the repository of society's constraints upon women's assertiveness, an attitude that is beginning to change, due in part to research findings and in part to economic and political developments. While some researchers have found that boys tend to be more aggressive than girls and receive more scolding and restraints from teachers (Maccoby & Jacklin, 1974), others have found that boys also receive more attention than girls (Serbin, 1978).

In order to encourage all children's desire to explore and be creative, to be independent and assertive, as a teacher you should notice and communicate your appreciation of these characteristics in girls as well as boys. Researchers have found that teachers who give only directions and favorable comments to girls may encourage conformity to less adventurous behavior (Fagot, 1975; Lieberman, 1977; Paley, 1984). There are techniques, however, that teachers have used to reverse these unintended outcomes. For example, both girls and boys changed their sex-role perceptions after only six weeks of an intensive intervention curriculum that emphasized career opportunities for girls and that contradicted stereotypes about job roles (Guttentag, 1978).

Avoid excessive use of gender as a category. Children can get their jackets from the wardrobe by color of clothing, birthday month, or many other characteristics besides gender. Analyze how many times you use "boys and girls" to address children. Good alternatives to words that are gender-specific include such terms as *everybody, people, class, thinkers,* and *friends.* Instead of "Atta boy/girl," use "Thoughtful job," "That's progress," and "You're really thinking/concentrating."

Increasingly, materials for children have become egalitarian and gender-neutral. Consider the hidden or missing messages in books you read to children. Be sure that career opportunities for all children are kept open and that assertiveness and adventures are depicted equally as possibilities for girls and boys. We want to enlarge children's great expectations for their lives while they are in the kindergarten.

Countering Racial Prejudices

There is agreement among many researchers that children's self-concepts develop parallel to their understanding of language (Clark & Clark, 1939; Goodman, 1964). In our society, black children learn to perceive themselves as black somewhere between 3 and 6 years of age (Clark & Clark, 1939). Children who are not black are believed to perceive these differences around age 4 (Goodman, 1964).

Sociologists have found situations where the "lower-class parent aligns himself with the child against the teacher on grounds of class antagonism" (Davis & Dollard, 1940, p. 42). They also learned that the child often "finds that neither his parents nor his teachers expect a person in his social position to go far in school" (p. 286). You might substitute the terms *race* or *ethnicity* for *social position,* with some degree of accuracy. In turn, these attitudes can be used as an excuse for nonachievement (Horney, 1939). Children need educational role models, available through literature and resource visitors as well as through your caring for and highlighting the unique contributions of each child in the group.

Although children of color come from a variety of economic and cultural backgrounds, many of them have experienced economic hardship. And teachers' perceptions of all racial backgrounds need examination. It does not do for us to dilute or deny differences; on the contrary, they must be accepted and appreciated. Otherwise, "if an individual has low personal self-esteem, he may project this onto his racial group" (Porter, 1971, p. 183). There is no substitute for a sense of competence and acceptance. You might engage in direct discussions or intervene in discussing feelings and expletives. You might provide varied colors of crayon, paint, or Band-Aids that reflect the range of flesh colors (Derman-Sparks, 1992). Whatever provisions you make, it is important that they be integrated into the social life of the school throughout the year rather than telescoped into "Brotherhood Week," Martin Luther King's birthday, or Native American Day.

Attending to Bilingual and Bicultural Children

The bilingual and bicultural child may feel particularly isolated in school. Current programs are attempting to support the retention of cultural heritage, notably in parts of the country where there are relatively large Spanish-speaking, Native American, or Asian-American communities.

Controversy around the bilingual aspects of educational programs reflects a collision between the "melting pot" and the "pluralistic" views of the mission that society assigns to schools. Current public funding for subject matter instruction in the child's at-home language, alongside instruction in English-language skills, is a break from the tradition of the melting pot; pluralistic approaches in the past had been privately funded.

Bilingual education can strengthen children's self-concepts as they see themselves progress in meaningful subject-matter areas in their own native language while simultaneously acquiring English language skills. Kindergarten children seem to be quite adept at functioning with two languages and often acquire a second language within the school year.

You can ease the problem of code switching for children who come from different cultures by building in divergent language materials. The "language experience" and "process" writing approaches base initial writing-into-reading upon the children's own spoken language structure or dialect. Therefore children do not face the problem of translating the syntax of typical printed material. Bilingual and bidialectal children have a greater chance to feel competent and successful with this kind of material.

Teachers who work with children from bilingual and/or bicultural homes also need to consider children's assumptions and expectations about social behavior. Some Native American children, for example, initially may feel more comfortable observing demonstrations and working in cooperative rather than competitive ways, while retaining a sense of privacy in relation to the group (Little Soldier, 1992; Locke, 1978; Teacher Corps, n.d.). It helps when you smile, slow down, listen, do not expect small talk or "thank you/pardon me," and show respect. Some Native American as well as Asian or Latino children may show respect by avoiding direct eye contact or not questioning an adult.

There are hundreds of distinct Native American communities with varied ways of life and belief. It is important to keep in mind that we need to counteract media stereotypes by helping children meet contemporary Native Americans—directly or through literature and other media—who live in modern houses, hold jobs, go to schools and supermarkets, and so forth. Consider the contradiction of advocating for a here-and-now curriculum while providing isolated, decontextualized historical and stereotyped symbols of some Native Americans and European Pilgrims. We can do better by providing socially and personally meaningful celebrations of harvest festivals from around the world as well as the North American Thanksgiving. Consider incorporating the study of, among others, the mid-September harvest festivals in China and Ghana, the Jewish Sukkot, Canada's Thanksgiving, World Food Day, and Norway's Potato Day in October (Spiegelman, 1966). Kwanzaa, an African harvest festival, is often celebrated in the United States in December. For young children, the meanings are more important than the dates (Ramsey, 1987).

You initially will need to engender trust in order to encourage involvement of bilingual/bicultural families. In addition to serving as resources of knowledge, skills, and modeling, family members can serve as storytellers and translators as well as contributors to, and participants in, educational celebrations, fairs, and meetings. Teachers have asked parents to teach them what the parents teach their children at home about such phenomena as kinship structures, immigration stories, legends and myths, and ways to categorize materials. Then teachers can help children relate their at-home learnings to the perspectives of their new societal context.

Using Inclusionary Materials, Language, and Practices

It is useful to analyze books, toys, and other materials in order to provide educational experiences that avoid racism, sexism, ageism, and handicapism. Select literature and pictures that include images of physically challenged people. Children also need direct and indirect contact with thoughtful, verbal people who may be in a wheelchair or who may be elderly yet lead productive, sensitive, and caring lives. Career models and role models need to be available that show all genders and a range of ages, abilities, pigmentations, and cultural backgrounds.

Consider developing a bulletin board montage of elderly people who are working or have just discovered new talents (Grant, 1977). Other displays might include people who have a disability and work at interesting careers or women and men in nontraditional careers.

There is a growing movement to include children with certain disabilities within mainstream classrooms. Before a child with special needs enters a class, it is important to provide orientation programs for teachers as well as for the other children. Part of the orientation should focus on ways to welcome, include, and accommodate to the mainstreamed child. Another part of the orientation should include specific preparation that can help you anticipate the possible needs for curricular adaptation and material, physical, and social provisioning. Many of the suggestions for curriculum development throughout this book provide an adaptive, flexible, and appreciative stance in relation to human variability. Chapters 2 and 4 offer specific organizational and interactive suggestions. In addition, the succinct suggestions in Figure 5.3 offer an overview of curricular accommodations for working with children who have varied disabilities. Such neat presentations notwithstanding, we need to keep in mind that each child will present a unique profile of behaviors, needs, experiences, and strengths.

Sociodramatic play is the ultimate integrator of children with special needs as well as children with other diverse experiences. Through play, children negotiate the dynamic themes that are based on their event knowledge, drawn from their distinct multicultural contexts. They collaboratively represent their experiences in an oral form of play writing and learn to communicate with others as they learn from each other. In these ways, sociodramatic play is a multicultural form of representation.

CYCLICAL CHANGE: A PERCEPTUAL MODEL/DYNAMIC THEME APPROACH

The holidays and seasons form part of the common cultural experience of kindergarten children across the country. The weather is another apparently safe topic in the universal culture with which schools deal. I propose that both the culture-free, competition-free universal attention to the

FIGURE 5.3: Accommodating Children with Disabilities

Language delay
- Expand on what child says; talk about what you are doing; model the correct usage and pronunciation instead of correcting.
- Provide frequent visual or concrete reinforcement.
- Keep directions simple; encourage child to repeat them for reinforcement.
- Explain new concepts or vocabulary.

Attention problems
- Start with short group sessions and activities.
- Provide visual clues (e.g., define floor space with tape).
- Offer a limited number of choices.
- Provide positive reinforcement for sustained attention.
- Help child quiet down after vigorous play.
- Plan for transition times, including arrival and departure.

Developmental delays and learning disabilities
- Allow for extra demonstrations and practice sessions.
- Keep all directions simple, sequenced, and organized.
- Offer extra help in developing fine and gross motor skills, if needed.

Emotional/social problems
- Provide extra structure by limiting toys and defining physical space for activities.
- Allow shy child to observe group activities until ready to participate.
- Help aggressive child control behavior through consistent enforcement of rules.
- Observe dramatic play for important clues about feelings and concerns.
- Help child learn how to express feelings in appropriate ways.

Mental retardation
- Establish realistic goals for each child.

- Provide frequent positive feedback.
- Sequence learning activities into small steps.
- Allow adequate time for performance and learning.
- Encourage cooperative play and help the child move from independent to parallel to group interaction.

Impaired hearing
- Obtain child's attention when speaking; seat child close to voice or music.
- Repeat, rephrase as needed; alert other children to use same technique.
- Learn some sign language and teach signing to the entire class.
- Provide visual clues (e.g., pictures or .. — .. — — to represent rhythm).
- Demonstrate new activities or tasks.

Impaired vision
- Ensure child's safety at all times without being overprotective.
- Provide verbal clues for activities.
- Introduce child to equipment and space verbally and through touch.
- Use a "buddy" system.

Physical disability or poor coordination
—ACCESSIBILITY
- Organize physical space to accommodate child in wheelchair.
- Use tables that accommodate wheelchairs or provide trays on wheelchairs.
- Use bolsters or other supports for floor activities.
- Provide adaptive equipment for standing.
- Learn about the availability of assistive technology and devices.

—MANUAL DEXTERITY
- Use magnetic toys to facilitate small muscle activities.
- Attach bells to wrist or ankles for musical activities.
- Use adaptive scissors or spoons as needed.

Source: Reprinted with permission from Dodge & Colker (1992), p. 34.

weather and the sterilized ritual study of holidays ought to become more controversial, or at least be considered more seriously.

In this section we will deal first with several points of view about the weather and holidays. On the basis of the perceptual model of cyclical change, we will explore a variety of selective activities using multiple ways of working. (Other relevant activities are integrated within other sections of this book.) Continuing within the framework of that model, we will then look at what children can learn about time, growth, and temperature as they use a variety of methods of study.

Young children first begin to perceive cyclical change directly through their eating and sleeping schedules and through seasonal changes. Since change is a constant factor in life, children engaged in a variety of activities may build toward inductively understanding cyclical change, even if only a part of a cycle of change is reflected in an activity. Kindergarten children have worked playfully in activity forms reflecting cyclical change, such as role playing and creative dramatics; building with blocks, mud, and clay; oral history; and examining artifacts and replicas from different times and places.

The perceptual model, by suggesting the possible connections between concrete, diverse experiences, also suggests alternative ways of sequencing activities. Using this approach, different children engaging in different activities at different times can have equivalent experiences.

Weather

There is sufficient reason to reassess the school's preoccupation with weather, if only to break out of a morning ritual of "Today is Monday. It is cloudy and raining. We will have indoor lunch." Educators must reconsider those activities that are taken for granted and accepted because they are the way things always have been done, that is, because they are the folklore of the school.

Teachers usually view weather as a science study—a study of the rain cycle, the related study of seasons, and of growing things. However, weather conditions represent social as well as scientific issues. You can introduce the children to the social aspects of weather in the context of its impact on food supplies, transportation routes, and the possibility of settlement.

It is worthwhile to look at weather as part of, rather than the focus for, the study of cyclical change. Viewing cyclical change as a basis for sequencing and juxtaposing events can provide a broader range of options and activities. As we saw in Figure 3.2, there is a natural flow of imagery that connects the perceptual model of cyclical change across disciplines. This imagery unites the weather, life cycles, animal migrations, holidays, cultural evolution, ecology, outdoor education, measurement, poetry, and economic issues such as the food cycle.

You can also have the children develop surveys based upon the cyclical changes that they observe. They can measure whether there were days without rain in a week or in a month.

Holidays

Since most of our holidays are dictated by the calendar, it is easy for some teachers to remain seduced by a kind of ritual calendar worship, often represented in trivial, color-coded paper cut-outs. Holiday study is more worthwhile when the focus is on human efforts or struggles for safety, sustenance, justice, and freedom. Young children, after all, have had personal experiences with power, frustration, and struggle that parallel cultural experiences.

Some kindergarten children have engaged in role playing and dramatic activities that provided a truly social study of various holidays. For example, they have celebrated Martin Luther King's birthday by role-playing Rosa Parks's initiation of the Montgomery bus boycott; they have observed St. Patrick's Day by dramatizing the potato famine; and they have expanded the feast of Thanksgiving by acting out the story of the peaceful strivings of the Iroquois nation (Ellen Ray, personal communication, 1981). Social scientist Donna Barnes has worked out some concrete activities around the Thanksgiving theme that reflect the role of colonial women.

On the surface, the study of holidays looks different from the study of the weather. On a deeper level, however, holidays commemorate the cycle of struggles in individual human lives and societies (*dialectical process*—children know about bullies and tyranny) and celebrate such times as a plentiful harvest in contrast with drought and famine (children know about unlimited wants and limited resources).

Time

Time is an important element in cyclical change. It is also a constraint for teachers because young children are still learning to sort out time distinctions and sequences of events. Analogy as well as concrete experiences can help children deal with the distant in time.

Various representations of time can be used with kindergarten children. A timeline can be hung on the wall, containing children's baby pictures beside pictures taken of them when they began kindergarten in September. After a few weeks, the chart can be stored until May, when another set of even more recent photographs can be added. Children will notice changes, such as in hair length and sleeve length. Krauss's *The Growing Story* (1947), Jonas's *When You Were a Baby* (1982), and Frasier's *On the Day You Were Born* (1991) are books with which children can identify in this context, but it generally is more meaningful to introduce a book to children after they have had the related experiences.

Some children experience a sense of cognitive surprise when they see a photographic timeline of their teacher's life. They also have enjoyed trying to match current and baby pictures of all of the personnel who work in the school. In a schoolwide project, kindergarten children have voted as a group on which baby and adult photographs matched.

Kindergarten teachers have used a variation of the timeline by taking photographs to create a sequence of events during trips and various other group projects, including parties. Tape recordings of group events are other kinds of records that can contribute to a sense of temporal order. These kinds of visual and auditory records can contribute to the children's developing self-awareness.

The various rites of passage in early childhood help children to become more aware of themselves. The first day of school [see *Will I Have a Friend?* (Cohen, 1967) and *The Trek* (Jonas, 1985)] and finishing kindergarten are such events. Learning to ride a bicycle, receiving a first umbrella (see Yashima's *The Umbrella*, 1970), and acquiring a library card (see Felt's *Rosa-Too-Little*, 1950) are also such benchmarks.

The understanding of the duration of immediate time is enhanced when children wait patiently for pudding to cook, cookies to bake, a film to end, or a story to begin. They can take a survey of heart rate by tallying the number of beats in ten seconds both before and after running for one minute, or they can count the number of birds at a bird feeder during a three-minute interval. Such activities deepen their sense of time on a personal level.

Children can use clocks with second hands, mechanical timers, metronomes, sand "egg" timers, and such nonstandard measures of time as water wheels. Sometimes children are quite ingenious about suggesting ways of recording changes. In addition, they can keep records through communal or individual "books of changes" at their own levels of representation.

Growth

Human beings of all ages wonder what will happen when they grow older. For young children, visiting a family with an infant and talking to elderly people are important supplements in an age of nuclear families. Kindergarten children welcome the presence in school of babies and senior citizen volunteers. The stories told by older people, other people who have interesting and unusual careers, and parents of babies form an oral history and provide vivid experiences for children to use in creating a data base and making connections.

Activities that deal with animal and plant growth parallel these concerns. Children acquire useful data about social behavior through the analogies to be found in observing animal and insect behavior and their social communities. Children can also reinforce their social studies by comparisons with the cyclical changes in plant growth. A book dealing with earth, sky, moon, and the sun, *Thirteen Moons on Turtle's Back* (Bruchac & London, 1992), and a nonfiction book such as *A Tree in a Forest* (Thornhill, 1992) integrate cyclical change with beautiful illustrations. They lend themselves to reading over time, rather than at a single sitting. *Rain Forest* (Cowcher, 1988) encourages children to consider ecological issues.

There are also books for young children that deal with growth, generations, reproduction, birth, and death. A most sensitively written book that deals with warm family relationships, different generations, the loss of a significant family member, and a rite of passage in an aesthetically beautiful way is *Annie and the Old One* (Miles, 1971).

The notions of life, death, and extinction are important human concerns. Considering the limits of kindergarten children's grasp of time, it is a constant wonder to notice them wrapped up in dinosaur lore. It is hard to say whether dinosaurs have more appeal because of their lengthy and varied labels, which have prestige in the child culture, or because of their image as powerful monsters, which appeals to children's developing consciences. While cognitively distant in time, dinosaurs are emotionally present for children through their imaginations.

Some children have brought to school fossils that their families acquired on vacation trips. One group of kindergarten children collected "future fossils" outdoors (Wynne Shilling, personal communication, 1985). Then their teacher asked them to classify and predict which items would be likely to last and which would not last. They believed that rocks, metal bottle caps, and leaves would last (leaves were included because they had seen the dried remnants of a fern in a fossil at an earlier time). They believed that plastic and glass would not last because "they break easily." Nor did they believe that cigarette butts and rags would last. Using plaster of Paris, they first made impressions of the "longest-lasting" items and then later created imprints of the "would-not-last" items in a second layer. Making plaster-of-Paris handprints or footprints and making other prints with sponges, vegetables, and then words all build toward the fossil concept. Early exposure to these objects lays a base for later ties to geological changes and the interactions between living beings and their environment.

Temperature

Temperature change, reflecting the days and seasons, is cyclical. It is important to plan ahead for varied activities that explore these cycles, but unplanned opportunities also may present themselves: The rare excitement of an unexpected snowfall can be turned into a spontaneous aesthetic event that children can appreciate either from indoors or as an outdoor tactile immersion.

Woven through each day are such fleeting moments that hold the potential for deeper meaning when you take the time to appreciate them with children. Consider, for example, outlining a puddle with chalk (Dodge & Colker, et al., 1992, p. 53) or wire after a rain and then comparing its size after an hour or two of other activities. Children can also become aware of the physical impact of wind as the weather changes. As breezes occur, they can also appreciate aesthetically the changing appearance of the precisely balanced mobiles that they have built.

The Use of Analogies

We can help children to notice that one cyclical change leads to another, and since our discussion has come around again to snow and wind, we will use weather activities to illustrate two kinds of analogies.

Direct Analogy. Ask the children to imagine that the weather today is just the opposite of current conditions. Then continue:

- What would you (as children in Puerto Rico; in Jamaica) be doing?
- What do those clouds look like? Remind you of? What else?
- How is a rainy day like a jail?
- What animal is like a rainy day?
- Why is a laugh like a rainy day?
- What kind of weather is like a song? A dance? Like you?
- What makes you feel like a sunshine sky? Thunder and lightning?

Personal Analogy. Children can be encouraged to use their imagination to project themselves into familiar experiences in new ways. A good example of this technique is the following activity, adapted from Gordon and Poze (1968, 1972): Ask the children to imagine they are spiders trying to spin a web on a rainy, stormy day. As they try to feel what the spider feels, ask them:

- As a spider, what does the storm do to you?
- What are you thinking as the rain becomes heavier and the wind stronger?
- What other things might you do? Plan? Wish?

Notice that aspects of the perceptual model of cyclical change appear in particular concrete activities that kindergarten children have experienced. These experiences include, permeate, cut across, or exist outside separate subjects that schools have defined. The activities are within the teaching range and help children integrate learning in personalized ways.

REFLECTIONS

Social studies, along with science studies and perceptual models/dynamic themes, form the meaningful center of education. In contrast, teaching the three R's as "basics" is "boring" (Weininger, 1990, p. 53) and an oppressive "pedagogy of poverty" (Haberman, 1991). Keeping the "social" in social studies means focusing on significant human experiences to which young children might connect personal meanings. This means developing sensitivities to other people, not as objects or categories, but as persons who have both similar and unique experiences within families and communities, and within themselves. It is apparent that attempting to share these understandings takes place through activities that we have called science, mathematics, literacy, constructions, the visual arts, movement education, and play as well as social studies.

We can satisfy ourselves that children have made progress in their study of social events when they apply those learnings. Caring behaviors, authentic questioning, and integrity in debates are among the ways to assess children's skills. When they deal with such a question as, "What might George Washington think if he met a jogger today wearing yellow ear covers and a wire?" you have an opportunity to hear the diverse power of their thinking.

Sociodramatic play, a major provision for social learning in kindergartens, is another way to assess children's understandings. Other adults sometimes will need your help in interpreting its significance. Tell them, therefore, about the power of sociodramatic play as one of the sources of writing as well as of social development. Let them know how block building and other constructive play and movement activities also help children to develop mathematical concepts. Explain that multicultural education is for all children and that the study of social issues prepares children to be citizens. These are issues of concern to adults.

If you now have separate block and housekeeping areas, consider placing them next to each other and facilitating traffic flow between them, ultimately merging them. Consider reducing the housekeeping theme while offering props for other varied themes. Add props that represent varied cultural uses, such as a cradle board, wok for cooking, packages printed in several languages, dress-up articles that represent different work roles, and so forth.

Try to find out about the after-school activities of children in your class. Perhaps you might find one making change on a busy street and confounding all predictions about the development of economic concepts as he set prices to make a profit on the sale of shopping bags, and returned to his supplier to replenish his supply. It is apparent that an additive approach to curriculum development cannot work for him or other such children. There will never be enough time. Therefore, developing activities from a core of perceptual models/dynamic themes offers children and teachers a unifying alternative. We need to look at our next steps in relation to the children with whom we work and gradually transform our work accordingly.

6

Action-Centered
Science Education

Scientists view the various branches of science as attempts to study and understand the physical processes that touch upon human experience and imagination. Yet the sciences are often taught as if they were a set of facts and bits of information that are designed to be memorized. In this chapter, the study of the sciences is presented in the context of experiential happenings and potential understanding.

In keeping with this approach, ways of knowing in the disciplines of physics, biology, and chemistry are discussed in order to provide examples of ways to plan selected activities. Children move toward the learning of concepts as they participate in these activities. Since activities, when you develop them with children over time, suggest ties across disciplines, vistas are offered into how you might plan from inter- and extradisciplinary viewpoints.

THE SCIENCE AREA

Whether you plan to set up a separate science area or integrate science and mathematics materials, consider beginning to provide for a science area that might include the following:

Some things from the physical world, such as magnets, water, and pulleys or other simple machines
Some things from the living world, such as plants, cuttings, seedlings, insects, and animal life
Items to compare, classify, or sequence
Some things to manipulate and use playfully

Tools for measurement, such as rulers, timers, and a stethoscope
A table, chairs enough for six to eight children, and storage shelves
     that set off the area
Writing materials and relevant literature
A sign to identify the area as a science area

These kinds of provisions can be replaced, revised, retired, and renewed on a regular basis, as needed.

UNDERSTANDING PHYSICS
THROUGH THE INTERACTION OF FORCES

Physics has been defined as the science that measures how objects move through space and time (Toulmin, 1953/1960). If you begin to see physics in this dynamic, relative way, there are many ways that you can help children construct related concepts. Even though you begin to plan at the point of your own "fund" of knowledge, as you work with your children their actions will suggest ways of actively representing the underlying concepts. In this way, each transaction between you, your children, and the experiences will be a unique fingerprint in time.

For example, let us look at the case of a kindergarten group in which a 5-year-old, Kay, showed others in the group a "trick" with magnets (Fromberg, 1965). Kay laughingly showed how her magnet could attract a piece of paper and then gleefully explained: "It can't pick up the paper without the nail but it can pick it up with the nail." Since time was limited, the teacher planned to follow this new path the next day. She brought various nonmagnetic materials. Kay shared her "trick." The teacher then asked, "Can you guess which materials could be used for such a trick?" Among the carefully selected materials were copper disks. Children variously predicted whether or not each material could be attracted by the magnet before attempting to use it as an intermediate body. When a number of children felt sure that the copper could be attracted, the teacher took the time to explore their thinking before continuing with her advance plan to classify materials based upon their magnetic properties.

When you build on children's active contributions, continuity of learning is a kind of negotiated result. As you look at the concept of the interaction of forces in nature, it is possible to see how you might help tie activities together in this negotiated way. If you relate this concept of the interaction of natural forces to the interdependency of living beings, you can discern a clear base for interdisciplinary activity that builds from a unifying conceptual framework.

Interdependency and Interrelationship

Interrelationship has been proposed as a major concept in science (Craig, 1958). Some subsidiary forces that reflect the interaction-of-forces concept in nature would be gravitation, magnetism, air pressure, and centrifugal force. Figure 6.1 shows a conceptual planning map for using these forces to organize instruction. These forces can be translated into concrete activities and materials for young children.[1]

You do not need to plan activities that focus only on one force and pursue it to the ends of human knowledge, nor do you need to make explicit to children the interaction of these forces, regardless of children's receptivity. Plan concrete experiences as you go along, taking into account children's reactions. Bear in mind that, were any other group of children to begin with the same set of materials, the actual experience would most likely be different.

Now let us look together at some actual kindergarten experiences with gravitation, magnetism, air pressure, and centrifugal force. These examples are drawn from my observations of a single half-day kindergarten class over the period of a school year.

GRAVITATION

Since gravitation was a common experience for these children, their teacher planned some activities that might help them become more aware of this force. She planned to focus upon contrasting up and down and finding out why objects stop moving up. At about the same time, the children had watched a popular television program at home in which the hero was flying in a basket suspended from a balloon. They also had heard Lamorisse's (1956) story, *The Red Balloon*. The teacher drew upon these experiences by preparing materials that included helium-filled balloons along with paper cups, strings, air-filled balloons, rubber balls of various density, yarn balls, and shuttlecocks.

After briefly talking with the children about the story characters, particularly the child Pascal, their teacher asked them how they could solve the problem of getting the paper cup off the ground. When the children tried and saw that one helium-filled balloon was inadequate, they made guesses concerning how many would work and repeated the process after adding extra balloons. Following the children's exclamations of "Ready! Aim! Blast! Any minute!" and "Pascal, come down!", the teacher asked them to suggest ways of bringing down the cup.

> CHILD 1: Hey, we could put the wood in.
> TEACHER: What would that do?

FIGURE 6.1: Conceptual Planning Map—Interaction of Forces in Physics

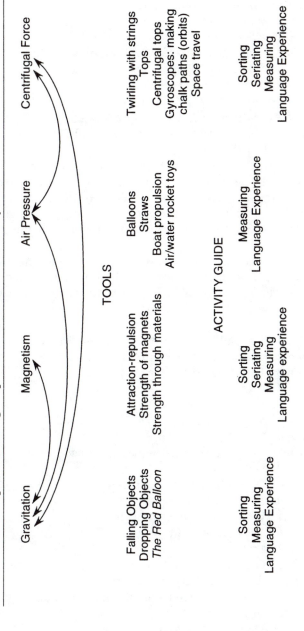

Gravitation	Magnetism	Air Pressure	Centrifugal Force

TOOLS

Falling Objects	Attraction-repulsion	Balloons	Twirling with strings
Dropping Objects	Strength of magnets	Straws	Tops
The Red Balloon	Strength through materials	Boat propulsion	Centrifugal tops
		Air/water rocket toys	Gyroscopes: making chalk paths (orbits)
			Space travel

ACTIVITY GUIDE

Sorting	Sorting	Measuring	Sorting
Measuring	Seriating	Language Experience	Seriating
Language Experience	Measuring		Measuring
	Language experience		Language Experience

TEACHER: (After several children have placed a block in the cup.) What happens now? . . . If Pascal is up too high, how do you think he might come down?
CHILD 2: Weight.
CHILD 1: How about a ladder?
CHILD 3: If he had a pin, he could pop it.
TEACHER: What would happen to the balloon?
CHILD 4: The air would come out . . . [2]

Notice that the teacher accepted each suggestion. She was in no rush to feed them a single "right" answer that would end the speculation. Instead, she asked them to describe the possible consequences of their actions. The teacher used the terms *gravity* and *force* casually, as they spoke. In this way, she began to build a pattern of guessing, observing, repeating, describing, and explaining that allowed the children to deal with a basic outlook of the physical scientist: defining the limitations (or context) within which a particular natural phenomenon could or could not occur.[3]

In an ancillary activity later in the week, the teacher asked the children to dictate statements concerning their prior group meetings, so that they could share them with a youngster who was absent. Some of the responses follow:

CHILD 1: The balloons and the cups went around the room.
CHILD 2: 'Cause they had helium in them.
CHILD 3: They lifted the cup up.
CHILD 4: Four balloons.
CHILD 5: We counted to four.
TEACHER: We had balls, too. What kind of balls?
CHILD 6: Little balls.
CHILD 7: (Moving hands.) They were shaped like this.
CHILD 8: Like a capsule.
TEACHER: (Reads back what is written.)
CHILD 4: They went up, up, up, up, up.
TEACHER: What made them come down?
CHILD 8: The air came out.
CHILD 7: Gravity.
CHILD 5: Because they have no motors.
CHILD 6: They don't have propellers or wings.
TEACHER: A bird can have wings and he can come down. Why does he come down?
CHILD 1: There's nothing to keep it up.

By recording the children's statements for the absent child, the teacher was able to assess what the children perceived. As they continued to be receptive to these exposures, the children added to their information and began to apply it. In contrast with these earlier experiences, notice the wider scope of their comments five weeks later, during an activity period. (They are looking at pictures of space travel on a bulletin board.)

CHILD 1: That's a rocket!

CHILD 2: My friend has a cardboard rocket that goes round and round.

CHILD 1: Hey, that rocket's upside down.

CHILD 2: I'm not crazy. The rocket is upside down.

CHILD 3: He's flying.

CHILD 4: He's standing on his head because there's no gravity.

CHILD 5: There's no gravity in space.

CHILD 6: If you get very far away the gravity can't pull the rocket down.

TEACHER: What if you were up in space where Meg said there's no gravity? How could she be kept from flying around?

CHILD 7: She wears a gravity belt.

CHILD 5: If she didn't have one she would be flying around.

TEACHER: What if she were flying?

CHILD 2: Just like upsy-daisy.

TEACHER: What if she tried to pick up her mommy?

CHILD 8: She could pick up her mommy.

CHILD 3: . . . because there's no gravity.

MAGNETISM

The teacher selected the force of magnetism as another focus for activities, since it contrasts with gravitation. Another consideration was that children can see and feel the effects of this force directly, thereby possibly strengthening their concept of force.

The teacher worked with two groups of four and five children at adjacent tables. She had set out the materials with enough magnets for most of the children. She limited group size so that there would be a maximum opportunity for children to use the materials. Also, in this way, she could be in touch with both groups. At other times, she worked with eight children as one group in order to stimulate discussion.

She provided magnets of different sizes, shapes, and strengths, along with a variety of magnetic and nonmagnetic articles. The teacher suggested that they guess into which pile each article might be placed. She encouraged the children to separate the objects into piles of those that the magnet attracted and those that were not attracted. After they finished sorting the objects, the children listed for each other the articles in their respective piles.

When the teacher asked them what the attracted materials were made of, some children variously mentioned metal and iron. However, after several different magnets were used unsuccessfully to attract a metal ring, children were left with a new classification to ponder until a later activity. New words such as *repel* and *attract* became part of the children's vocabulary in a functional way.

Another classification activity with the magnets was to differentiate them by size and strength. The teacher asked the children to notice which magnet the object was attracted to first when she moved magnets of different sizes toward an equidistant object on the table. She asked them to guess which magnet might be stronger than a larger magnet and to suggest ways of testing the magnets. In another activity to measure the relative strength of magnets, the group used paper clips. They saw which magnets could attract more and fewer paper clips, and they represented their findings graphically on a survey chart.

Approximately two months later, the children spontaneously applied these experiences to a situation with a gyroscope, in an attempt to change its direction of movement.

CHILD 1: I don't think the magnet will do anything.
CHILD 2: (Indicating the gyroscope.) I don't think it will spin. The inside will but not . . .
CHILD 3: (As child has brought a magnet.) Nothing happens. I'm going to use all the magnets.
CHILD 4: 'Cause it's going too fast.
CHILD 1: Maybe it's not metal or something.
CHILD 5: Maybe it's not iron, not iron, not iron . . .
CHILD 6: You sure it isn't the broken one?

They certainly were able to use their knowledge of magnets independently in this new situation. Independent work with the magnets as well as discussions with the teacher both contributed to this facility in applying their knowledge.

Kay's "trick" of attracting paper, described earlier, was turned into another session the following day. Children tested the magnet's power to attract through materials that were not themselves attracted. The teacher encouraged children to *predict* with each additional material, to test each *guess* in turn, and to *describe* and *compare* each occurrence.

They performed several tests to see how many pieces of cardboard could be "attracted" to the magnet through the use of a paper clip. Children held their breaths in suspense at the veritable drama that ensued as each piece of cardboard was added. They found that seven pieces was the maximum number through which a paper clip might be attracted by any of their magnets. A child who noticed that the paper clip had been attracted but that it did not go "zip" stimulated the group to think about the relative strength of the force. While to an adult it may seem to take a long time to find out about seven pieces of cardboard, one at a time, the children derive a direct, aesthetic satisfaction from such an experience.

AIR PRESSURE

Children can see and feel the force of air pressure directly. When the teacher planned the viewing of an astronaut's rocket launch, which relied upon jet propulsion, she felt that children who had been exposed first to the use of air as a propelling force might bring more associations to that later experience. She thought about what materials could offer experiences with air pressure. For example, she decided against using pressurized cans because children could not feel the pressure build up. Since they had used plastic bottles and squeezed air out of them at other times, she added model rockets designed for children to use outdoors because they require a combination of water and air pressure for their propulsion. The children could pour the water, attach the parts of the model rocket by themselves, and then feel the air pressure build up as they pumped.

Initially, the teacher encouraged the children to select balloons, blow them up, and play with them in whatever ways they chose. Some children blew them up and asked the teacher to seal them. They would pat and throw the balloons up and down and follow them around the room. Other children, who had difficulty blowing them up, tried to fill them with water. Still other children blew them up and let the balloons loose to enjoy the sight of them deflating and the sound of the air escaping. This last play became popular, and children also placed the deflating balloon against their cheeks. One child said to nobody in particular, "Can't see air, but you can hear air."

The teacher planned activities with balloons, drinking straws, and toy boats. She asked the children to tear off an end of the paper covering the straw, to suck at the straw and describe what happened, and then to blow out and notice what happened. The children had a grand time and compared this activity with others they had had.

CHILD 1: It stuck on.
CHILD 2: Kind of like a magnet.
CHILD 1: When I blow up paper it's like a balloon.
CHILD 2: He was the pump.

She asked the children to *predict* in which direction an untied balloon would move if it were released. The children pointed in a variety of directions and later *described* and *compared* the actual course. They *repeated* the procedure several times, and the teacher remarked, as she had done before, "Now you have to do things several times to see where they're going." In this way she was trying to make them aware of the need for repetition and tentativeness as a way of studying natural phenomena.

Then they discussed the plastic boats. A hole was drilled in the rear of each boat and a transparent dropper, from which the rubber cap had been removed, was set through the hole so that an end of the dropper would be below the water line. The teacher attached a balloon to the opposite end of the dropper that sat in the boat, and rubber bands held the apparatus together.

Children blew up the balloons in the boats through the dropper, set the boats in a large water-filled tub, and gleefully watched the boats being propelled by the air that was escaping from the balloon. As they repeated their activity, they talked together about jet propulsion:

CHILD 1: What would happen if it had two balloons?
CHILDREN: It would go faster.
TEACHER: What if we put three balloons?
CHILD 3: (A child who rarely spoke; smiling.) It would go faster.
CHILD 4: Round and round.
CHILD 1: Let's do it.
CHILD 2: If they were on the sides it would go . . . (Makes a zigzag motion.)
CHILDREN: (Laugh.)
TEACHER: That would be good to try. Hal thinks it will stay pretty still, wouldn't go in any direction.
CHILD 3: That's the problem. We really don't know.

The children seemed involved and comfortable in expressing conjectures, "not knowing," and extending the discussions. Yet, through the discussions and introduction of new materials, they were encouraged to be active and to inflate their balloons. This was similar to their ongoing use of magnets. The physical involvement with materials appeared to help them keep their thinking focused. They were simultaneously able to manipulate materials and to expand ideas.

CENTRIFUGAL FORCE

An understanding of orbits in nature requires some idea of centrifugal force. Therefore the teacher planned classroom experiences in which children could feel and see the effect of centrifugal force. To equal lengths of string, they attached a spool, cardboard square, small plastic toy, cork, or other small object; they then created a twirling motion by hand at the top of the string. As they did, they saw each object swing around and spin away from the hand. The following dialogue shows how the kindergarten children and their teacher interacted as they explored this force by predicting, observing, comparing, and attempting to explain their findings.

Predicting Stage

TEACHER: (Holding strings from which cardboard squares are suspended.) Look at what we have here.

CHILD 1: A merry-go-round.

CHILD 2: (Holding strings apart.) If it would stick out like this it would look more like a merry-go-round.

TEACHER: Is there any way we could make it go out?

CHILD 3: Sticks.

CHILD 4: Glue it out.

CHILD 2: You can push it around.

CHILD 5: Like blow it.

CHILD 1: You could twirl it.

Observation and Comparison Stage

CHILD 6: It's going faster.

CHILD 2: I saw the string going with it.

TEACHER: Is the cardboard under my hand?

CHILD 1: At the sides.

TEACHER: (With a meter stick.) How far off the ground is it?

CHILD 6: 18.

TEACHER: Yes, just about. Let's see if it goes down closer to the ground.

CHILD 7: No, higher.

CHILD 5: Lower.

TEACHER: Let's measure and see.

CHILD 1: 24.

TEACHER: Is 24 more than 18?

CHILDREN: (Nod.)

CHILD 4: 'Cause your arm is higher.

TEACHER: Let's measure if it goes higher without an arm moving. (They repeat the procedure until all are satisfied that they are repeatedly seeing the same thing.)

Explaining Stage

TEACHER: What might make it go up?
CHILD 1: Air.
CHILD 8: Your hand.
TEACHER: Does it go out by itself?
CHILD 8: When you twirl it the air holds it up.
TEACHER: Is it moving faster or slower?
CHILD 4: No, faster.
TEACHER: When it goes faster, what else is happening?
CHILD 2: It's going outer.
TEACHER: What makes it go out?
CHILDREN 2 and 4: Air.
TEACHER: Remember, when we drop things, what's the force?
CHILD 3: Gravity.
TEACHER: [Mentions forces of magnetism and air.] The force that makes the spool go out is centrifugal force. This is the center, and the force that's moving it out is centrifugal.

Notice the integrity of the children throughout these interactions. Children are saying what they actually see. They are not simply trying to guess what the teacher might expect or what a single "right" answer might be.

They followed a similar procedure after the teacher had added some transparent tops to the materials that children used during work periods. These "centrifugal" tops contained colored water, colored oil, and grains that separated into three rings when they were twirled. The children enthusiastically used some of them and acquired great skill at keeping numerous tops twirling simultaneously.

Meeting with half the class for a discussion, the teacher distributed the tops so that three or four children shared each one. The children identified the three materials in the tops—water, oil, and beads—and then compared the materials with regard to weight and color while the tops were at rest. Then, with the tops spinning, they described the color of the outside, inside, and middle rings and observed that the rings were always in the same order. That in turn led them to think about which of the materials was heaviest, and which was lightest. Their interchanges suggest that the children were becoming more careful observers. They seemed able to challenge the observations of others and to offer explanations for events based upon prior activities in the classroom. Their numerous earlier experiences with differentiating relative weight were essential to this activity. Over the next weeks the teacher planned several other related activities:

1. They observed the rotation of clay spheres rotated on pencils in the presence of a flashlight.
2. Children heard the story *Follow the Sunset* (Schneider & Schneider, 1952) while a globe lit by a filmstrip projection lamp was nearby. A globe had always been present in the classroom, and the children had often referred to it. The teacher's purpose was to highlight the notion that the earth moves continuously. This activity preceded a look at a large model of the sun and planets in motion.
3. They used chalk to follow the path of a gyroscope spinning on the floor.
4. Children launched their own toy rockets outdoors.
5. They watched a space launch on television.

Children were beginning to apply some of their learning and to try out their growing vocabulary, sometimes more accurately than at other times. They brought in newspaper clippings about the spaceship's orbit and discussed why the path was not straight up. The children were able to relate the path to the "round" earth. The youngsters communicated excitement. They were receptive to activities that dealt with the interaction of opposing forces such as gravitation and magnetism, centrifugal force and gravitation, and air propulsion and gravitation.

Measurement

In dealing with the physical world, we often deal with quantities. In their study, the children discussed in the previous section repeated their manipulations of concrete materials and measured changes when possible. For example, the meter stick was used repeatedly when children studied centrifugal force. The use of this tool was possible only because they had had prior experiences in the classroom measuring and seeing numbers written. They also frequently used rulers at the woodworking bench.

The children also had heard their teacher use terms that described the relative position of phenomena. They discussed angles in connection with the earth's axis as well as in their rhythmic movement and dance activities. Continuing with this same class as an example, let us look at some experiences kindergarten children can have with measurement.

These children tried different ways to measure time. They quickly noticed that counting was inadequate for timing the fall of objects because individuals counted at different rates. The teacher obtained a one-minute timer with a clock face; however, the children were confused by the representation of a whole minute in the space of half the area of the circle.

Further search in photography shops uncovered a small three-minute timer that had a clock face marked into seconds and minutes. The teacher acquired several and left them on a shelf, without comment. Several children who noticed the new timer recognized it as some sort of "clock with only one hand." One youngster said, "Hey, I know what that is! It's a countdown on rockets."

The children began to use the timers to time their cooking play, to find out how long their tops would spin and their rockets would fly, and to measure the length of time it took for a boat to sail a given distance.

When the children used the timer with their own jet-propelled boats, they talked a good deal about the "countdown"; however, the timekeeper had been counting up. That is, while several children seriously and patiently waited, the timekeeper set the timer and watched it go through its 3-minute cycle three complete times all the while counting off seconds by tens. Then he announced, "Blast off," promptly pocketed the timer, and enjoyed the boat race.

The children clearly were not yet able to coordinate their interest in the boats with the timer. Therefore, in an attempt to extend the children's experience with the timer beyond the "countdown" and "countup" phase, the teacher planned a short session in which they used the timer and the meter stick. The children's comments during this discussion revealed that several of them needed to clarify vocabulary and concepts about length of time as duration and length of meter stick as distance or height.

At the teacher's request, the children suggested various ways that they could make the boats sail. The children mentioned pushing, blowing, and fanning the boats, in addition to jet propulsion. They predicted and measured how far the boats would move and how long it would take when the methods of blowing, fanning with cardboard, and jet propulsion were used.

Then they compared which methods took the longest and the shortest time to move the boats the greatest distance. As each procedure was repeated, the teacher wrote their findings on a chart so that they could compare times and distances. The children were physically involved and attentive as they coordinated their manipulations of materials and their discussions of events.

Depth of Study

The study of the interaction of forces in the physical world can be spread over half or all of the school year, depending on the density of activity to which your children seem receptive. When children engage in related activities, rather than isolated one-time events, they can integrate new perceptions in individually meaningful ways. Depth in this sense refers to the personal involvement and the meaning level of a series of experiences that extend over time.

For example, look at erosion as an illustration of forces. You can speak of and observe the interaction of air, temperature, water, soil, wind, rock, and human-made structures. You can notice the relationships among forests, fires, rainfall, climatic conditions, and landforms, tying in human use of land as another interactive element. You can observe eroded sites; directly witness erosion during and immediately following rain, flood, or a thaw; and compare pictures taken before and after land development for construction, pictures taken before and after fires, and pictures taken before erosion and at a later seashore or riverbank visit. You can read about mudslides and avalanches in both adventure stories and the daily newspaper. You can create structures in the classroom or on school grounds and play at eroding them. You can see films, slides, and videotapes as possible substitutes for the real thing, but they are insufficient by themselves. Therefore, if a child were growing up on an Iowa plain, for example, without direct access to mountainous terrain, his teacher would attempt to plan a series of related experiences that reflect the interaction of human beings and nature in their own locale.

Measuring tools may differ. The plains child might measure wind, drought, or flood damage. The interplay of different tools and varied data can provide a large number of experiences of comparable quality. Here again, the nature and purpose of experience is to use knowledge to gain understanding and cultivate cooperation, with absorption of information being a by-product, not the end, of learning.

UNDERSTANDING BIOLOGY THROUGH CLASSIFICATION

As we teach kindergarten children, we need to remind ourselves that they will perceive best those things that they can see, feel, touch, taste, and smell in a meaningful context. We need to keep in mind also that humans can perceive things most clearly when two conditions are present: (1) movement and (2) contrast. Among these conditions, we might consider that a contrast is structural—for example, an unknown figure set against a known background, where the unknown figure represents a single new variable. By the same token, we might consider that movement is functional.

For example, when there is a sufficient contrast between the figure and ground structures, children can perceive the interrelation of these structures as movement. For biologists, function and structure are undergoing continual change and self-regulation because they are both processes:

"What are called structures are slow processes of long duration, functions are quick processes of short duration" (Bertalanffy, 1960). Regulator genes, for example, function as "stable, self-consistent patterns" (Waldrop, 1992, p. 107). Making these processes explicit for ourselves can help us to plan activities so that children can learn about biology by experiencing contrasts between figure and ground, between slower and quicker phenomena.

Among the major concepts in biology are cyclical change, adaptation, and variety; these are broad categories that lend themselves to many types of activities; indeed, numerous volumes have been written on the subject. The purpose of this section is to share some of the approaches and activities that represent these categories, in the form of experiences to which kindergarten children have been receptive. Figure 6.2 provides a conceptual planning map for using the concepts in biology instruction. It is clear that we have an overwhelming array of activities from which to choose. Several criteria that can be used in deciding which activities to pursue are presented in Figure 6.3.

Plants

Plants in the classroom provide a periodic activity that represents elements of *cyclical change* and variety for children. It is useful to provide more than one sample of each of several types of plants, such as cactus, moss, green leafy plants, geraniums, elodea in the aquarium, peas, and bulbs. Beyond

FIGURE 6.2: Conceptual Planning Map in Biology

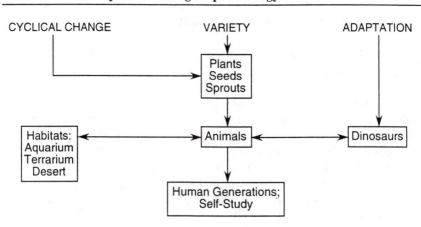

FIGURE 6.3: Criteria for Selecting Biology Activities

Gregariousness. Which processes or concepts can be investigated with the most gregarious activities? More gregarious activities are the most likely to help children to suggest and generate possible ties with other related activities.

Appeal. Which activities are the most exciting and attractive to pursue? For example, it is ridiculous to initiate a study of snakes or mealworms if they make your stomach dance. Hatching chicks, peeper frogs, or fish provide equivalent opportunities for studying growth concepts.

Resource Availability. For which activities do you have the most ideas, materials, and resources?

Children's Receptivity. In which directions have your children shown greatest interest and capacity? To what activities do you estimate they will be most receptive?

Opportunities for Participation. Are there opportunities for different children to engage with different degrees of involvement and commitment?

Representativeness. Which activities most clearly represent an underlying perceptual model or part of a perceptual model?

labeling the plants, there are various actions that you and your children might take and then compare the different types of plants:

- Vary locations in relation to light sources
- Measure the amount of water that different plants require each week
- Vary water quantities for a few samples of the same plant
- Vary temperature
- Record actions that you take
- Measure plant growth with direct, continuous, nonstandard measures such as yarn or paper strips, and place them on a chart and in individual science/mathematics notebooks as relevant

Cyclical change is represented easily in activities with seeds. In northern climates, one popular activity is an autumn trip to a pumpkin farm, scooping out the pumpkin seeds, drying them, sometimes eating them, and cooking the pumpkin itself. Some teachers have saved some of the pumpkin seeds until the following springtime and helped the children to plant them in used milk containers. It is advisable to plant seeds in several containers, for this practice both increases the likelihood that something will grow and provides an opportunity to vary some of the growth conditions.

Other activities with seeds involve collecting a variety of seeds, some of which you can collect from fruit and vegetable snacks. These can include choices from among fruits and vegetables, including sprouts. Potatoes, wheat berries, mung beans, rice, and lima beans are other types of seeds that you might collect. The following are some ways the children might use them:

- *Classify* seeds according to one contrasted variable at a time, such as texture (rough/smooth), color (green/yellow), shape (curved/pointed), or size.
- *Create collage patterns* with seeds. Children can write or dictate descriptions of the products.
- For peas, *predict* the number of seeds in a handful of pods, shell them, and list how many peas you find in your set of pods, the largest number and the smallest number in a single pod, and the most frequent number.
- When you cut open the fruits and vegetables, the children can *note any symmetrical patterns* and chart which seeds were or were not aligned symmetrically.
- You can offer a *collection of other objects that look like seeds* and ask children, "What might these be?", "How do we know they are seeds?", and "How do we know that they are not seeds?" Children might plant the various samples, attaching a sample to a stick with transparent tape so that it stands in the soil where you planted the sample. Accept all responses.

Sprouts grow very quickly from such seeds as alfalfa, mung beans, sunflower seeds, and peas, as do plant cuttings such as carrot tops, turnip tops, and sprouting sweet potatoes. You can vary several other growth conditions, such as

- *Medium*—grow seeds in water, dry soil, and damp soil, as well as on paper towel or sponge
- *Distance*—plant seeds close together and farther apart
- *Depth*—vary how deeply you plant the seeds
- *Direction*—using two transparent containers, plant several seeds in the usual way, but turn one container on its side and turn another upside down
- *Moisture*—vary the amount and frequency of watering
- *State*—see what happens if you plant half of a seed or a frozen pea
- *Measure*—predict, compare, and measure the growth of different varieties of sprouts under different conditions
- *Record*—use a chart to represent the findings

Whichever of these activities you decide to use, do keep in mind that the major purpose is to keep open the questions, the wonder, the imagination, and the excitement, rather than to provide a predigested set of statements for children to hear and repeat.

Animals

Children enjoy animals in the classroom, and there is much important learning connected with the play, care, observation, comparison, classification, measurement, and description that take place. Caring for animals creates an opportunity for children to develop feelings of responsibility, nurture, and reverence for life.

Kindergartens have housed hamsters, gerbils, and rabbits successfully, with families taking turns in caring for these pets over the weekend. Children can learn about feeding habits, water consumption, elimination, growth, reproduction, illness, unique behaviors, and even death. They can survey and chart what a particular insect or animal will or will not eat. Measuring the girth and the length of a young animal every two weeks for about two months is another exciting survey activity. Two or three months is ample time to study a single animal. If resources are limited in your school, perhaps you can exchange animals and findings with another class, and revisit them later in the year.

Local ponds in the springtime are a source for tadpoles that grow into peeper frogs. These have been raised easily on crumbs and fish food in an aquarium. Children take great pleasure in watching them develop into peeper frogs, after which time they need to live out of the water. Children have developed their own booklets of drawings and raised many significant questions when they observed these dramatic events. As children share and discuss their drawings in small groups, they have an opportunity to increase their perspective-taking skills.

Alternative activities can include raising mealworms from a local pet shop, raising sanitary land snails from a scientific supply company[4] in a terrarium, or incubating chicken eggs with equipment available from the local 4-H Club. Children predict, observe, classify, compare, measure, write, draw pictures, model in clay, and talk about their experience with animals.

The study of contrasting life forms can highlight an understanding of adaptation to different environments. Studying fish in classroom aquariums is another way of learning about adaptation, cyclical change, and variety. It is most useful to have more than one aquarium, in order to be able to compare events resulting from different variables. One well-tested and adaptable environment includes guppies, snails, plants, and pebbles.

When the water needs to be changed, the replacement supply should be left at room temperature for a day before use.

Children can classify elements in the aquarium according to their own criteria, including:

> Living things (plants, animals); nonliving things (water, a liquid; and pebbles, a solid); once-living things that are no longer alive (waste products)
>
> Large and small objects
>
> Slow-moving and fast-moving things
>
> Animals that have fins or shells

You can control the environment for such variables as the location or absence of plants. Children in a small group can predict and then count with pegs or numbers, depending upon their skills, the number of times in a minute that a fish flaps its gills for breathing. They can then compare their findings with the breathing rates of other classroom pets as well as humans.

A terrarium in the kindergarten is another environment that permits children to study adaptation and change in plants and animals. Soil, rocks, various plants, earthworms or snails, and moisture are a sufficient beginning for study and comparison with the aquarium environment, as your group uses many of the same investigative processes. Moreover, the observation of water condensation is particularly apparent in the terrarium habitat. You can even place a transparent plastic bag over a seedling long enough to see condensation form. A related activity could be comparing changes at different spots in the schoolyard throughout the year (Russell, 1990).

Animals in the Classroom is an Elementary Science Study (1970a) publication that describes the establishment of a desert habitat and classroom study of the kangaroo rat, the pocket mouse, and the desert iguana, a type of lizard whose scientific name, *Dipsosaurus dorsalis*, kindergarten children love to use. This habitat provides a fascinating contrast with the terrarium and the aquarium. You will find other exciting classroom-tested science topics of particular interest to kindergarten children listed under Elementary Science Study Teachers' Guides in the bibliography.

In addition, kindergarten children enjoy the study of dinosaurs, whether you call this study history or biology. In the biological sense, dinosaur study illuminates the concepts of physical change, adaptation, and variety. Kindergarten children certainly are motivated highly enough in studying dinosaurs to differentiate and label them with rather complex names, such as pterodactyl, brontosaurus, and trachodon. They enjoy classifying the different limb structures, teeth, and running capacities of vegetarian as opposed to flesh-eating dinosaurs. One knowledgeable kindergarten group even voted for their favorite dinosaur. Children's fascination with dinosaurs is an example of how emotional and aesthetic concerns influence motives for cognitive attention. Kindergarten children can deal with the subject of dinosaurs both playfully and for purposes of classification within the context of their own imagery.

Humans

Focusing on different generations of people also can help kindergarten children to reinforce the elements of *cyclical change*. It may work out well in your classroom to ask parents to send baby pictures of their children. Throughout the year, you will have many reasons to record class events and photograph the children. Whether some of the children create "A Book about Myself," using these photographs, or you decide to develop a bulletin board chart, there are interesting comparisons to make.

You can invite a parent to bring in a baby early in the school year, then at midyear, and at the end of the year, so that the children can create a chart of the baby's growth. Perhaps you can weigh her, measure her length with nonstandard as well as standard measures, list the food she adds to her diet, and notice the behaviors she develops over time.

You might compare varied sorts of care that parents give their offspring and observe differences between classroom animals and humans. For example, children might notice differences in gestation. Do be prepared for their possible curiosity about fertilization. It makes sense to be ready rather than to offer unsolicited or inadequate information. This attitude is also useful when dealing with questions about death.

When dealing with intergenerational study, consider inviting a well-prepared elderly resource person who might bring photographs and stories about how things used to be. The best preparation for this is for you and the resource person to plan the activity together. Perhaps you could consider this visit to be part of your social studies program, since this information is social as well as biological. This case is a good example of the futility of trying to draw strict lines between disciplines.

Children also enjoy learning more about their physical selves and what they can do. There are many measurement activities, using nonstandard methods, that relate to the children's own selves and can be enjoyable cooperative mathematics activities. Here are a few ideas to suggest to the children that have been adapted from Science 5/13 Project materials (Richards et al., 1976a, 1976b), rich sources for activities:

- Measure your height, weight, and girth.
- Measure the length between your knee and the ground.
- Measure the length of your cubit (elbow to middle fingertip).

- Compare the length of your left and right feet.
- Count how many beads, pegs, or other objects you can pick up in your right hand. What about your left hand?
- How much water can you displace in a transparent container with each hand in turn immersed to the wrist? (Mark water line with tape before and after immersion.)
- Tally your wrist pulse or heartbeat, briefly using a stethoscope.
- Compare the different hair colors of people in the classroom.
- What colors can you see at the greatest distance?
- What colors can you see in the dark? What difference does sunlight make?
- What can you see when you look at a ruler in a transparent jar full of water?
- What can you see through Jell-O?
- What can you see when you look at a leaf or newsprint through a magnifying glass? Through a drop of water? Through a drop of oil? Through (how many) layers of plastic wrap?
- Compare and sort out transparent and opaque objects. Which objects are easier to see? Where? With a flashlight?
- How can you change the way things look with mirrors? (This activity might tie in with earlier explorations of symmetrical patterns of seeds in fruits.)
- What can you see with a periscope?

You can also help the children create a horizontal or vertical graph of the relative distribution of eye color among the children in the class, using a standard-sized index card for each child.

Other sensory studies of children's own capacities include smelling and hearing. Children enjoy identifying different smells such as soap, perfume, vinegar, dry cheese, and so forth. They enjoy identifying sounds of objects when they are dropped, such as a coin, comb, rubber toy, plastic spoon, and so forth. They also feel powerful when they can guess that another child is pouring water, rubbing sandpaper, or blowing bubbles through a straw. It is intriguing to wonder and compare whether it is easiest to hear when an action is taking place to the right, left, front, or rear of you.

A standard Montessori material consists of covered cylinders that are filled with gradations of grains. Children can seriate by size as they shake the cylinders, listen, and project an image of the grains, guessing, for example, whether they are sand grains or pea-sized grains. Of course, as with any seriation activity, it helps when you begin with a single contrast between two containers and then add each new variable gradually.

As children look at and compare body coverings for their own selves as well as for birds, classroom pets, and other animals, they can consider different ways that living beings keep themselves warm or cool. This may even lead to exploring the school's heating and cooling systems, tracing pipes or other conduits. Some people may say that we are too far from classical biology, but it is my belief that understanding in its broadest and most useful sense is achieved best through such networking and exploring of connections.

UNDERSTANDING CHEMISTRY THROUGH SYNERGY

Chemistry really concerns cooperation among the component elements of matter in such a way that chemical processes often seem to become more than the sum of their parts. This is known as *synergy*. For young children, cooking is a familiar activity in which they can see transformations of the parts into new forms, whether apples become applesauce, dry corn becomes popcorn or sprouted corn, or heavy cream becomes whipped cream and eventually butter. Of course, sensitive teachers will try to tie such experiences in synergy to other activities. A visit to a dairy where children can see cows at milking time is an exciting first step in following the food chain, which will lead ultimately to a market, where they can buy cream. In some families, butter may not be a usual food item, so making their own butter for a school snack with crackers can have extra meaning for the children. Here again, we are crossing strict disciplinary boundaries, to touch briefly on economics.

These activities also lend themselves well to recording with photographs, audiotape, drawing, and experience charts. Teachers and kindergarten children can develop recipe charts that integrate pictures and words and become part of the literacy program. They also can develop stick-figure directions on task cards for use in the science area.

Figure 6.4 shows a conceptual planning map for chemistry instruction that reflects synergy. It includes cooking activities, usual in kindergarten practice, and extends to other more or less chemistry-related activities. (Refer back to Figure 3.2 to locate some connections between chemistry and other disciplines.)

The Evaporation/Condensation Cycle

Particularly when we approach the study of the behavior of particles that we cannot see unaided, we need to integrate the study of chemical properties with concrete activities. Children are intrigued by the evaporation/

FIGURE 6.4: Conceptual Planning Map for Chemistry Instruction

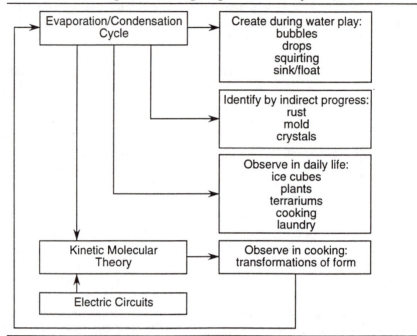

condensation cycle. As with the study of cyclical change through physical and social activities, children's experience with only a part of the cycle will help them to build toward broader understanding. Also, as in all investigative activities, it is useful to develop and use open-ended questions:

- What do you see? (This is worthy of lots of time.)
- What happened when . . . ?
- When might it not happen that way?
- What do you suppose will happen . . . ?
- How might we find out?

Water Play

Since water is the most familiar form in the evaporation/condensation cycle, water play is a good, concrete place to begin. Ice cubes are fun for young children. Consider having some available at the snack table for children to use from time to time. When it seems to fit, after children have had many occasions to savor the ice, you might discuss when the ice seems to melt most quickly or to last the longest. You might even have occasion to try different coverings on the ice cube container, such as a cloth towel, aluminum foil, or Styrofoam, in order to see which material keeps the ice frozen longer.

If you have a snowfall in your area, take the opportunity to look carefully at the snow outdoors; bring some indoors and try to find different ways of keeping the snow frozen longer or of melting it. Consider developing a survey chart during a week in which you measure the height of the snow, then the water, each day and record the amount with a length of yarn. As children compare the lengths of yarn, they manage to raise important questions. At another time, mark the height of the water in a transparent container at the same time each day, to add both drama and precision, as you predict and compare each day. If you heat the snow or ice in a pot, consider using heat-proof glass with a cover so that the children can see the steam and the condensation form. Even if you do not have a glass pot, you can always open the pot for the children to look at the steam, which looks "cloudy," and then see the "rain" form on the cover and the sides of the pot when it cools.[5]

As children carefully observe water heating in a transparent pot, you can help them build toward the drama of the "phase transitions" from still water to simmering to boiling water. Consider asking four or six children to signal the moment of change with a rhythm instrument. At other times, tossing pebbles in a pond, or looking at clouds, or connecting light switches all offer similar moments of phase transition, which you might highlight as contrasts. These kinds of activities begin to create for children a sense of the frontiers of scientists' studies today in the fields of *chaos theory* (see Gleick, 1987) and *complexity theory* (see Waldrop, 1992). Indeed, when you give them a chance, they will share with enthusiasm their observations and ideas concerning the nature of such changes.

As part of your plant studies, you might consider whether there are some places in the room where moisture lasts longer and other places where evaporation is faster, such as near heating vents or in direct sunlight. Consider placing transparent containers of the same size, containing the same amounts of water, in these places as well as in a closet or near an outside door. You might consider putting salt and sugar in some containers, to see if they make any difference. Do take the opportunity to see what happens after all the water has evaporated in the salted or sugared containers. In all such activities, *predict, observe, talk, compare,* and *record.*

If the occasion arises at birthday parties, you might ask the children to describe what they see as they look at the candles. Just observing is an adequate activity, as long as you accept what you hear from children.

Clothing does become wet in school from time to time, and there are occasions when children might launder sociodramatic play clothes. If there is a reasonable moment, ideally not planned grandly ahead of time, you might take the time to consider with the small group involved in the activity which fabrics seem to dry more quickly. It would be good to have cotton, nylon, silk, corduroy, wool, and plastic items handy.

This activity can lead to a written chart that has a sample of each labeled item, in the order of drying time. You can record statements, such as "The silk dried faster than the cotton shirt," "The nylon was the first to dry," and "The wool sweater took the longest to dry." Another language-related activity could include asking a small group to describe and list how various wet and dry objects feel (Richards et al., 1976a).

Making *bubbles* with water is another favorite activity. Richards and associates (1976a) recommend asking the children, "How many ways can you make water bubble?" The children's suggestions might include clapping hands under water, moving a large cloth, blowing through a pipe, blowing through a drinking straw, and blowing up a balloon and letting out the air under water. Have at hand such items as various wires, bubble wands of different size, sieves, and kitchen basters. As children learn to blow large bubbles, ask them to share their findings and describe what happens as they blow harder and more softly, when a bubble pops, and what colors they see (Department of Education & Science, 1989). Children might collaborate in blowing bubbles with straws from the same container, classify bubbles, measure them, catch their wet impressions on paper, and write and read about them (Charlesworth & Lind, 1990). Children also can compare the bubbles that they create with soap, vinegar, oil, or milk (Elementary Science Study, 1971a). The aesthetic aspects of bubbles and the social metaphor of imagining yourself seated or moving inside of your own bubble reflect still other perspectives. These activities represent the roots of experiences that may grow toward the adult scientists' and mathematicians' study of the stress points and phase transitions of bubbles.

As another activity, children have compared density, smell, color, and viscosity of water with corn syrup and vegetable oil and have observed what happened when objects moved through different liquids (Sprung, Froschl, & Campbell, 1985). Kindergarten children also enjoy playing with the "grabbiness" property (surface tension) of water as they fill a cup beyond the top with an eye dropper—one suspenseful drop at a time. They also enjoy moving objects through water by blowing into transparent plastic piping (Nichols & Nichols, 1990). A particularly dramatic activity uses two half-gallon plastic bottles, held together at the openings by duct tape or vinyl tubing. Enclose water or colored water and a different object, such as a toothpick, button, or pebble, in each connected pair of bottles. Ask children to predict which object will descend first or last as the bottles are turned over at the same time (adapted from Wilmes & Wilmes, 1991). Children also enjoy creating spiral "storms" with these attached bottles. In all of these activities, build expectancies by encouraging predictions, observations, and comparisons. There are other sources for additional activities (Bird, 1978; Kamii & DeVries, 1978/1993; Sherwood, Williams, & Rockwell, 1990). As you select activities in order to design a sequence, consider matching activities with the multiple perspectives by which children may integrate perceptual models.

Other water exploration activities that might be classified more readily as physical rather than chemical knowledge are worth mentioning in this context. Certainly, seeing which objects sink or float is an involving activity that represents the underlying *dialectical* perceptual model. It is most useful when children predict whether or not an object will sink or float, try the object, and become puzzled to find their prediction unfulfilled. For example, young children tend to expect that larger objects will sink. When a larger object floats or a smaller object sinks, they experience a moment of cognitive dissonance, which jars their learning, just as happened with magnet sizes.

Sometimes children discover on their own how to alter the surface area of an object, or use clay or aluminum foil in ways that help an object to float or sink. While you can provide a variety of materials for this classification activity, ask children to suggest others. It is most useful to record children's findings after plenty of exploration. You might either list the objects that float and those that sink or develop a cooperative collage or drawings of the sunken and floating objects; or survey and chart the predictions and findings for each object.

Other water exploration activities include squirting water into a tub, using containers of different shape, size, and size of opening. Encourage the children to observe the following:

- Notice which openings water squirts out of more quickly.
- Determine how high the container needs to be before the stream either becomes wiggly or turns into droplets.
- Notice what differences are seen when funnels, straws, eye droppers, and syringes are used.
- Watch what happens when two streams meet as they fall.
- Using a balance scale, weigh different liquids such as water, juices, oil, and milk (Elementary Science Study, 1971a).

While we have moved some way from the beginnings of the discussion about the evaporation/condensation cycle, it is worth mentioning one other role of water that you might study, that is, water as an aspect of the weather. You can compare quality of precipitation, such as heavy or light rain, drizzles, or snow.

Temperature

Children need to understand the notion of density somewhat if they are ultimately to understand temperature as well as evaporation–condensation. Concepts of density grow from their daily experiences with balance scales and water play.

The child who has time to study a straw sinking into a thick milkshake and says, "Oh, look; like quicksand," is learning about density just as she did when she took delight in slopping through mud. Experiences with foods, plant textures, the bathtub, and blowing soap bubbles are related, as are rush-hour train trips, packed elevators, and popular buffet tables.

Kindergarten children can survey and seriate food and plant densities using straws and lenses. They can survey traffic density and crowd density at different places and times and chart them. Their observations of heating and cooling processes further contribute to building a notion of density. One of the most time-honored activities is to heat in a pan of water a cooled bottle whose opening is covered with an attached balloon. As the water heats, children become excited to see the balloon expand; when the bottle is placed in a pan of ice cubes, they watch the balloon shrink. This demonstration is a dramatic example of the *molecular-kinetic theory*. In effect, heat speeds the movement of molecules and causes them to expand away from each other, whereas cooling slows the movement of molecules while compressing them. For children, the value of such an experience may lie in the process of wondering and the questions that are beginning to form.

Bear in mind that kindergarten children can gain more when they actually do things physically in ways that grow out of their inquiries, rather than merely observing a demonstration. A worthwhile activity is worth repeating for others, as they become receptive. At the same time, not everybody needs to have participated in each activity.

Because temperature is a more abstract and changeable condition to measure than something like length, it is helpful to use nonstandard representations and analogy. An example of nonstandard representation would be marking a large thermometer by color designations such as red for hot, yellow for medium, and blue for cold. Varying the sizes of the thermometers is another way to do this.

When you introduce a personal analogy, children have a chance to learn about temperature personally and aesthetically: "When you get into bed at night and the sheets are cold, what does your body do?" and "When you get into bed and it is a hot, sticky night, what does your body do?" The mercury in the thermometer thus becomes more accessible to the young child, as children empathize their way toward understanding.

Electric Circuits

Kindergarten children's earlier experiences with magnets can help them to appreciate the concept of forces in electricity. They are quite comfortable setting up electric circuits that work to operate a light or bell. Children can assemble a battery-driven circuit themselves when they have clamps that they can easily squeeze open and shut in order to attach the wires, light, switch, and battery. These inexpensive materials are available in hardware stores.

The concept of closing and opening circuits for the transfer of energy is a fruitful one. Children can draw pictures and write experience charts, with your help, about the activity. They can use the light as stop and go signs in their sociodramatic play. Parents and other adults in the school usually are pleased to see children using such sophisticated-looking material.

Although kindergarten children do not grasp the underlying concept of unseen electrons in an adult sense, anymore than they might accurately imagine the transformations in the evaporation–condensation cycle, they are receptive to these activities inasmuch as they can feel successful. This is an opportunity to help all children, regardless of gender, to feel comfortable as they handle technological materials and hear related vocabulary. In these instances, we defer assessment of information learned and instead focus on assessing a child's willingness to compare and risk thinking critically.

The Whole Is More Than the Sum of Its Parts

Besides cooking, there are other chemical transformations that you can look at through concrete classroom activities. There was mention earlier about looking at the results of evaporating liquids that contained salt or sugar. Evaporation, as well as electrical conduction, is one of a number of means for identifying materials indirectly. Crystallization is a sophisticated chemical process that children may encounter in their later studies. Their work in building with blocks, playing with mirrors, stringing beads, building patterns in their artwork, and classifying objects and changes can build toward an understanding of these concepts.

There are other chemical changes that children will notice around them, such as rust, decay, and mold. It is relevant for them to question these changes and to see what happens over time, as well as when conditions vary. Here are some examples:

- If you sandpaper rust off your bicycle, will it rust again?
- Does wood rust? How can we find out what rusts?
- Will objects rust in a plastic bag? On a shelf indoors? On an outdoor window sill? Before/after they are painted? When they are refrigerated, frozen, or heated? When they are buried in soil?
- What happens if you change the environment of rusty objects? (Elementary Science Study, 1976c.)

Similar questions can come up when your pumpkin molds, when children notice that bread dries and crumbles and crackers become soggy and taste stale, and when molds of different colors appear on foods. All these changes reflect the cooperation among parts and the processes that contribute to the chemical transformation of matter.

REFLECTIONS

In all these sample activities that emphasize the physical, biological, and chemical sciences, the main work for us in the kindergarten is to create experiences in which children can be physically active, questioning, and touched by awe.

Acting and wondering together are at the heart of the study of science. Talk comes at the end rather than the beginning, and some things just never need words. There are numerous books written for young children that deal with "science" topics. If you do use any of them, you will want to apply your best criteria for selecting literature for children and will save the books until after children have had the experiences.

Activities provide the possibilities for children to perceive the kernel models that extend beyond a particular datum of experience. A particular activity, in itself, conveys no magic; a particular tool, in itself, carries no insight. It is the children, through experiencing inductive possibilities, who can construct their own perceptions, connections, and insights.

As a teacher, if your initial responsibility is to plan meaningful activities, your ongoing responsibility is to appreciate children's unique ways of making connections, being flexible, and expressing their receptivity to activities. This understanding of how the children experience things can then become the basis for planning future work.

In the sciences, as in all areas of study, there is certainly plenty that each adult does not know and about which adult scientists today still wonder. When your teaching raises many new questions with children, you are helping to keep them open to exploring the unknown and preparing them to find excitement in the challenges that they will inherit. When children raise "why" questions, it is worthwhile to appreciate that, "Questions are themselves mini-theories, and a theory means that the child already has the cognitive wherewithal to relate two or more facts" (Forman & Landry, 1992, p. 190).

New cognitive learning often grows out of pleasurable, social, physical, aesthetic, and perceptual pastimes. All too often, however, the public categorizes as "frills" those activities in school that involve artforms and concrete experiences with natural phenomena. In times of fiscal austerity, funding for these ways of learning can fall prey to the financial guilt felt among uninformed lay groups who understand only the linear thinking and disconnected information contained in traditional textbooks. However, richness and variety of experience and coming at things from varied perspectives are principles that support human, functional learning.

When we base activity plans for kindergarten children upon an appreciation of the unique ways in which workers in the domains of physics, biology, chemistry, earth science, and so forth study the world, we find that the division between domains becomes secondary. What is primary are the active, concrete experiences that wrap themselves around data from many perspectives. Isolated "cognitive" learning is not the only way to learn. The physical, emotional, social, and aesthetic residues of experience form the roots of early images from which children can build the networks of associations and connections that nurture later forms of understanding. Therefore, we expose children to activities that can have some degrees of personal meaning to them and that appeal to some of their motives to feel competent. They extend and employ imagery, social skills, language skills, art skills, and mathematical skills in their study of the sciences. The multiple ways of working, the processes of inquiry, become content for kindergarten children. In the course of their activity in the full-day kindergarten, children acquire the pure information, knowledge, and attitudes that lead to further understanding and cooperation.

7

Cooperative Mathematics

Mathematics is a discipline that usually is regarded as a tool or a skill. Children can learn mathematics as they apply it to the study of many social and physical phenomena; however, it is often taught as if it were an end in itself. In this chapter, mathematics is presented so that it can be used as an applied body of constructions and activities. Educators agree that a meaningful integration of mathematical study helps children to develop a positive disposition to learning and using mathematics (Atkinson, 1992; Commission for Teaching Standards for School Mathematics, 1991; Jensen, 1993; Stoessinger & Edmunds, 1992). Inasmuch as children come to school with plenty of quantitative event knowledge, the teacher's job is to build bridges from children's informal mathematics and solving of real quantitative problems to the conventional language of mathematics, grouping, and representation. A parallel development occurs in the inductive ways that children learn to speak, read, and write, as discussed in Chapter 9.

One of the big problems in kindergarten is finding a way to teach mathematics that will satisfy parents that teachers are doing serious business, even though workbooks and ditto sheets are not used as the core of the program. As I emphasize throughout this book, early education can be a public relations nightmare because intellect develops through physical, social, and aesthetic means. In order to communicate the seriousness of our purpose, we as teachers must present our program so that parents and other educators can understand that we are engaged in mathematics education through a variety of forms.

Toward this end, it is useful to establish a mathematics area that includes many of the components we will discuss in the following section.

THE MATHEMATICS AREA

Physical Setup

There should be a physical space set aside and labeled as a mathematics area. It should contain

- Concrete materials (see list that follows)
- Mats upon which to use each set of concrete materials, in order to define work space for many small pieces in a set
- Storage space
- Writing materials (consider including a date stamp)
- Standard measures such as a cup, ruler, meter stick, and tape measure
- Two tables and six to eight chairs
- Floor space as an alternative area for using materials

Concrete materials often include the following:

- Beads and laces
- Pegs and pegboards (rubber bands and sometimes geoboards)
- Parquetry blocks
- Balance scale with accessories, such as labeled boxes of buttons, pine cones, wooden cubes, washers, and so forth
- Sand/water table and accessories
    Containers (ideally, the containers are transparent and include different shapes that hold the same volume)
    Measuring cups (transparent) and spoons of varying sizes
    Transparent funnels, transparent tubes of varying length and diameter, squirting bottles, and a rotary beater
    Sponges and cloths
- Unifix cubes and Stern arithmetic blocks
- Sequential pattern cards (Developmental Learning Materials Teaching Resources, 1985) or *Geoboard Activity Cards: Primary* (Barson, n.d.) (suggestion: to keep the cards in sequence, punch holes in them and secure them in a ring binder)
- Commercial and teacher-made games such as board games and card games

Less usual manipulative materials that are worth having, even if you build your stock by adding a few each year, would include:

- Attribute Blocks and People Pieces (Elementary Science Study, 1974a), or their generic equivalents
- Cuisenaire rods
- Nonstandard measures such as drinking straws, yarn, and strings of differing thickness and texture
- Centimeter graph paper
- Dienes's multibase arithmetic blocks

- Tool tote trays for holding together related materials so that they can be moved easily to a place where children will use them, whether to a table, a mat on the floor, or outdoors

Aids in Teaching Mathematics

Mathematics Notebooks. Each child should have a personal mathematics notebook labeled as such, with the child's name. These notebooks are stored in the mathematics area, next to writing materials. The notebook can begin as a set of blank, unlined pages with an oaktag or construction paper cover.

Content might include drawings, photographs, and attached lengths of yarn, straws, or paper with labels. Many kindergarten children can copy a line of text early in the school year, and most of them feel comfortable using invented spelling to record their experiences. A folder or word cards containing words that are related to a particular activity may be stored in the area. Do keep in mind that mathematics is an applied tool and many activities will be related to children's measurements and other quantitative studies of physical and social events.

Mathematics Homework. Each child should be encouraged to bring home a zip-lock plastic bag, labeled "Math Homework," each week. The purpose of this bag, in addition to providing children with a worthwhile activity, is to involve parents. Develop ideas cooperatively with other kindergarten teachers and use them optionally. You might send home different homework with different children. Send parents photocopied homework instructions. Some homework samples are

> Dear Parent,
>   We have used the piece of yarn in this bag to measure some objects in school. Please help your child find things at home that are the same length as the yarn. Please send two objects to school that are the same length as the yarn.

You can use the same technique in studying family size over generations, and the result is often a truly engrossing kindergarten social science research project. Again, send letters home to the parents to enlist their cooperation, such as the following:

> Dear Parents,
>   We are making a survey of families at school. Please have your child make a mark for each brother and sister that you have.

Mother's brothers: _____ and sisters:_____
Father's brothers: _____ and sisters:_____

Dear Parents,
We are comparing generations of families at school. Please have your child make a mark for each brother and sister of his/her grandparents.
Maternal grandmother's brothers:_____ and sisters:_____
Maternal grandfather's brothers: _____ and sisters:_____
Paternal grandmother's brothers: _____ and sisters:_____
Paternal grandfather's brothers: _____ and sisters:_____

Begin with the data from the children's immediate families, graphing the results of the survey and then describing the findings. Then you can graph and describe the results of the parent's families and then the grandparents' families. Did the sizes of families in different generations in your class change or remain about the same? Children might also create an individual family comparison as well as a group study of generations. What patterns exist in different families?

In these kinds of surveys, you are applying mathematics to social science research. You are also integrating writing skills by describing your findings.

Do be sensitive to the possibility that you may have parents who are unable to read English and/or their native language, reflect alternative families, or are otherwise uncomfortable with messages from school. Be sure to talk about the homework task with the children beforehand and read the precise message to them at school before they take home their homework bag. "Backpacks" serve as an additional way to involve parents. Chapter 9 describes the use of backpacks developing verbal literacy. Teachers have adapted similar procedures for cooperative mathematical projects.

Bulletin Boards and Displays. The findings of your class's studies and homework surveys can be represented in graphic forms and displayed on classroom and hallway bulletin boards or in display cases, as well as in children's mathematics notebooks. For example, you might label a hallway display, "Kindergarten Math Study in February," and present a concrete format in which one or more groups of children have been involved.

Activity File. Keep a personal card file of cooperative mathematics activity ideas. When you have one idea on each card, it is easy to add new ideas and to sequence activities.

Camera. Photograph children when they are engaged in cooperative mathematics with concrete materials or as they record findings in their notebooks. Share these prints and slides with parents at meetings or on bulletin boards and in hallway displays.

While funding is sometimes difficult, most school districts have a system whereby teachers can request small grants for special projects. Parents' associations are another source for funds. You may even find that your building principal has some discretionary funds that you can use for buying and developing film. You can also ask the school district's public relations representative to come into your classroom to take photographs when you have accumulated several surveys and children can demonstrate some of their activities.

Parent Involvement. Let parents know what you are doing in mathematics education at meetings and parent conferences, as well as with occasional notes. Notes to parents need not be any more complicated than this example.

Dear Fiske Family,
    Ray weighed and measured the hamster today and wrote it up in the Math Book. It was exciting to see Ray's enthusiasm.
                                        Sincerely,
                                        Lee Allen

The math homework projects, described earlier, also involve parents.

COOPERATIVE MATHEMATICS

Kindergarten children learn mathematics best when they engage in concrete activities with other children. Working together, they use mathematics as a tool to solve the natural problems that arise in their encounters with the physical and social worlds. There are two important, interrelated assumptions for teaching contained in this approach that influence kindergarten mathematics activities.

The first assumption is that kindergarten children should have legitimate opportunities for social interaction in connection with their active learning of mathematics. They learn about quantity as they compare and contrast physical relationships, and many of their activities with other children revolve around these experiences. As they encounter one another's varied viewpoints, they extend from their own view and decenter from it.

The second assumption is that kindergarten children should have opportunities to participate in activities that create cognitive dissonance. Indeed, children's social interactions create more opportunities for cognitive dissonance as children predict, observe, and compare their views with those of others. Kindergarten teachers can provide conditions in which cooperative mathematics can flourish when they plan activities for children to pursue independently in dyads and when they work with children in small-group activities that use contrasting materials.

Gender Differences in Mathematics Achievement

Inasmuch as boys and girls come to school with different patterns of socializing and game preferences, it is no surprise that researchers are finding that boys seem to achieve better than girls in mathematics after the elementary school years (Maccoby & Jacklin, 1974; Serbin, 1978). There is a general acceptance that boys' superior visual and spatial skills are largely responsible for this difference, whereas girls generally perform better at verbal tasks. This appears to be consistent with the fact that as many as 90 percent of the children in school remedial reading programs are boys. While most schools offer such programs, few schools, in striking contrast, offer remedial mathematics programs.

Contrary to popular belief, researchers also find that boys seem to be at least as social as girls, but in a somewhat different way (Maccoby & Jacklin, 1974). While boys will often congregate in larger peer groups, beginning as early as nursery school, girls tend to engage in one or two social contacts at a time and are found in smaller social groups.

These are general research trends that summarize an immense number of studies and are subject to some exceptions. It is useful, however, to plan instruction that will counterbalance these factors and help prevent handicaps later in school. It makes sense to plan for all children to have visual-spatial experience and for those who need it to have extra help. It also makes sense to plan for all children to have experiences in large-muscle group games that require collaborative planning and afford opportunities to practice alternative strategies.

Organizing and Grouping for Instruction

If you want to create the best possible learning situation for all your children, then you will offer mathematics instruction to small groups and individual children, based upon their needs, just as you do in reading or science instruction. The full-day schedule provides time to organize in this way while leaving time for other worthwhile experiences.

FOUNDATIONS IN MOTOR ACTIVITY

Mathematics concepts depend upon visual-spatial relationships that children experience in the physical world. Children develop visual-spatial skills when they have many and varied motor experiences, including music and movement, large-muscle games, and building activities in which they explore three-dimensional space.

When teachers notice some children who need more exposure to these kinds of activities, they can find ways to extend the time that children will spend in an area. They can encourage participation by (1) inviting the child or children to work with the teacher in a particular motor activity at a specific time and (2) physically moving near the child or children who are in an area that is helpful for improving visual-spatial skills.

The floor-block building area, part of the sociodramatic area, is one place where girls and other underrepresented children need teacher encouragement if they are to gain some of the large-muscle, three-dimensional skills usually associated with mathematics. It is also worthwhile to have large hollow wooden building blocks outdoors, either stored in a shed or rolled out each day. The playground and gymnasium are other places where you can encourage more reticent children to participate.

Games can help children to build visual-spatial skills, including games with balls and hoops, climbing and jumping games, and group games requiring collaborating with others, free from the pressure of hard competition. Various group games, skills games with marbles, and tag games have been used successfully (Cratty, n.d.; Kamii & DeVries, 1980).

Particularly in a full-day kindergarten, it is important to schedule more than one opportunity for such large-muscle activity each day. Some settings offer locations for such activities both outdoors and in a large indoor playground–gymnasium.

Motor experiences take place as children use concrete materials for mathematics education. Five-year-olds readily play with place values and the concept of base when they have concrete referents. For example, the Dienes (1969, 1973) multibase arithmetic blocks (Educational Teaching Aids, 1985) and a home-made die or dice can easily become a place-value game using bases between 2 and 10. It is much easier for young children to work with base-2 blocks than with base-10 blocks, simply because 2 has fewer variables.

The original Dienes blocks are calibrated pieces of natural wood in which the cubic-centimeter unit block has the value of x^0; the long block, x^1; the flat block, x^2; and the "block" block, x^3. In base 2, the wooden blocks have the relationship shown in Figure 7.1.

In base 3, the long block is equal to three units, or three cubic centimeters, and the long block in base 10 is equal to ten units. If a player collects ten units in throwing the dice, then she can trade them for a long block in base 10. However, if using base 3, these ten units are worth one flat block and one unit block (see arrows in Figure 7.2).

FIGURE 7.1: Dienes Multibase Arithmetic Blocks—Base 2

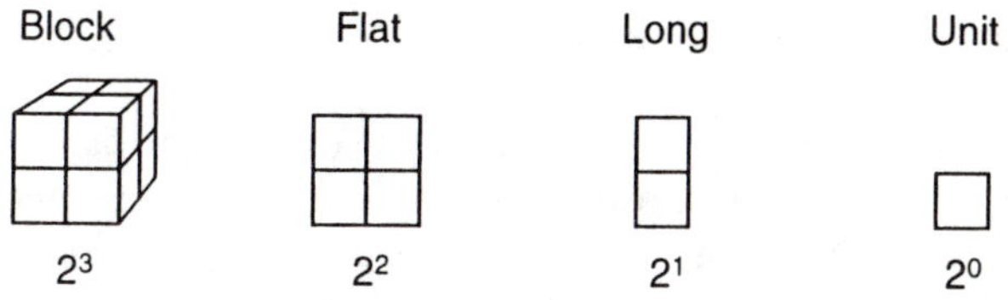

It is a delight to see 5-year-olds' enthusiastic absorption as they trade two units for a long when they play in base 2, or three units for a long when they play in base 3, and four longs for a flat when they play in base 4, and five flats for a block when they play in base 5. In base 10, ten units (ones column) can be traded for a long, ten longs (tens column) can be traded for a flat, and ten flats (hundreds column) can be traded for a block (thousands column).

Initially, children (and many adults) need to physically remove from the storage box the exact units that they have drawn, match them with their existing collection, and then trade up to the next-larger-size wood in the base. After a while, the children learn to anticipate a trade "in their heads" and trade up by exchanging part of their existing collection, eliminating the intermediary motion. When you see this anticipation taking place consistently for a few children, you can try providing centimeter graph paper on which they can record their final set of wood, marking the equivalent cubic-centimeter squares. Adults who despaired of ever comprehending bases, or who thought they understood but in fact had only relied on memorized formulas, have found authentic understanding of the concept after playing with Dienes blocks.

On another level, children understand multibases when you provide a model that they can complete:

FIGURE 7.2: Dienes Multibase Arithmetic Blocks—Base 3

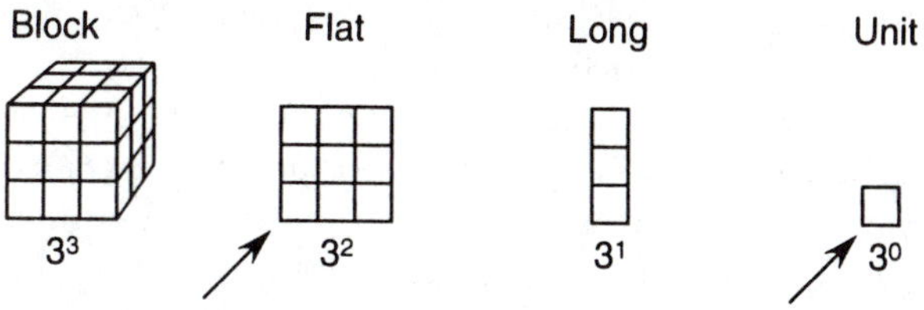

Teacher: If this is a grain of sand (unit) and this is a pebble (long),
then this is a rock (flat) and next would be a . . .
Children: Mountain! Boulder! Hill! . . .

Beginning to use the blocks must come only after many prior activities with one-to-one correspondence and concrete experiences with concepts, including larger than, smaller than, any, some, either–or, biggest–smallest, pairs, groups of two, sets of two, and simple seriations. After a few weeks during which many small groups have played in base 2 and some children seem ready to move ahead, it makes sense to bring out base 3 for them. Do be particularly sensitive to the more timid children who may not select this activity during the integrated activity periods. Invite them, set a time with them, and be with them when they need encouragement.

FOUNDATIONS IN RULES

Mathematician and philosopher Alfred North Whitehead (1911/1958) contends that mathematics consists of establishing rules and understanding their relationships. The "gambling–counting–trading" game with Dienes multibase arithmetic blocks and simple ball games help children build toward a sense of codifying rules. Elementary Science Study's Attribute Blocks (1974a), Color Cubes, and colored loops are useful also as children build a notion of rules. Kindergarten children can establish their own rules and try to guess the rules that their friends create with the Color Cubes and the colored loops. Figure 7.3 describes a sequence of activities for building rules.

These activities involve classification in a cheerfully charged, suspenseful atmosphere of, "What's going to happen next?" The teacher models, the children predict, the children replicate, and then the children construct their own rules so that other children and the teacher can try to guess them. In this activity, children are dealing in very concrete ways with class inclusion, intersection of sets, and class exclusion. Each session involves five to ten minutes of instruction and some flexible follow-up time when children can play independently, on their own and with one another.

In setting rules for others, including the teacher as well as other children, the children experience a healthy sense of power. They are also on the way to dealing with placing the same number of cubes in each "playground," beginning with a one-to-one correspondence, then by counting, and then by adding and subtracting. Clearly, different children will demonstrate by their use of the materials that they are ready at different times for the next steps. The loops and cubes also lend themselves to "community planning" kinds of activities, as they represent zones and functions.

FIGURE 7.3: A Concrete Activity Sequence for Building Rules

Build a Cognitive Map. Shake a covered box of Color Cubes and ask children what they think might be inside. Take out one cube and ask, "What do you see?" "Guess what else might be inside." At a separate time, it is useful to follow the same procedure with the Attribute Blocks and the People Pieces, which also vary in size and shape as well as color.

Build Sets. Lay out a red loop and a blue loop so that they do not touch. "Let's pretend that this is a red playground and that this is a blue playground. I have a rule that I can put red cubes in the red playground and blue cubes in the blue playground. Here are two loops. What cubes can you put in the green loop? In the yellow loop?" (Children place cubes.)

Build Intersecting Sets. Lay out the red loop and the blue loop so that they overlap each other in part. "I can put red cubes in the red part and blue cubes in the blue part. Now, there is this part (overlapping) which is both blue and red. Let's put cubes in it. Which ones can be there?" "Now use the green and yellow playground loops."

Build Class Exclusion. Lay out the red loop and the blue loop. "Guess what rules I am using." (Place blue cubes in the red playground loop and red cubes in the blue playground loop.) "Here is a green playground loop and a yellow playground loop. Place the green and yellow cubes, using the same rule that I just used." Then, "Make up your own rule and let us try to guess what it is." After building these activities over several sessions, you might place cubes outside, but adjacent to, the same-color loops. A "People Sorting" game uses a similar procedure (Downie, Slesnick, & Stenmark, 1981, p. 28). Children themselves enter, or leave, a large loop of yarn laid out on the floor. They base their movement upon some attribute such as wearing something green or not wearing glasses. They guess each other's rules.

Any activities with simple mazes, including large-muscle obstacle-course versions, help to develop rule-building skills. The perceptual model of *indirect progress* is represented in these activities, which sharpen children's visual-spatial skills in challenging ways.

Playing with color matrices is a helpful parallel activity. Children might begin by looking at a pattern of cubes, having someone remove a cube, and then guessing which cube is missing. Reversing two cubes in a matrix, children can attempt to locate the change for one another. In addition to playing with rules, children are also developing scanning skills.

Since mathematics is a rule-bound occupation, as are group games, children need to have opportunities to explore and test rules in many games that they play. Research indicates that children develop an understanding of rules as they live through repeated social interaction and get feedback from their peers (Piaget, 1965). Often cognitive dissonance is involved when children experience such feedback.

Five-year-olds use rules in games, but they apply them incompletely, although with confidence. Therefore children need repeated opportunities to test the rules, to see how they work, to make and play with rules, and to see how their actions affect other people.

The parallel between the rules of children's games and the rules of mathematics is too important to ignore. This is particularly true with respect to boys, who traditionally have been more involved with group sports, building with large floor blocks, and woodworking, activities that tend to improve their visual-spatial development. Kindergarten teachers need to be aware of these factors and plan for girls as well as boys to build with large blocks, engage in group sports and rule-bound games, and continue their woodworking and other problem-solving activities. Teachers can use regular planning sessions and the times that they circulate around the classroom as opportunities to encourage the participation of all the children in cooperative mathematics.

FOUNDATIONS IN RELATIONSHIPS

One might infer that mathematics is to discursive, logical forms what music is to nondiscursive, imaginative forms. As an expressive form, each discipline uses unique abstract symbols and deals with relationships.

In mathematics, you are helping children to understand relationships in space, shape, and size and to develop the ability to represent these relationships through symbols. However, learning mathematics is more than acquiring a rapid command of "number facts" and basic arithmetic computation. Machines are able to do that better than people.

The standards of the National Council of Teachers of Mathematics have moved beyond only technical, rote approaches to encouraging teachers to help children develop

> mathematical power . . . [which includes] the ability to explore, conjecture, and reason logically; to solve nonroutine problems; to communicate about and through mathematics; and to connect ideas within mathematics and between mathematics and other intellectual activity. (Commission for Teaching Standards for School Mathematics, 1991, p. 1)

The Council's definition of mathematical power is congruent with the integrated and meaning-based approaches to curriculum design that include perceptual models and the seven conditions of learning outlined earlier in Chapter 3.

Other ways in which the Council standards are compatible with this book's outlook include their egalitarian concern that "every child" have access to a respectful learning environment in a decentralized setting where children's voices are present along with the teacher's voice. The Council also underscores the importance of helping children to develop a disposition to engage in mathematics.

A disposition to engage in mathematical (or verbal) literacy activities makes the difference between seeking out opportunities to use literacy skills or avoiding them in school and thereafter. One researcher found that children whose teachers felt comfortable with mathematics were those children whose achievement in and attitudes toward mathematics prospered (Karp, 1988). Consider your own mathematical autobiography, present attitudes, and what enthusiasms you convey. Consider how you can relate to the notion of mathematics as a body of games with rules, games which mathematicians both play and create: "The really profound changes in human life all have their ultimate origin in knowledge pursued for its own sake" (Whitehead, 1911/1958, pp. 19–20). Play, the arena in which children feel empowered, is "pursued for its own sake." If the roots of your discomfort with mathematics begin with the sense of "required work" rather than playfulness and choice, then perhaps you need to reflect on your playfulness index.

Children will need help in building positive dispositions and expectancies, in understanding how and when to use the tool that mathematics is, and in applying computational skills where they are relevant. Objects, task cards, and books, whether employed separately or in combination, do not insure that children will learn. You need to juxtapose elements at the proper times, with adequate preparation and appropriate follow-up activities, in order to help children gain an enriched sense of the world.

The Nuffield Mathematics Project (1967), developed with children, offers a framework that is useful with young children and is integrated into the discussion that follows. Other approaches, in addition to the Dienes multibase arithmetic blocks and the Attribute Blocks, include activities that use Cuisenaire rods, the VeriTech materials, and Cruikshank, Fitzgerald, and Jensen's (1980) analysis of an early childhood measurement sequence. You will find relevant activities to adapt and selectively sequence that reflect the framework of relationships discussed in this chapter in such approaches as *Mathematics Their Way* (Baratta-Lorton, 1976), *Box It and Bag It Mathematics* (Burk, Snider, & Symonds, 1988), and *Math Excursions K* (Burk, Snider, & Symonds, 1992). As you adapt ideas from such enthusiastic collections, you might consider giving priority to those activities (1) that you can integrate with real, rather than contrived or "cute," activities and (2) that provide children with opportunities to figure out their own strategies. You might view with healthy hesitation tasks that require you to cut out lots of patterns.

Children learn about relationships among space, shape, and size by active participation. Relationships are relative; therefore children need contrasting experiences, some of which will be detailed in the following sections.

Space

Kindergarten children explore space in a variety of ways. Visual and plastic arts, building with blocks, and construction activities provide them with data. When they try to fit into boxes, tunnels, toys, last year's coat, father's shoes, or an area near the teacher, they learn about space.

Topology is a good way to study spatial properties. Mathematical topology studies the "existence of permanence in the midst of change" (Guillen, 1983, p. 153), whether in the arts, psychology, politics, economics, or physics. For example, the sizes of markings made on a deflated balloon will change when the balloon is inflated, but the topological relations—relative ordinal positions among any set of points on the markings—remain the same. Children learn this kind of spatial order through repeated transforming actions that bend, twist, or stretch, just as they learn to recognize a particular person intuitively on the basis of a profile view (Copeland, 1984; Piaget & Inhelder, 1956/1963; Sauvy & Sauvy, 1974). Both the social and the physical components of this development have their roots in the baby's development of object permanence.

Some of the activities that help children build this intuitive sense of spatial order include work with clay, yarn, rubber bands, and other malleable materials. The actions children perform with these materials—molding, tying, sewing, weaving, stretching, compressing, and so forth—foster the acquisition of early geometric concepts upon which projective and Euclidian geometry can develop.

Children also reconstruct concepts of *enclosure* and *boundary* through some of these activities, as well as through building with blocks, puzzling over mazes, and engaging in various mapping activities, such as those that involve Color Cubes and colored loops. Experiences that call upon the child to differentiate by categories such as part of/not a part of, inside/outside/on, and before/after/in between provide excellent opportunities for inductive learning of these ideas.

Proximity and continuity concepts can develop through countless daily activities that involve tying knots, stringing beads, and various science activities with evaporation and condensation. Such learning grows whenever an experience calls for being close to or far away, in front of or behind, above or below, and to the left or right.

During kindergarten, children's sense of topology will develop intuitively before their sense of relative length and number of surfaces or angles emerges. For example, the notion of continuity, which is required in order to see a line in geometry as an infinite set of points, is beyond the usual kindergarten child's sensorial or perceptual experience. You help children to extend and deepen their topological experiences when you provide concrete materials that children can transform and plan activities in which they can feel and see contrasts in texture and appearance. Children also need a chance to talk about what they are seeing and feeling as they are using materials.

Examples of topological activities are given in Figure 7.4. These activities focus on contrasts and changes. For example, pouring is a most concrete example of change. It is especially important to provide children with containers of varied shapes and sizes as well as a series of containers of standard size gradations, which will help children learn about volume. Children acquire the concept of conservation of quantities with objects only after many experiences in which they have observed and have themselves created transformations of shape, size, and space that are reversible in real, social settings.

Shape

Children can explore shapes in a variety of ways. When children match and compare similar and different shapes, and series of shapes whose sizes vary, they build discrimination skills. When they fit shapes into corresponding openings, they have shown readiness to solve two-dimensional and, later, three-dimensional puzzles. They move from creating rubber band designs on pegboards to geoboard activities.

Geoboards. Geoboards that are circular or triangular as well as square can be used by kindergarten children. Wherever possible, it is useful for two or more children to work together when they are independent of the teacher. Sharing sequenced teacher-made or selected commercial picture task cards, they can work on parallel, equivalent geoboards and later on boards that have different proportions, an experience in topology. Then the children can compare their parallel work, another occasion when they are likely to encounter cognitive dissonance.

Children can explore how many different three-, four-, five-, or six-sided figures they can create on the geoboard. They can replicate street

FIGURE 7.4: Topological Activities

- Tie, twist, or weave yarn or raffia that has two adjacent colors or two adjacent textures. These activities help to sharpen the sense of proximity.
- Build patterns cooperatively with a friend using beads, blocks, stickers, or geoboards, first back to back and then comparing patterns, a potential cognitive dissonance experience.
- Touch an unseen object and match it with corresponding pictures to sharpen images of boundaries.
- Engage in large-muscle creative movement activities with props such as hoops, ropes, discs, and cloth, to help develop a feeling for boundaries, enclosures, and proximity.
- Rotate shapes and objects and play with symmetrical signs to stimulate relative thinking (Waters, 1973).
- Pour water, sand, or beans through funnels, sieves, and tubes, into containers.
- Play "hide-and-seek" in relative-location games with dioramas. For example, Karplus and Thier (1967) use a toy figure, "Mr. O," who functions as a puppet, describing to anyone trying to find him whatever he sees from wherever he is located whether or not he may be moving or seated on a moving vehicle. Kindergarten children and their teacher can play with the observer notion, placing objects in front of "Mr. O," and setting him on both stationary and moving vehicles. Young children can deal with an imaginary observer on much the same level as an imaginary friend who can be blamed for misdeeds. The outside observer points up for children that, depending upon your viewpoint, there may be more than one way to describe a situation. The cognitive dissonance in this tension between viewpoints is an important turning point in learning. Lavatelli (1970) also suggests activities that develop relative spatial concepts. She uses table settings and house, garage, and tree dioramas, often in connection with pictures. You might try dioramas with three-dimensional materials.

signs such as the octagonal stop sign. When used to compare shapes and sizes, geoboards lend themselves to the study of perimeter and area concepts, beginning with nonstandard measures. Children can rotate a figure on a matching geoboard and compare them (Burton et al., 1991). When they bisect a geoboard shape with another rubber band, children build up their sense of division and fractions. As children select geoboard shapes for drawing, they add to their representational repertoire. Related activities would include walking, hopping, crawling, skipping, and jumping around shapes outlined on the playground or floor as well as representations with a "turtle" using LOGO on the computer (Burton et al., 1991).

These various ways of exploring shapes also include considerations for patterned shapes. Patterns of shapes might range from children in alternating sitting and standing formations, to geoboard rubber bands, to pattern blocks or cubes, to fractals.

Fractals. Fractals is a relatively new kind of geometry that deals with branching, in which one constant feature repeats itself on different scales, as is the case with jagged shorelines or broccoli. Computers can generate such branches—fractals—thousands of times on a tiny scale. Children, however, can see and make many of these patterns with three-dimensional materials when working with you in a small group. Mathematician Sharon Whitton Ayers (1993) suggests starting by making designs, such as the following:

• *Branch design.* Children can make a tree, for example, with toothpicks (or other materials). Each branch adds one, then another, branch, like a "frac-ture" or break (See Figure 7.5). They can also cut drinking straws on a carpeted surface and create branches and halves in size. The fractals, rather than size, are the predominant feature. As participants count paths and extend two more each, they are able to see the underlying pattern. The resulting tree diagram makes it easier to organize varied forms of data. These activities also help children to prepare for probability theory.

• *Amish quilt design.* Some children, using a paper square, can mark the midpoint on each of the four sides. Using a straight edge, they line up these midpoints and then draw diagonal lines connecting them. By folding along the lines they have drawn, they create a square within a square. Coloring each set of patterns with a different color highlights the pattern.

FIGURE 7.5: **Branch Design**

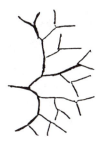

• *Snowflake design*. Children can use an equilateral triangle of paper and mark the midpoint on each side to create three line-segments. Coloring each set of patterns with a different color highlights the pattern. The latter two designs adapt easily to LOGO computer programs.

Tangrams. In contrast to branching patterns, tangrams are puzzles composed of seven shapes that children can assemble in numerous ways. They require children to move outside of preconceived frames of reference and proceed through indirect progress, using trial-and-error manipulation. These puzzles are difficult to do when children begin with the seven pieces and try to replicate the preprinted patterns. The Elementary Science Study (1976b) has developed a sequential approach to learning tangrams that begins with two shapes rather than seven. Using a series of cards, the puzzle proceeds with controlled variables until children reach seven shapes.

In addition to controlling variables, there are a number of steps that help children to develop the *indirect-progress* skills that make it possible to work with all seven shapes. The following steps, adapted from the Tangrams cards (Elementary Science Study, 1976b), can also be used with such materials as the Developmental Learning Materials' (1985) cubes, cards, and parquetry blocks:

1. There is a one-to-one correspondence between the printed pattern outline, which has been demarcated, and the pieces. Pieces are placed on the outline.
2. There is a one-to-one correspondence between the printed pattern, which has not been demarcated, and the pieces. Pieces are placed within the outline.
3. There is a one-to-one correspondence between the outline and the pieces, and children assemble the pieces next to the outline.
4. Children replicate the pattern of shapes that are the same in configuration but different in size.

When you control the variables and increase them gradually in these ways, most kindergarten children can move into the third step. Some children may be able and interested enough to pursue the less concrete fourth step.

Particularly for children with perceptual difficulties, it is very important to control variables and analyze tasks so that they have an abundance of experience similar to the first two steps. Kindergarten children enjoy the Tangrams cards immensely and move through them with increasing enthusiasm and often with incredible speed.

Mini VeriTech. You can increase children's sense of independence by providing self-checking devices and a buddy system of children who have different skills. For example, the Mini VeriTech (1977a, 1977b) booklets contain printed patterns that children compare and categorize. They are sequenced and self-checking when children place patterned block pieces in a boxed frame and compare them with an overall pattern. Children who use these materials enjoy recording their own progress by marking a card each time they complete a page. The catalogues of companies such as Developmental Learning Materials and Educational Teaching Aids include various similar self-checking devices that help children to "appreciate" themselves.

The VeriTech materials appeal to the perceptual skills of kindergarten children. As with Tangrams, many children become obsessed with these materials, perhaps because the VeriTech materials, like Tangrams, are sequenced very gradually. Unlike Tangrams, however, the VeriTech booklets begin at a visual rather than a physical stage; moreover, because they are self-correcting, they have a kind of problem-solving potential. Children can review their work if it is not matched, and try alternatives to create a match. The single-correct-answer quality of the materials, however, could be seen as a limitation when compared with a deeper view of problem solving, which classically involves the possibility of coming up with alternative solutions. Because these materials are visual, you will need to help kindergarten children "bridge" this imagery to ideas that grow out of their physical and social activities.

Attribute Blocks. The Attribute Blocks have been mentioned in previous sections. They are blocks of different shapes that also vary in color and size. When you plan to have children study shape, it is useful to control other variables by using the same color and the same size in order to focus on shape as the only variable. This method is useful whenever you want children to perceive an individual variable, whether in the study of mathematics, reading, or science. When trying to teach a new shape, the Montessori technique of using an a:b:b:a pattern is helpful, for example:

> This is a rectangle (a) and this is a parallelogram (b). This is a parallelogram (b) and this is a rectangle (a). Please, you take a rectangle . . . and now a parallelogram (handing each in turn to the child). And take a parallelogram and then a rectangle. Please give me a rectangle . . . and now a parallelogram. First, please give me a parallelogram . . . and now a rectangle.

However, even before children have labels for shapes, they can sort them into the same or different categories. As they do so, you can use the names. Children will probably learn most labels easily in this incidental way if you control the number of variables at any single time. Your control of new variables creates "figures" that contrast with children's "backgrounds."

Size

Relative size and absolute size form still another relationship for study. Kindergarten children become involved with such phenomena as the size of a group of children or a portion of strawberries, the length of a truck, the height of a building, and how much is enough money for ice cream. They are concerned with being bigger than or smaller than; having more than and receiving less than or fewer than; and having the least or the most. These concerns reflect their daily activities in school and at home and pave the way toward understanding numbers and counting. Researchers, for example, have noted that 96% of kindergarten children can solve quantitative problems when they are couched in terms of their experiences—for example, "How many won't get . . . ?" as compared to the 25% who responded correctly to "How many more birds . . . ?" (Hembree & Marsh, 1993). I suggest that this is one way that children reflect their personalized grasp of the economic problem of scarcity in a mathematical sense.

In the course of solving problems of size, children can use nonstandard measures to find out more about themselves—their height and weight, the length of their feet, and the length of their strides. They can use strings, blocks, crayons, a favorite doll, or other objects of their choice as nonstandard measures. They also can compare size and density by using balance scales, performing float-or-sink activities, predicting distances and rolling objects along varied inclined planes, and using a meter stick to mark the arc of a pendulum. These activities flow into graphic representations.

Your role as teacher is to integrate each new variable gradually and to help children with the needed language as they engage in activities. Gross observations and approximations become refined through predictions, repeated observations, trying out new actions, and revising views. When children have opportunities to work in this way, their cognitive development progresses via the healthy tensions of cognitive dissonance.

Using a balance scale is one such activity. A teacher and 4- and 5-year-old children can sort heavy and light objects by touch (Biggs, 1971), observing the balance scale's movement for feedback. The teacher can ask them to guess, for example, which will be heavier—a small metal object or a large piece of Styrofoam. When they look at the Styrofoam, they may well predict that it will be heavier; but when they test it on the scale they will find that the smaller metal object is heavier. They can verify their observations by repeated testing. When contrasts take place between appearance and performance, children notice and raise questions. These same kinds of contrasts may be evident in their science study, for example, when they use magnets or compare flotation in fresh and salt water. Kindergarten children have been able independently to graph a comparison between their predictions and their findings after balancing objects on the scale.

Using the balance scale is also a physical manifestation of the concept of equality (=), just as are children's intuitive balance experiences on a seesaw. Through these active experiences, children build their isomorphic understandings. Number lines do not substitute for such direct opportunities to construct the meaning of equality; and when children learn the equal sign before building understandings, they perceive it to mean "action to be completed" or "the end is coming up" in relation to calculations (Ginsburg & Baron, 1993, pp. 12, 14).

Other experiences help children to construct their understanding of size. As they classify materials and have many experiences with one-to-one correspondence, their seriation skills can grow. Here are some useful activities for children to do:

- Match keys to padlocks. As the number of items increases, you can encourage children to seriate, beginning at first with large and small locks, then with three locks, and adding materials as children seem ready for more.
- Decide how much water, sand, or grain to pour into transparent cups and then seriate each in turn. (This is different from asking a child to fill the next cup with a bit less or more. It is best when a child can decide independently how much to pour and thus experience a degree of control. Then he can make comparisons as he seriates.)

These various physical problem-solving activities help children cross the bridge into numbers and calculations. Estimations and probabilities continue the process.

Almost any activity can begin with estimations. Children have estimated/predicted such issues as how many red, yellow, and green apples might be in a basket; how many unifix cubes tall might be a popular classroom material; or whether a guinea pig's girth was longer or shorter than a length of yarn. Teachers begin with smaller quantities and gradually increase the variables. Children have graphed their predictions and compared their findings by counting.

In general, coming to think of numbers in groupings (sets) helps to advance children's sense of number as they approach problem solving with numbers. A recommended sequence for solving problems with numbers includes beginning with tallies; then changes in quantity; then parts in relation to the whole; then equalizing and comparing; and then changing the unknown (Baroody & Standifer, 1993). A recommended sequence for solving problems with words includes beginning with children's natural language descriptions; then concrete/pictorial materials; then mathematical language; and then written symbols. Games, discussed in a later section, are helpful in constructing such activities. In this regard, consider that calendar rituals may bypass children's need for real meanings—such as how many days it is until an important event; to count the days until such an event, rather than counting days simply for the sake of counting, makes much more sense. Children, in effect, best develop their number sense and counting within real contexts. In kindergarten, as well as grades 1–3, there is currently considerable engagement in counting the 100 days of school and then celebrating with many collections of 100 objects. Reflect on how much of an enjoyable thing is enough.

Representations in the Development of Relationship Concepts

Understanding the concepts of space, shape, and size, therefore, is an important foundation on which real comprehension of mathematics can be built, not an end in itself. The activities that follow will help children to progress along this path by giving them further experience with these concepts and encouraging them to represent and manipulate relationships through symbols.

SURVEYS

Surveys grow naturally from classifying and seriating activities and are good ways for investigating size as well as other factors. The survey is a useful activity because children can be active, work cooperatively, set problems, suggest ways to represent findings, and use both nonstandard and standard measures, as they are able. Children from diverse backgrounds can learn similar concepts and receive practice through various forms, whether you classify the content as science or social science. Surveys are an essential way of integrating mathematics with meaningful content. Various survey ideas that have been used successfully with kindergarten children appear in Figure 7.6.

While kindergarten children enjoy participating in and collecting data for surveys, not everybody will need to participate in every survey. Having the entire group sit while each child places a marker next to his or her

FIGURE 7.6: SURVEY ACTIVITIES

- Birthdays each month among children in the group.
- Bedtimes.
- Family size. (This activity has been discussed in greater detail in an earlier section.)
- When I grow up I would like to be …(career choices).
- Favorite or preferred …
- Food in general, or cookie, or ice cream flavor, or snack in school
- Television program
- Story book this week
- Writing implement (pencil, marker, pen, crayon, etc.)
- Vehicle to drive (truck, automobile, spaceship, motorcycle, etc.)
- Activity area in school
- Age (older, younger, same)
- Color (in general, or sneaker or shoe color, etc.).
- Number of pieces of mail received at home on Monday. (This is a useful homework activity.)
- How many cards can you hold in each hand?
- How high can you leap to place paint from your hand onto a chart?
- How many cars of each of several colors are in the parking lot? Which color is the least present? Which color is the most popular?
- Number of teeth lost by children this month, or to date.

- How many cars, trucks, motorcycles, and so forth, pass the school during several five-minute time samplings? Use pegs or a tally to keep track. (This is ideal for a collaborative small-group independent activity.)
- Number of children wearing long or short sleeves today.
- Ways that mother or father travels to work (walks, takes automobile, train, bus, motorcycle, bicycle, etc.).
- Ways that children in class travel to school (walking, bus, automobile, etc.).
- Parents who smoke or do not smoke; adults in the school who smoke or do not smoke (or other yes-no sorting).
- Changes over time, for example, pet length and girth, baby visitor, plant growth, container markings where water has evaporated each day, shadow lengths at different times during the day outdoors. (See chapter 6 for additional ideas.)
- Which containers hold more? (adapted from Burk, Snider, & Symonds, 1992, p. 144)
- Graph children's actual snacks such as fruits, vegetables, or baked goods on a large floor graph, also known as "real" graph.

birthday month or favorite snack can take a very long time, during which most of the children could be doing more productive things than watching the seemingly eternal repetition. Many teachers have found that working with a group of about eight children provides enough repetition to represent the communal process, while it avoids too much waiting, which creates demands on the teacher for managing children's inattentive or disruptive behaviors.

After your children have made a variety of surveys, pairs of children might be ready to cooperate in collecting data independently, after you plan together the purposes of the survey with the partners and discuss their suggestions. For example, if the survey involves asking individual class-mates in which area of the classroom they prefer to work, the children would need some guidelines about when they should approach another child or when it would be intrusive. They will need to have agreed upon the answers for the following questions before they begin:

- How will we keep a tally (marks, moving pegs)?
- Who will do what? In what order?
- Will the same person do each task throughout the activity? If we take turns, how do we switch roles?
- When will we have enough samples?
- When will we be finished?

When developing a survey with a group of children, it is useful to ask them to *estimate* what they are likely to find. Realistic estimations will be phrased in terms of more than, less than, the most, the fewest, and so forth, rather than actual numbers. Solicit their suggestions for ways to record their predictions. After all, there is documentation that children invent their own symbolic representations well before kindergarten and use picto-graphic and iconic representations (Atkinson, 1992). After *recording* their predictions, the children enjoy the anticipation that builds until they can *compare* their original projections with the actual results.

In addition to recording predictions, you and the children will need to select a way to *represent* the findings in graphic form. In addition to collaborative suggestions, consider varied ways in which to represent your activity, for example, using a horizontal or vertical bar graph format in which each segment represents one response. If you and the children de-cide to use this technique, be sure that each segment—whether it is a card, sticker, tooth outline, marking, or photograph of a child—is the same size for each datum. This is important so that anybody who looks at the graph or chart can make comparisons easily. Figure 7.7 is an example.

The next step is to develop a language experience chart of some sort that describes and analyzes the survey. For example, charts summarizing surveys on family size and eye color might look like this:

Ali has two people in her family.   (2)
Bob has five people in his family.   (5)

FIGURE 7.7: Graph of a Survey of Lost Teeth

Lost more than 1 tooth	⊔ ⊔ ⊔ ⊔ ⊔
Lost 1 tooth	⊔ ⊔ ⊔ ⊔ ⊔ ⊔ ⊔
Not yet lost a tooth	⊔ ⊔ ⊔ ⊔

Cal has seven people in his family.   (7)
Di has the same number as Bob.   (5)
Ev has the same number as Ali.   (2)
Fran has four people in his family.   (4)
Cal has the most people in his family.   (7)

Three people have green eyes.   (3)
Six people have blue eyes.   (6)
Fifteen people have brown eyes.   (15)
Most people have brown eyes.   (15)
The fewest people have green eyes.   (3)
Many people have blue eyes.   (6)

Before you know it, the children are using, writing, and comparing numerals. While estimations and surveys are one form of activity in which numbers burst into life, in addition to Dienes multibase arithmetic blocks and Attribute Blocks, there are a number of other approaches that nourish this development.

MEASUREMENT

Various measurement activities, using nonstandard and then standard measures, can become parts of larger surveys. In themselves, measuring activities, because they employ some tool, prove to be active and involving for kindergarten children. These activities are powerful foundations for building children's understanding of quantitative relationships.

Cruikshank and colleagues (1980) suggest measurement activities in various categories, along with a useful sequence of difficulty. Such sequencing begins with direct measures and continues with indirect measures, first using nonstandard measures and then standard ones. Another sequence begins with the measurement of length and continues, in turn, with area, volume, weight, time, and temperature. Ideally, these activities are tied to meaningful social and scientific studies as well as reading and writing activities.

Since measurement defines the relationship between a phenomenon and the measuring tool, a direct, nonstandard measure is the most fundamental form, that is, $a = b$. Many examples have been mentioned already, and some others would be, "What is longer than this book?" or "What is shorter than this rod?"

You would need an indirect measure, however, to test the relationship between a bookcase and a closet, since it is unwieldy to move the bookcase each time you might want to establish the nature of the relationship. Will the bookcase fit into the closet? Rather than remove all of the books and move the case, the children might be able to come up with a suggestion for using an indirect continuous measure, such as a length of string; thus, $a = b : b = c : a = c$. The area of a surface might be measured in a similar way by cutting a paper outline of an object and comparing the outline with a second object.

In order to create cognitive dissonance, consider suggesting that children select a set of nonstandard items with which to measure a particular length or area. If different children use smaller or larger items in their set, then there will be discrepancies in their findings, which they will discuss. This is a way in which they might come to see that few and many units make comparisons difficult when measuring the same length or area (Wilson & Rowland, 1993).

Two activities in which children use direct measures and can experience cognitive dissonance about the conservation of quantity appear in Figures 7.8 and 7.9.

Cuisenaire Rods

Cuisenaire rods use visual, spatial, and tactile senses. They help young children to move from the concrete manipulation of materials to dealing with quantitative relationships and actions with numbers. This process takes place only after they have experienced many of the active uses of relative quantity in their daily pastimes.

It is useful to nail an edge of quarter-round molding onto one table in the mathematics area, so that the Cuisenaire rods will not slide off too easily. It makes sense to use this area for small-group instruction. After five or ten minutes of instruction, you can leave children with ten to twenty minutes of follow-up activities that are both independent and cooperative, while you circulate.

At the outset, children need plenty of time to explore freely and build usual and unusual structures with the rods, which should be set out in the

FIGURE 7.8: Cognitive Dissonance in the Direct Measure of Volume: I

Purposes. Encourage children to predict, observe, and compare. Create
  possibility for cognitive dissonance.
Materials. Transparent jars of different sizes and shapes, measuring cup, paper
  strip taped along the length of each jar, rice, and marker
Organization. A small group of 8–12 children work with the teacher.
Procedures. Pour one measured cup of rice into a jar, shake it down, and mark
  the height on the paper strip. Repeat for each jar.
  Ask children what they see when they compare the lengths on the markers in
    different jars. Why are some the same and others different? Accept
    answers and consider them seriously.
  Repeat estimates and measures a few times. (This is important because some
    children may not be able yet to conserve a quantity when it changes in
    appearance. Repetition gives children the chance to discover that the
    discrepancy does not exist because of incorrect measurement.)
  Children can record their findings in their math notebooks as drawings and
    direct measures of tape length.

Adapted from M. Baratta-Lorton (1976), *Mathematics their way* (Menlo Park, CA: Addison-
Wesley), p. 136.

mathematics area for several weeks or longer. During that time, some children may sort them by color intuitively, and some may notice that the rods
of the same color are also of the same length. When you have observed
any pattern building, you might begin with one group of those children
to play a grab-bag game in which each person has a brown paper sack, as
follows:

> Pick up a white rod, feel it, and place it in your bag. Now, pick up an
>   orange rod, feel it, and place it in your bag.
> Shake them up. Now you will be able to see with your fingertips. Pick
>   out the white rod. Put it back. Now pull out the orange rod. Put
>   it back. That was easy for you.
> Next, pick up a red rod, feel it, and place it in your bag. Shake it well.
>   Now, pull out a white rod. Put it back. Now, pull out a red rod.
>   Look at that! You can see with your fingertips.

The orange rod is the longest, equal in length to ten white rods. The
white rods are the shortest. The red rods are equal in length to two white
rods. When you use this sequence, first the white and then the orange rod,

FIGURE 7.9: Cognitive Dissonance in the Direct Measure of Volume: II

Purposes. Encourage children to predict, observe, and compare. Create possibility for cognitive dissonance.

Materials. Two eight-ounce transparent containers, one low and broad, one tall and skinny; brown paper sacks; beads or marbles of the same size

Organization. A small group or 8–12 children work with the teacher.

Procedures. Place a brown paper sack with a hole in the top over each of the containers. Ask a child to drop a bead from each hand into each of the holes in the paper sacks, at the same time.

Ask the child, "Are you putting the same number of beads in each jar?" (Children may deny that both containers have the same amount of beads when they can see the beads, but invariably give conservation responses when they cannot perceive the inequality of the level of the beads in the containers.)

Repeat a few times, occasionally alternating using the paper sacks and leaving the containers uncovered. Eventually the discrepancy between the responses they give in the two situations becomes apparent to them, and they say excitedly, "It's got to be the same; I put the same in each jar! It doesn't matter how it looks."

Adapted from C. S. Lavatelli (1970), *Piaget's theory applied to an early childhood curriculum* (Cambridge, MA: American Science and Engineering), p. 112.

you provide the greatest possible contrast and children build a tactile and visual image of quantitative relationships.

Fingertip retrieval with these three lengths of rods may be enough for one instructional episode. Keeping it brief and seeing that children feel successful means that they will look forward to the next session in which you begin the same way and then gradually add the yellow rod (half the length of the orange), the green rod (equal in length to three white rods or a red and a white), and finally the purple rod (equal in length to two red rods).

At a separate time, after reinforcing the tactile relationships with the grab-bag game, you might ask children how they could tell somebody who was not in the grab-bag group their methods for tactile retrieval. As relevant, the following questions are helpful:

- What can you build with these rods?
- What can you build with the purple rods? (Ask about other colors.)
- Which rods are the same length as one another?

- Which rods are longer than the green? Shorter? (Ask about other colors.)
- If the green rod were a train and you used red rods and white rods as cars in the train, what different patterns of cars could you make?
- If the purple rod were the length of your train, what different combinations of cars could you use to equal the length, to be the same length, as your purple train?
- What if the yellow rod were the length of your train? (Ask about other colors.)

Five-year-olds have comfortably spent as much as half an hour substituting two rods for one. They are ready to hear you describe this process: "When we put these together, we call it adding their lengths." As children compare and contrast lengths, it is clear that there are differences among individuals. Some children may need more time than others to handle the rods at each phase. Some may need weeks, while others may take months of exploring and making patterns with the rods.

The materials may help, but they do not substitute for the children's personal construction of the relationships. The ultimate recognition is in the child and not in the materials.

At the very least, it makes sense to offer varied materials and activities. When you and the children have explored many possibilities with trains, you might have some centimeter graph paper and colored markers or crayons handy so that each child who wants to do so can pick her or his favorite train to record in the mathematics notebook.

At this point, the children are on the threshold of manipulating numerals, if they have not already done so spontaneously. The use of graph paper as a discontinuous form provides children with a contrast to the continuous form of the rods. You will find many suggestions for using graph paper with the rods, for playing with "trains," and for engaging in cooperative games in P. S. Davidson's (1977) *Idea Book for Cuisenaire Rods at the Primary Level*.[1] Your children may experience a touch of cognitive dissonance in the game "Filling Spaces with Rods." In this activity, two or more children can completely fill an area with rods, transform the rods in that area so that they lie end to end, and then compare their patterns at various stages with those patterns that other children have made.

Whenever children can predict, transform materials, and compare and contrast their results, they have an opportunity to make new connections. Materials provide an additional benefit because children can arrive at their conclusions through contrasts and the basic problem-solving technique of trial and error, in this case with some inevitable inductive discoveries. You will notice that children who have more opportunity for inductive learning also acquire a stronger sense of power. Their findings are not based on an authority figure decreeing a "correct answer," but on their own constructed understanding, which they can verify by returning to the materials.

After manipulation, train construction, and other active pursuits, some children may be ready to consider addition. While they add, they can use the Cuisenaire rods as a self-checking device that confirms whether or not the mental construction is true. You may find that a few kindergarten children are able to engage in this concrete activity rather late in the school year.

Initially, children will spend plenty of time playing out the combinations of plus-one and doubles of numbers (Kamii & DeClark, 1984). At each new phase, it is useful to begin instruction with the rods and then to have them available for self-checking. You will find that it is easy to individualize instruction within your mathematics instructional groups because you can pose different problems to different children. This can be helpful for individuals who are returning to school after an illness or for those who need more time or special help with a procedure.

COMMERCIAL AND TEACHER-DESIGNED GAMES

Games are also useful in building toward numbers and the operations of addition and subtraction. There are several "syntaxes" or varieties of games that kindergarten teachers have used successfully. Among these are card games, action games, and board games with cards, spinners, dice, or markers. Children's stories, such as *Rosie's Walk* (Hutchins, 1968), have also been adapted to game form with a die, predictions, and comparisons (Skinner, 1990). (Teacher-designed games are discussed at greater length in Chapter 9.)

Ordinary adult playing cards can be used by kindergarten children and can be adapted for different levels of use. Teachers usually begin with part of the deck. When children can identify the numerals, two children at a time can independently play a more-than or less-than game variation of "War." (Some teachers prefer other names for the game.) In this game of chance, players match pairs of numbered playing cards to see which is greater. Kamii and DeClark (1984) describe a game of "Double War" in which each first-grade child plays with the sum of two cards, using a deck limited to values up to four. With either numerals or suits, children can play "pairs" games in which they seek pairs that are alike after the cards have been placed face down. While both of these games are designed for the person who achieves the pair to keep the pair, you might consider "Pairs Bank" in which pairs can be placed communally, reducing competition.

"Go Fish," in which children ask each other for a particular card by number in order to collect and discard pairs of cards, is another simple card game that children can play cooperatively with discontinuous teacher supervision, once they have had instruction. Dominoes requires that children match equivalent sets of dots on wooden or plastic pieces, although you can sometimes find domino cards. Games with bowling pins also use counting.

An African game, commercially available as "Kalah," encourages children to plan ahead. You can make this game board easily out of a regular twelve-hole (two-by-six) egg carton, with an attached "bowl" or box at either end made from two halves of the upper part of an egg carton. To begin the game, three or four beans are placed in each of the twelve "pots," six of which "belong" to each of two children. On each turn, one player empties one pot from her side of the game. Moving clockwise, she drops one bean into each pot, her bowl, or into one of her playmate's pots. The beans in the bowl are no longer in the game. The person who ends up with empty pots on her side wins. African children play this game using pebbles and holes in the ground (Zaslavsky, 1973). You can make the game easier by using half the egg carton and fewer beans. As children play, they learn to anticipate strategies and intuitively begin to add and subtract.

In another game, teachers have used lima beans or other items, painted on one side, to play with probability and adding: (1) Toss five (later more) lima beans, painted on one side, on a tray. (2) Predict the pattern of colors before tossing, and place colored stickers on a chart. (3) Compare findings with the prediction. (4) Represent the finding with colored stickers underneath the prediction, with a 1:1 correspondence (Baratta-Lorton, 1976; Burk et al., 1988, 1992; Department of Education & Science, 1991). Children can play out possibilities and record their findings in pairs or independently.

BLOCKS, COMPUTERS, AND OTHER CONSTRUCTIONS

Kindergarten children can construct many important quantitative concepts and put various relationships in fresh perspective as they play with commercial and teacher-designed games that stimulate them to focus on controlled variables. These experiences, many of which we have just discussed, help children to move into counting with numbers and toward performing operations with numbers. We will discuss several more such activities in this section.

The one material that serves best as a multidisciplinary concrete tool for learning is undoubtedly floor blocks, typically found in most kindergartens and only rarely in primary classrooms. Floor blocks help children to experience a range of mathematical relationships that include classification, seriation, spatial relationships, and number concepts. Through collaborative use of blocks, children face the need to appreciate another person's viewpoint. Children might, for example, use the same number of identical blocks to create different structures to compare.

The computer is another type of generic equipment that serves science and mathematics education at the same time that it has uses in language and the arts. Computers are beginning to be present in kindergarten classrooms, and it is likely that their use will increase. It therefore makes sense to consider how they are being used and what relevant decisions you may need to make in kindergarten work as you approach the end of this century.

Blocks

Wooden blocks for young children have been used in schools since Froebel introduced them in the nineteenth century. The most frequently used wooden floor blocks today have a 1:2:4 relationship with each other, as opposed to the original Froebel blocks with a 1:2:3: . . . :12 relationship. The Montessori blocks and the comparatively small Cuisenaire rods have a 1:2:3: . . . :10 relationship.

These internal relationships are worth mentioning because they all reflect the concern of their inventors for children to be able to construct relationships. As a kindergarten teacher, it makes sense for you to be aware of relationships represented in available materials. While children will build most of these relationships inductively as they use the materials, it is worthwhile for you to be open to the fleeting moment when you can raise an appropriate question that can promote problem solving:

- Why do you suppose that is happening?
- What else have you tried?
- Which one is just the right length? The same length? Shorter? Longer?
- If you could invent a block that would be perfect for that part, what would it look like? What other objects in our room might you substitute?

Children need to use problem-solving skills when they build with blocks. This activity is an opportunity for children to identify their own real problems and then to work out possible solutions. Since the materials allow the children to set the parameters themselves, they can feel successful and autonomous. The process of using blocks evolves through a number of activities (Provenzo & Brett, 1983):

Beginning explorations
Attempts to build up and out
Creation of patterns
Exploration of balance and symmetry
Attempts at bridging
Learning about enclosures
Decorating and designing
Dramatic play with structures

Children learn varied solutions, such as that placing larger blocks under smaller blocks improves balance and that bridging requires adding onto a structure after excluding smaller and equivalent pieces. Because this medium is so versatile, children can use their imaginations and build creative structures. Encourage this imaginative tendency with occasional suggestions: "Close your eyes. Imagine what your structure will look like. When you open your eyes, try to change it to fit your imagination." The floor blocks particularly suit dramatic play because children can create enclosures into which they might fit or in which they can use accessories (see Chapter 5).

The Patty Smith Hill blocks nurture sociodramatic play because they can be held together with metal rods and bolts, enabling children to build tall and large enclosures that are sturdy. Quadro components (Children's Playgrounds, Inc.), a contemporary version, are a system of plastic pipes to which children attach bolts. Large hollow blocks, which are readily available, serve a similar purpose. In contrast are the smaller types of building materials such as Lincoln Logs, Tinkertoys, Bristle Blocks, Lego, and Construct-o-Straws. Both the large blocks and the smaller construction materials stimulate problem solving and skills in managing three-dimensional space. It is important, therefore, to be conscious of which children have been underrepresented in the block activity and to encourage them with your presence and appreciative comments when they are using the materials.

Woodworking

Woodworking is another activity in which you may need to encourage underrepresented children to participate. Working with wood and real adult-sized tools serves to develop many skills. Adult-sized tools are easier to use because the weight and size of the tools help children to achieve more balance and control as they work.

In addition to learning how to use carpentry tools and apply measurement skills to real problems, children learn to plan a few steps ahead. Some of these steps reflect the perceptual model of *indirect progress*, which children can apprehend as they try out different approaches. The simple tools connected with woodworking also represent indirect activity—the way in which simple machines function. For example, consider the following:

- *Hammer.* Children learn to apply leverage when they extract a nail with a hammer.
- *Brace-and-bit.* The brace-and-bit drills holes with an indirect motion.
- *Screwdriver.* Some of your children can also apply the leverage used in screwdrivers.
- *Saw.* Children learn that they need to draw the saw across the wood, held in a vise, toward themselves about three times in order to establish a groove. Then they can learn to apply a downward motion to saw into the wood, which should be carefully selected soft pine lumber.

When children use tools, they have direct experiences with the principles of physics. As with other acquired skills, some children will need more direct help than others.

In the beginning, children are quite content to hammer nails into a single block of wood. Later on, when they use more pieces and varying sizes, they face the problem of finding just the right sized nail to hold the pieces together. If you have precut wooden wheels, you create another reason for children to measure carefully in order to attach the wheels so that they will turn together. They need to measure lengths of wood that can help them execute their plans, however simple they may be. While kindergarten children usually build up or out with woodworking, a few of them create enclosures.

Offer children dignity and respect for their work. For example, you can provide sandpaper so that they can have a smooth product. Sandpaper is easier to use when it is tacked to a hand-sized block of wood or attached to a commercial sandpaper holder. Another way to show valuing of their products is to have a nail-set available to sink nails below the surface of the wood and help give a finished look. Sometimes children like to paint their work. You might also consider displaying finished pieces on a colored-paper or cloth background.

Woodworking is an activity that needs continuous teacher supervision; therefore it should be scheduled when you are not committed to direct, continuous instruction elsewhere but can be nearby, aware, and available. The workbench should be placed out of the way of traffic, so children can concentrate safely. The use of adult tools is prestigious and certainly a privilege that can be available only to those children who show that they can use them safely. As with block building or any other construction work, some basic behavioral expectations are reasonable. Materials should be handled carefully, not thrown, and children need to respect the work of other children and treat it carefully to avoid damage. The historical use of woodworking in kindergartens anticipates a current trend to develop "design and technology" curricula (Department of Education & Science, 1991).

Computers

Kindergarten children can learn to become comfortable around computers. Computer familiarity, rather than literacy, is a realistic goal for kindergarten children.

In some kindergartens, Big Trak (Milton Bradley Co.) is available (Swett, 1984). This is a vehicle with a number board on top that children can program in order to move the vehicle in different directions in multiples of its length. Teachers and children can measure the toy and place tape marks on the floor at intervals equal to the toy's length, creating a kind of nonstandard, numberless number line. This is an example of a direct, continuous measure. They can also engage in estimating and comparing where the computer will stop the vehicle. Playing with Big Trak can be an enjoyable and worthwhile activity, but some teachers are disturbed by the military-type insignia and have painted over them in order to deemphasize this aspect. The computer software for LOGO is a two-dimensional extension of these three-dimensional activities. Young children also can engage actively in the LOGO graphics package that uses a hand-held programming device, called a mouse, and requires that children estimate, explore, and compare their representations.

Since some ability to identify numerals and to differentiate at least a few keys on a keyboard is necessary for these activities, it is a good idea to have the children work in pairs. Most schools also have an aide available. At the very least, you will need to provide an intermittent adult presence. Indeed, one way to gauge whether or not an activity is too difficult for your children is to observe the degree to which they can work with some independence and increasing autonomy.

Whatever you plan in the way of computer experiences for children, monitoring their attentive or off-task behavior will help you know when the activity is relevant or appropriate. For example, when you find that children need repeated reminders to return to the task, you might suspect that the activity is beyond their comprehension or too restrictive. The computer can serve your human purposes in the kindergarten only if you are a critical user.

REFLECTIONS

You will note that mathematics suffuses diverse activities through isomorphic imagery. Whether engaging in routines for getting coats with one, two, or three friends in Chapter 4, mapping in Chapter 5, recording how many wet footprints you can create before the water evaporates in Chapter 6, clapping syllables or counting patterns for movement activities in Chapter 8, or classifying book sizes in Chapter 9, quantitative issues are integrated. You find quantity integrated in general children's books and books that combine multicultural concerns and number, such as *Moja Means One* (Feelings, 1971) or *Count Your Way Through Japan* (Haskins, 1987).

Throughout these many forms and transformations, young children build their imagery and increase their sense of number and sense of space. Their expanding imagery and growing awareness continually strengthen their capacity to solve problems in daily life and then by using the conventional forms of mathematical representations.

Our job as teachers includes the need to reflect about choosing and organizing activities. For example, mathematics specialists often focus on whole-group instruction. If your children engage in "tubbing," for example, select some activities in "tubs" for integration with other classroom areas, rather than having all the children use tubs at the same time. Take the time to find out how children reached their conclusions, rather than stopping discussion to settle for the "correct" answer. We appear to be willing to accept invented spelling as part of the process of constructing verbal literacy: What is the worst thing that might happen if you let an "incorrect" quantitative answer remain untouched? Continue exploring the children's strategies even after a "correct" answer—for example, "Who did it in a different way?" The quality of your interaction is more important than expensive manipulatives for which you might substitute generic everyday materials from outdoors as well as household supplies.

Even in the longer kindergarten day, there is not enough time for all that you may want to do. You will therefore need to make choices with children in your setting. The most worthwhile activities encourage kindergarten children to be active and autonomous and give them the chance to modify their environments. When you use mathematics as an integrated tool, you can feel secure in the knowledge that children can be active in their own learning. When you offer opportunities for the powerful learning process of cognitive dissonance to occur, and provide contrasts through materials and games, children "break out" into numerical and other relationships with comfort and energy—and develop a comfortable attitude toward mathematics.

8

Aesthetics, the Arts, and Playfulness

The capacity to have aesthetic experiences and to appreciate and create artforms is part of what defines us as human beings. When we talk about, criticize, and trace the history of artforms, we engage in an indirect activity, which is different from the aesthetic experience of art. An aesthetic experience of, or creation of, something is a direct way of knowing.

Aesthetic experience is available to all people as part of the broad range of ordinary human experience as well as in exposures to artforms. For John Dewey (1934/1958), "Even a crude experience, if authentically an experience, is more fit to give a clue to the intrinsic nature of esthetic experience than is an object already set apart from any other mode of experience" (p. 11). Aesthetic experience exists within, but also beyond, the "artistic" disciplines such as music, the visual arts, dance, and literature, including drama. These as well as all other artforms have the potential for helping us to have an aesthetic experience and to see the "familiar" in "strange" ways (Dewey, 1934/1958; Gordon, 1961). The experience is not guaranteed in the form itself but in the readiness of a consuming human being.

There are no guarantees, however, that we can have an aesthetic experience unless the artist has successfully created a form that can help us share some of the artist's experience, based upon our own past experience as well as our present motives for perceiving (L. Rosenblatt, 1969, 1978). Philosopher Martin Buber (1923/1958) proposes that there is an aesthetic experiencing for both the artist while creating and the connoisseur while appreciating, a direct relationship between the two human beings in a particular moment, which he terms an "I–Thou" relationship. Another philosopher, Suzanne Langer (1953, 1957), suggests that there is an opportunity for enrichment and fresh "insight" in a work of art.

In this context, aesthetic experience, including the "formed" arts as well as ordinary life, is available in some way to all people, regardless of age or intellectual capacity. Art is neither elitist nor a "frill," but an intrinsic perspective that is possible in all human activity. This chapter deals with the aesthetic emphases in children's representation of experience through varied media—music, movement, language, and the visual and plastic arts. There is also discussion about ways in which teachers have helped children to appreciate as well as to create.

AESTHETICS AND EDUCATION

Human insights can be communicated and perceived in varied forms. Even though a work may use several media, a "primary" realm (Langer, 1957) will stand out. When we look at "dance theater" or multimedia "concept art," it is clear that one is basically kinetic, dealing with motion, and the other is basically visual.

Suzanne Langer (1957) proposes four major types of art products: plastic (visual), musical, balletic, and poetic. People perceive one or another type of form as it stands out as a figure against the background of a larger activity. These nondiscursive (sensory, emotional, surreal, imaginative) processes can reflect a rich range of perceptual models (underlying ways of connecting experiences) that would be less fully knowable if only discursive (logical, linear) tools were employed. Indeed, Howard Gardner (1983) suggests that people have different proclivities for appreciating aesthetic experiences or representing meanings through various media. In his view, some people tend to find kinetic or visual or musical or linguistic experience more accessible, although opportunities for exposure, practice, and cultural valuing help to enrich their learnings.

For children to be exposed to a full range of meaning-rich experiences and forms of representation in school, therefore, they need to have opportunities to use the artist's nondiscursive tools (ways of knowing) as well as the discursive tools of scientists, mathematicians, and others. You can integrate the nondiscursive tools across the range of children's experiences, in order to provide opportunities for flexible thinking, problem setting and solving across media, and the creation of new connections. Many of the children's aesthetic experiences will come as they play with materials and with one another. "In a field where there are no 'right answers,' individuals learn that art can be a celebration of diversity, a celebration of individuality for its own sake" (R. Barnes, 1987, p. 16).

Kindergarten children can create insightful forms, even if those forms are somewhat episodic rather than closed. Their coordination and skills will grow. Beginning with random approaches, they create forms with varying degrees of purposefulness. Researchers have identified a progression, for example, in their two-dimensional representations (Gardner, 1980) as well as their three-dimensional constructions (Reifel, 1984). In addition, you might notice that experience influences representation, for example, when the urban child illustrates trees that are shorter than houses, whereas the suburban child's trees are taller (Shelley Saunders, personal communication, 1992). Part of the teacher's role will be to recognize the child's perspective, support succeeding levels of challenge, and communicate an appreciation of small benchmarks. Some suggested roles for the teacher have been mentioned in Chapter 5, in the section on sociodramatic play, as well as elsewhere throughout the book. Others involve:

- *Sensitizing.* Provide a verbal description and appreciation of what you perceive is a child's intentional combination of materials, a kind of "verbal harmony."
- *Modeling fluency.* Elaborate on symmetrical or unusual structures.
- *Modeling originality.* Create original work of your own, such as an occasional bulletin board, decorative program, or haiku poetry, in the children's presence.
- *Flexibility.* Create new forms or explore aloud alternative ways of framing and solving problems.

The additional time of the full-day kindergarten permits teachers to work in greater depth in the arts and to broaden all program areas as children integrate them with artistic activity. Most kindergarten teachers take major responsibility for the arts in their own classrooms. Occasionally, a kindergarten teacher who is particularly skillful in music education will share these skills with another teacher, providing a special music time that can supplement, but should not replace, music as a regular part of classroom experience. It is unfortunate that music appears to be an area in which many teachers feel a lack of confidence; however, there are varied activities that teachers can do with children that do not require extraordinary skills.

In cases where a specialist teacher in the arts can be requested, teachers tend to prefer a music specialist. In the early childhood center of one public school, the staff gave priority to a specialist teacher of creative rhythmic movement and music. In another full-day kindergarten center, where many teachers played the guitar or piano, there was an instrumental music teacher who taught groups of children to play the violin by modeling and ear training, using an adaptation of the Suzuki method. Where separate special education classes exist at the kindergarten level, programs involving teachers who are specialists in music, movement education, or physical education have helped to include children with special learning needs.

It is rare, however, to find an art specialist in full-day kindergartens. Most kindergarten teachers have included art activities as a major program component and feel comfortable using specialist resources in other areas. The visual arts in particular have always been the major form of symbolic representation in kindergartens. This chapter, therefore, highlights ways of working in the arts that supplement practices in the field that are already widespread. In kindergarten education the major role of the arts is to build on a strength that children bring to school—their capacity for successful aesthetic experience.

MUSIC

Representation through music and movement is part of the communication continuum of which language is a part. Before and after mathematics instruction, children move themselves and objects through space. Before and after speech development, they represent experiences in movement. Before and after writing, they represent experiences in drawing. Before and after reading print, children decode the meanings of human emotion and behavior. Before and after all of these, children represent their feelings, experiences, meanings, and imagination in play.

Music is a nondiscursive symbolic repository of perceptual models in its perceptual immediacy, direct involvement, and connectedness. One philosopher has seen "mathematics as conceptual music and music as sensuous mathematics" (Polanyi, 1963, p. 38). There is a sense in which "only music can achieve the total fusion of form and content, of means and meaning, which all art strives for" (Steiner, 1970, p. 29). Music can communicate basic human feelings to a baby before he understands words.

Music has long been a part of school life. In addition to creating music, children can listen purposefully to different musical genres and music from different cultures. No matter how long or how well someone describes music, we will never really grasp it unless we hear it directly.

Creating Music

Instruments. Individually and in groups, children can explore rhythm directly through body movement and using percussion instruments, including such items as drums, triangles, Chinese gongs, shakers, "rhythm" sticks, African rain sticks, tambourines, and everyday objects. Melodic and harmonic patterns are available through singing and playing other musical instruments. Children experience the *dialectical* perceptual model directly through musical counterpoint, part singing, and rhythm instrument orchestration.

It is important for you to intersperse plenty of free-form exploration with instruments each time that children use them. It will be easier for you and the children to listen if you begin with a few instruments of fine tonal quality and gradually add to this stock. Before the children receive the instruments, make sure they understand your visual signal to "stop and place instruments on the floor." In that way you can arrange to stop and share ideas after they begin to play.

Children can classify and counterpose instruments of different pitches and music of varying rhythms and tempos. Since they frequently confuse volume, pitch, and tempo, children can profit from your help in providing direct contrasts of these different variables. After they have heard models, they can intuitively counterpose the musical concepts. With increased awareness, children might be able to take turns providing musical accompaniment to favorite stories, poems, or creative drama. In addition to percussion instruments, children might look at string instruments, comparing them with woodwind and brass instruments that older children might demonstrate.

An experimental attitude on your part will encourage experimentation—for example, the variations in echos made by the human voice, objects, and instruments. You can also empower yourself and the children by communicating your acceptance of the notion that everyone can be expressive and creative with sound.

Song. One of the most available and versatile of all music-making instruments is the human voice. Singing songs can turn an ordinary moment into something filled with expectation and camaraderie. The important element for children is their feeling of belonging and participating. Rather than trying to "teach" a song precisely, line by line, try to "infect" children with songs by singing them spontaneously as well as on planned occasions. Folk songs and some contemporary songs, with their natural repetition, are especially relevant for kindergarten use. For the child who has limited English proficiency, singing along or being encouraged to sing "tra-la-la if you don't know the words" is a private way to practice new language in a group sing-along. Folk songs in languages other than English offer an additional opportunity for the bilingual child to teach or participate more fully at the same time that English-speaking children expand their range of language. The folk song format, with its repetitive structure and rhyme, lends itself to revised wordings that children gleefully compose, for example, "Put Your Finger in the Air" (Guthrie, 1963). It is no surprise that children's musical creations combine easily with their sociodramatic play and creative dramatics, increasing their richness and expressiveness.

If you are among the many people who believe they cannot sing on pitch or carry a tune, perhaps you have noticed that young children are unaffected by this. Thus you may feel comfortable accompanying activities with a song or chant, whether at the beginning of a whole-group meeting or during transitions.

Appreciating Music

Children can appreciate as well as create music. In either case, music is a symbolic form, and some elements require instruction so that they can become figures standing out against a background of sound.

Children learn to appreciate music when you systematically attempt to build their perceptions. You can set the tone through scheduling and creating a climate for listening. Sometimes controlling lighting or using a fragrance can set a tone conducive to listening.

You can control variables in other ways. You can play recordings or arrange for live performances in which children hear individual instruments and then the instruments in combination with others. Sometimes you might contrast melody, rhythm, tempo, or mode with another musical element.

Hearing brief samples of music from different cultures is another way you can highlight and contrast unique forms. Kindergarten children can distinguish among European, African, South American, Asian, Australian Aboriginal, and North American First Peoples' music. When children hear a story or see a videotape about people in other regions, hearing their music, before or after the story or videotape, can augment that activity.

We have been culturally conditioned to expect certain music to evoke certain kinds of images. Working with young children who are not as fixed in their connections, you may be able to keep open their appreciation by encouraging them to select, from a large collection of varied pictures, those that remind them of music they have heard. When they see that you accept a variety of alternative associations, they build confidence in your support of diversity.

MOVEMENT EDUCATION

People have a veritable need to move, despite the fact that, as they grow older, they have movement socialized out of them. Moving through space and observing the movements of other people and objects are both direct aesthetic experiences. Incidentally, experiences with movement are the foundation for mathematics and the development of science concepts.

Children may apprehend the perceptual model of *dialectical activity* as they have experiences related to studies in math and science as well as in music, movement, and the visual arts. Creative rhythmic movement is also a starting point for dramatics, which is part of poetic language experience as well as an outgrowth of sociodramatic play.

Children enjoy many activities with rhythm and rhythmic movement. Rhythms are varying interrelations of tempo and pulsations that we perceive as patterns. These rhythmic patterns are repetitious signals that we perceive as "wholes" that are more than their "parts." Much of musical experience reflects this quality of transposing "emotive" wholes, a direct experience with the perceptual model of *synergy.*

It is valuable to do movement activities and play with rhythm alone as well as with melody. In order to keep open their opportunities for new discoveries, you can use a drum to accompany the children rather than ask the children to keep in step with it. With more experience, children can try to adapt to rhythms initiated by the teacher or other children.

These practices extend and support children's imagery processes. Body movement is a medium that is a primary source for symbolic expression and can, when carefully developed, become an important additional way in which to legitimize and develop children's representations. If possible, consider videotaping children's efforts as a way of providing them with both appreciation and feedback.

To begin, you can encourage children with these invitations:

Come to me in any way you like.
Come in a new way. Come in a different way.
Come in a high way. Come in a low way.
Come as if the bottoms of your feet were covered with glue. As if you were wearing a heavy crown. As if you were carrying an injured bird. As if you were very angry. As if you were on the moon . . .

You can ask individual children to isolate and variably combine parts of their own bodies: "Move only your elbows. Your shoulders. Your head." They can isolate levels: "Move in as high a way as you can. In as low a way as you can." You can ask them to control their direction: "Move in the straightest way you can. The most curving way you can." "Move in the flat, as if there are transparent walls in front of and/or behind you." "Move in the deep as if there are transparent walls on either side or both sides of you." When teachers emphasize the validity of finding alternative ways to move, children can directly experience the perceptual model of *indirect progress.*

The possibilities for discussion and moving are vast. The children's use of space and rhythm are kaleidoscopic. They enjoy the challenge of "coming to you" in different and creative ways. They enjoy using such props as hoops, ropes, scarves, costume parts, and labels. One group of kindergarten children explored the use of their bodies in space, both alone and with partners. The sampling of activities shown in Figure 8.1 took place over a period of many weeks.

These movement education activities encourage individual children to be creative and independent problem setters and solvers. Game songs, such as "Clap, Clap, Clap Your Hands," or "Looby Loo," or "The Wheels on the Bus" suggest movements that you can use to continue to pursue this purpose or to restrict it, depending upon what you emphasize. The teacher's role is to appreciate and encourage kindergarten children to explore new contrasts and to elaborate their movement activities.

CREATIVE DRAMATICS: A POETIC ART

Creative dramatics grows out of children's rich experience in music and movement activities, sociodramatic play, and children's literature. Such activity is at once social, emotional, substantive, verbal, and aesthetic.

In sociodramatic play, children's favored, repeated plays in the form of informal oral "scripts" may become more formalized as creative dramatics. The drama can continue to retain an evolving, episodic format when centered around this kernel of common experience and interaction. These plays express actions, feelings, and problematic issues. It is a group authorship in flux, as it were.

> Social pretend play involves the development of scripts that evolve collaboratively. The negotiation processes provide a scaffolding similar to that of an editor and author. These images suggest that young children's increasing oral language skills are the foundations upon which they build their skills as writers, learning about how to communicate with an audience and what voices to use. (Fromberg, 1992, p. 65)

Such play may never be written down or, with help from older children or adults, may evolve into written form.

Music can also enter into creative dramatics as children collaborate in exploring space through rhythmic movement activities and experiment with the interplay of sounds. In one kindergarten, a teacher noticed that a few children's rhythmic movements complemented one another. While

FIGURE 8.1: Movement Activities

Angles
- When your feet stay in the same place without moving, your body can lean. That's very special.
- Now try a different way to lean. Take a partner and try leaning with him or her.

Bubbles
- Imagine that you are inside a bubble. Show how you could move so that the bubble won't break, so that you can stretch part of the bubble, ever so gently now.
- As you move inside your bubble, show how you can pass other people in their bubbles without touching, then with touching.

Moving
- Move toward somebody.
- Move away from that person in a new way.
- Meet somebody else in a new way. (Repeated) (Adapted from P. Press, personal communication, 1974.)
- First, imagine how you will move.
- Partners take turns walking, skipping, tapping, or running on one another's shadows.

Directions
- With a partner, try moving together toward the labels on our wall, first toward the north, holding hands.
- Hold your partner by the elbow and move in a very tall way toward the west. [Oh, Alan has found an interesting way to hold Jan's elbow. Betty is making a new line with her head. Jo is showing us the west side with her ear also. It's beautiful to see so many different ways.]
- Move toward the south with your partner in a very low way, as if there is a low tunnel. Find a new way to move together. You're leaving that tunnel in so many different ways. [Danny, that's a new way that you never tried before–very clever idea. Evan, how original. Pam looks so relaxed and

comfortable. Hal looks as if he's done a great deal of hard work.]

Mirrors
- Next, let's be mirrors. Take partners and decide which of you will begin. It could be whoever is nearest the east side of the room. Now, one of you move very slowly as you hear the drum begin. Partners, try to copy that person. [What nice new movements. Slowly, carefully now. Ian and Lil, move there so you have more space.]
- Now, the lead partner, change, and be the mirror to your partner. (Repeat.) (Variations on this activity include using hoops which children can roll to one another, with one another, move around and inside of, or jump in and out of, faster or slower, abruptly or smoothly, heavily or lightly.)

Personal Analogy
- Everybody go to the end of the room. Now, come to me in a new way. [That's fine, so many different ways–some high, some low, somebody sideways. Oh, it's good to see you.]
- Try a new way now, and move backward to where you started. Try a new way to come sideways. Find a new way to return sideways. [So many new ideas. Martin was really following his neck. Nora, what an original way to use your shoulder.]
- Let's rest for a minute and talk. What were you thinking of that can move sideways? What else can move sideways? (pointing to four children). Try to be that thing. (Repeat procedure.)
- Let's think together about some things that can move backward. Yes. Uh-huh. Interesting. What a fine idea. The objects can bend and stretch? Let's try (pointing to six children) to move backward as those things do. Become those things. Let's move as if we're in water, on mud, in a crowded hallway/bus.

the remainder of the group observed with her, several children developed partner, trio, and quartet movements. As they enjoyed this cooperative effort of using space together, they began to develop pantomimes. They pantomimed and guessed episodes of trips that they had taken to a zoo, a bakery, and a bottling factory. Pairs of children planned together and "became" inanimate objects, sharing their interpretations with the group. They "became" parts of cooking processes, electrical experiments, and appliances and pantomimed volcanic eruptions. Some of the pantomime activity evolved into sounds and dialogue.

As the activity grew increasingly elaborate, the emergence of dialogue marked its transformation into creative dramatics. These explorations spanned a period of several months, during which three or four sessions lasting from 10 to 25 minutes were held each week. In some classes, children with limited English proficiency have been able to participate successfully in such collaborative processes along the movement–pantomime–speaking continuum.

Kindergarten teachers can highlight elements, variable forms, original efforts, and growing sensitivities and skills. They provide opportunities for children to participate most of the time, with brief spectator periods. They notice when children's actions become more spontaneous and authentic or when they are contrived and restrained. In order to help children become as spontaneous and authentic as possible, teachers let children know that all sincere expressions are acceptable; and they recognize and appreciate each child in relation to his or her own progress.

A contrasting source for children's creative dramatics comes from the outside in, as compared with the more internal evolution just described. For example, the folk-song game "Up on the Mountain" involves partners first swinging each other and then becoming "frozen" into statues (Landeck, 1950). Teachers can emphasize the variety, originality, and specific elements of these "frozen" statues. Incidentally, children may directly experience centrifugal force before they "freeze." A great deal of such tacit knowing takes place when they dance and use playground equipment such as swings, seesaws, and slides. Thus their three-dimensional imagery builds in many ways.

Some poems and cumulative folk tales lend themselves to dramatization that is heavily improvisational. "The Three Billy Goats Gruff" is an all-time favorite. Children find high drama, suspense, and glee in stories with this sort of manageable threat.[1] Increasingly, children elaborate their play, adding simple costumes and props. *Ramona the Pest* (Cleary, 1968), the story of an amusing mischief maker with whom children identify, and "The Pied Piper" (Jacobs, 1968) are the sorts of stories that kindergarten children can dramatize. Everyone can have a role in "The Pied Piper." Siks

(1958), Ward (1960), and McCaslin (1980) are among the sources for specialized techniques and materials.

Researchers have found that role playing helps to improve story recall and comprehension (Pellegrini & Galda, 1982). Kindergarten children, however, need guided practice in role playing. In order to encourage their expressive language, teachers can begin by taking roles themselves (see also Chapter 2). Whenever young children attempt to "become" a role, they need to have a background of experience sufficient to fuel their imagination and identification. For some children, asking them to take on career-based roles, for example, is asking too much. On the other hand, roles that fall within their own experience—such as a child who is trying to persuade a parent to acquire a pet or change a rule or persuade a sibling to share television time or a toy—are more likely to develop with meaning.

It is important to create space in which to move. If there is one area in the classroom where whole-group meetings can take place, it may be possible to enlarge this area for children's creative rhythmic movement and creative dramatics activities simply by moving furniture. Pairs of children can take turns moving the chairs and tables to the side, perhaps stacking them. It is helpful and safer when everybody knows which furniture needs to be moved, where it needs to go, and how it should be carried.

THE VISUAL AND PLASTIC ARTS

Creating Visual and Plastic Arts

Space for the visual and plastic arts can be set aside near a water source, thus cutting down on traffic and mess, and would be labeled as an arts area. It would contain the following materials:

- An easel and brushes of varying thickness so that children can choose their own style; each child should have a fresh set of tempera colors, at least two or more of their own choice, in order to provide contrasts.
- A pencil hung from the easel or the table painting area so that children can sign their own names
- A drying rack
- Plastic aprons
- Table space for six to eight chairs
- Storage shelves, including shoe boxes of uniform size, shirt boxes, huge ice cream cylinders, and/or packing crates

- Newspapers for covering table or floor surfaces, in order to cut down the washing up of markings, glue, and clay residues
- Colored pencils, crayons of varied thickness, markers, and pastels as well as papers of varied size, color, shape, and texture
- Clay and varied accessories, including dowels of varying diameters for rolling; jar covers, cookie cutters, sticks, and a stylus for marking; and plastic knives and wires for cutting; pine cones and other large, textured seeds can be used for pattern making
- Collage materials, including shop window dressings, discarded wallpaper books, close-out fabric sample booklets, merchants' discards, wrapping paper, candy wrappers, packaging materials and containers, discarded buttons and trimmings, feathers, yarn, washers, screening, mesh, wires, and wire ties

Materials can be outlined and stored on shelves or pegboards. Scissors and marker tops can be stored in wood or Styrofoam holders for easy retrieval, return, and inventory. Tool carriers and a low rolling cart are also useful. Bulletin boards and displays can include framed openings to hold children's two-dimensional work; and with the children, you can create attractive arrangements on which to display three-dimensional work. Hang hoops, wire, or twine to accommodate mobiles and other hanging displays.

You may find it helpful to keep a personal card file containing varied visual and plastic arts projects. You should also keep a camera on hand for photographing children at work, as well as their projects.

Three-Dimensional Arts

The three-dimensional arts deserve a closer look since they are produced less often by kindergarteners than drawings or paintings. The visual-spatial skills that children strengthen through problem setting and solving in three-dimensional artwork also affect their mathematical skills. Many more kindergarten children need to have access to molding materials such as clay, sand, plaster of Paris, papier-mâché, wire and foil, and pipe cleaners. They also need to spend much more time using construction materials such as floor blocks and carpentry materials.

Woodworking. Woodworking can be used in kindergarten, often by midyear, when routines are well-established. In the full-day kindergarten, there are more opportunities to plan for this activity. One project might involve children in the creation of a "design board" by hammering nails and then creatively stringing yarn or rubber bands (Kohl, 1985). There is additional discussion of woodworking in Chapter 7. For detailed ideas, see also Skeen, Garner, and Cartwright (1984).

Clay. Clay may be one of the most popular of the plastic arts. One research study reports that 5-year-olds spend more time with clay sculpture, an average of 19.7 minutes per session, than any other art medium (Haskell, 1984). Other research connects children's cognitive and affective development when they use clay in a structured, supportive environment (Smilansky, Hagan, & Lewis, 1988). Clay provides sensory comfort as well as a sense of power. Where possible, children's finished work can be fired in a kiln. One class received additional inspiration when a sculptor, the grandmother of one of the children, worked in their room one day.

Sewing and Weaving. Another category of three-dimensional art activities includes mesh weaving with yarn or combinations of cloth strips, rope, and negative space; sewing designs that children have drawn, first on cards and later on felt fabric; simple macramé; and cooperative rug murals or quilts. Patchwork quilts lend themselves to celebrating many occasions and enrich or prepare children for a book such as *The Quilt* (Jonas, 1984). Children can work with supermarket food trays that, using a hole punch, you string as a loom or a sewing card. Plastic grid berry baskets also serve as looms. The "Cat's Eye" weaving around two crossed dowels, which you tie firmly for children at the center, is another kind of loom that they use with various yarn colors and beads. Kindergarten children have woven with paper clips and paper straws and made potholders with jersey loops. (Parents often find that the potholders with asymmetrical patterns and skipped stitches come in handy for many years!) Such sewing and weaving activities begin with patterned bead stringing and double- and single-sided sewing cards that children make. Paper weaving, however traditional, appears to me to create more frustration than fun.

Mobiles and Built-Up Sculpture. Kindergarten children also create mobiles and built-up sculpture. They make mobiles from coat hangers, hoops, and other items. Constructions built from a clay or Styrofoam base with interesting collections of clean junk provide an opportunity for children to experiment with various materials. Children also design, glue, and then paint collections of small boxes, cardboard cylinders, wood scraps, and/or rolled up newspapers. They face challenging problems with balance as well as design and texture.

Collages. Paper strip sculpture is a type of collage. Collages have three-dimensional as well as two-dimensional aspects, as children fold, twist, crumple, loop, fringe, and layer materials. For these as well as other activities, teachers would do well to become selective junk collectors. In addition to materials already mentioned, children can use wood shavings, toothpicks, onion skins, various dry beans, eggshells, and a variety of macaroni products. Making puppets and masks extends collage activities with such materials as paper plates, paper bags, Styrofoam, stuffed socks, covered balloons, sticks, and clothespins. Masks in particular lend themselves to representing the festivals of diverse cultures or to children's need for a sense of power and playfulness.

Two-Dimensional Arts

Variety. Variety is important if you want to keep interest fresh and create new problems to solve in the arts area. For example, at different times during the school year, you might offer string or shadow drawing, sand-painting, and printing with a range of implements: textured materials, spools, jar lids, or potatoes with children's original designs. Children enjoy using luminous colors of paint and crayon on dark paper, and they also like to engage in face or arm painting, especially when they can decide on elbow-, foot-, or hand-printing. Provide paints that are more or less thickly mixed, multiple hues of two primary colors, and opportunities to mix colors and to add color to white paint (R. Barnes, 1987; Schirrmacher, 1988). When you provide repeated, well-spaced exposures to materials, you will observe different outcomes, due to children's intervening experiences, their growing coordination, and their ability to plan.

Some teachers encourage children to bring drawing materials on trips in order to draw what they see, adding a creative dimension to this experience. Both actual and imagined drawings are acceptable and offer opportunities for ongoing revisiting (Edwards et al., 1993). In a parallel way, pairs of children have illustrated a song (Quinn, 1992) or story.

Film. Film techniques are part of some kindergarten programs. Children can use felt-tipped pens to draw directly on 8 mm film. They can take photographs of objects, or parts of objects, with inexpensive cameras and display their pictures. This work might help to demystify the power of film.

Donated Materials. If you run out of paper for painting, grocery bags and classified columns of newspapers can serve as great substitutes. Freezer wrapping paper or barber-chair paper rolls are less expensive substitutes for fingerpaint paper. Lumberyards have provided soft-wood scraps suitable for carpentry or collage, printers have provided surplus posterboard and paper, and merchants have donated dated wallpaper rolls or fabric scraps.

Diverse materials, in general, can encourage diverse, personal use. This use is quite different from static pattern-making, picture-coloring, or copied cutting-and-pasting pastimes. There are unlimited possibilities for materials to be used artistically when you and the children learn to see the strange in familiar surroundings. When that happens, your major problem may be to find space to store everything.

Appreciating Visual and Plastic Arts

Just as kindergarten children listen to different genres of music and literature from different cultures, they have been able to enjoy and contrast different visual and plastic art products that represent different genres and cultures. Kindergarten children have viewed Monet's, Hokusai's, and Rivera's as well as Pollack's paintings, and created paintings that are distinctly related to the respective styles. In a similar way, they have explored ways to represent the styles used by children's book illustrators (Raines & Canady, 1992). Children have seen self-portraits of artists from different cultures and done self-portraits themselves. You might consider collecting self-portraits at several times during the year for children's portfolios (Foote, Stafford, & Cuffaro, 1992). After drawing a friend's name out of a grab bag, they have painted the friend's portrait (Marion Silberman, personal communication, 1993). They have come to understand the terms *positive space* and *negative space* and to take for granted the nudes in art books (Joyce McGinn, personal communication, 1993). Children have played concentration games with fine arts cards from which they have induced the style of artists (Linda Davey, personal communication, 1993).

When teachers provide contrasting bodies of work done by different artists, children induce the underlying aesthetic unity of each artist's style. This takes place without adult expectation that children will create a particular product, and it makes us aware that kindergarten children do perceive isomorphic imagery that they are able to represent directly. Exposure to, and welcoming, many kinds of art products is the antithesis of copying, tracing, coloring in, following patterns, or other forms of trivial "busy work." *The Art Lesson* (de Paola, 1989) is a book that underscores the political need of artists to create their own forms.

A nonfiction work for children that focuses on some accessible elemental contrasts in visual art is *Lines* (Yenawine, 1991). It can help kindergarten children to become more aware of the styles that illustrators employ in other books. Our understanding about what children might perceive as they have such diverse experiences is an ongoing process.

REFLECTIONS ON TEACHERS' ROLES

As you work with kindergarten children in some of the varied roles discussed below, you have an opportunity to use their artistic representations as a lens through which to see the perceptual models that they share. As you do so, do keep in mind that aesthetic experience is part of daily life as well as a distinct experience with art media.

Supporting Exploration

Kindergarten children need many opportunities to explore the visual and plastic arts, music, movement, and sociodramatic and creative dramatics activity, as you encourage and highlight their original expressions and helpful, collaborative intentions. You might, for example, observe occasions for adapting rhythm to accompany a child's needs as you focus on smaller or larger forms of representation; dancing with scarves may extend the possibilities for a child who has coordination problems.

Different children need more or less practice in holding pencils, chalks, crayons, brushes, and scissors. Occasionally, a child, perhaps one with special learning needs, will need help in applying glue. You might find it useful to hold a child's hand when he is using glue or scissors so that he can see how it feels. For children who are left-handed or have special needs, provide left-handed or four-fingered scissors. If a child is beginning to use the scissors with two hands, use masking tape to attach an end of the paper to the table, so that the child can do the cutting as independently as possible.

It is important to offer consistent opportunities for exploration, even if the representations take place in what you might consider to be science study. If you were to offer kite-making materials during the study of wind, for example, provide children with varied materials and encourage them to try out different shapes with both three- and two-dimensional forms, instead of pre-cut, uniform materials. Your children can appreciate the relative movement and efficiency of angles and aerodynamics from the aesthetic standpoint of design and body movement before they are ready to understand the technology.

Engaging in Conferences

Your major job is to encourage children to use materials in imaginative ways, including multimedia work. With careful questioning and the use of analogy, teachers sometimes, but not always, can help children to extend their ways of working in the arts. In order to represent experiences, children need to make decisions about the content to which they feel committed. Just as you engage in writing conferences, you would also confer about children's role play, visual artwork, movement activity, and creative drama, because they all require children to think and attempt to solve problems in representing meanings. These contacts are times to appreciate and encourage as well as ask children to share their preferences and joys. They are also times for you to plan for activities that might extend skills and expose children to varied media.

The purpose of instruction, after all, is to build independent skills and a sense of confidence as well as to avert frustration and defeatism. Your observations can also point to the need for sequencing particular skills, such as helping children move from random printing, to patterned printing, to planned patterns, and so forth (R. Barnes, 1987).

Planning

Any time you find yourself feeling that absolutely every child must use a particular material or create a particular product, you might suspect that a truly artistic experience is missing. Remember the teaching assumption: Different children doing different things at different times can have equivalent experiences. Also consider planning for children to work together on visual art projects as well as on movement and dance or creative drama projects.

It is all right to revisit a medium or activity after a few days or weeks. Some children experience revisits as a novel experience because they have grown since the last exposure.

Encouraging Connoisseurship

Finally, you can serve as a museum curator when you frame or mount children's artwork and written work with dignity and display it on walls, the backs of room dividers, and the spaces between windows. You can cover boxes with contact paper, wallpaper, or cloth and stack them to provide a three-dimensional display area for children's constructions, clay work, artifacts, and collections. One educator suggests displaying children's unit-block work on a turntable that can be rotated, in order to add to spatial awareness (Haskell, 1984). Another way of valuing children's work is to shine a lamp on such a turntable display or on some other three-dimensional arrangement so that you can create interesting shadows.

String wire or twine across a corner, or across a room from wall to wall or corner to corner, and hang up such things as hangers and hoops for making mobiles as well as displays of splatter painting, puppets, weaving, straw sculpture, or children's own poetry, dictated or copied. Sometimes you can move a storage shelf or screen to set off a new area, so the contents of that area become a new focus for the children's attention.

Children themselves can help create such "museums," which become an integral part of their experience of success rather than an alien form. These personally involving experiences provide a readiness for trips to a school exhibition or art fair and to school- or library-based hands-on museums. School librarians, collaborating with teachers, are working increasingly to develop these kinds of experiences. You are indeed fortunate if there are such collections of activities or hands-on museums nearby. Model sites such as the Please Touch Museum in Philadelphia or the Exploratorium in San Francisco are uniquely endowed extensions of more modest local efforts.

Communicating with Parents

Hanging photographs, with captions, of children's construction work, face painting, costuming, and movement activities dignifies their efforts and affords delight to them and their parents. Dating samples of children's artwork and related photographs, as relevant, can help you to communicate with parents about the progress that children are making in their representational skills. In parent conferences, it is worthwhile to highlight the creative ways in which a child has solved the problem of representing three-dimensional space in a two-dimensional medium. There are cases, for example, of children depicting both the inside and outside of houses, or the four sides and top of an automobile (Gardner, 1980), similar to adult artists who have lived in different epochs and regions and solved similar problems in similar ways (Gombrich, 1957). Such documentation also communicates to parents and others the significance and variety of your activity.

9

Language and Literacy Learning

Language teaching and learning can be a natural part of most activities that are rich in content. Language is a tool skill that grows out of, and adds meaning to, human experiences. The repetition and practice that are necessary for acquiring skills and using a tool can occur naturally in various forms that are integrated throughout the full-day kindergarten.

In this chapter we will consider what language and literacy learning look like in a full-day kindergarten. The views presented here are consistent with a "whole-language" outlook in that children learn literacy skills inductively in the integrated context of daily life, which includes the negotiated development of meanings reflected in children's perceptual models. These views value the multiple learning processes that grow out of the unique personal cultures of children, as well as their unpredictable products.

We will discuss the knowledge bases of a literacy program, focus on ways in which children learn language skills, and outline the components of a literacy program for kindergarten children. There are four essential, integrated components in a systematic instructional program: (1) oral language development, (2) reading, (3) writing-into-reading, and (4) phonemic instruction. These components should be practiced flexibly for different children.

INDUCTION AS A WAY OF KNOWING LANGUAGE

Any one of us can look around and see that normal children are learning the language that they hear around them, yet most adults do not remember learning to speak. It just happened comfortably for most of us, without self-awareness. Theoretically, it should feel no more difficult to learn to read and write than it was to learn to speak. After we look at some basic ways in which children learn to speak, we can consider how to extend these methods as children learn other language skills.

In a nutshell, children learn to speak through the process of induction. First, they perceive a model that is repeated in daily life settings. After lots of touching, seeing, and hearing a word and object together, children begin to approximate the sounds, to great acclaim and appreciation. They imitate the sounds, receiving adult feedback, until they are able to expand an utterance to approximate the whole word.

A similar process takes place as children begin to use and learn sentence structures (syntax) within daily life situations. A kind of rubber band stretching takes place. The "rubber band" image fluctuates as the child reduces the adult's syntax. The adult in turn expands the child's statement. With continuing interaction, the child begins to expand her syntax, stretching toward the adult's fluent, more complex syntax.

Some researchers have identified a continuing process of adult–child "expansion/reduction/expansion/lesser-reduction" (Brown & Bellugi, 1964). Scholars of varied viewpoints have underscored the power of contrasts and analogies in the child's active construction of language (Bruner, 1966; Cazden, 1972, 1981; N. Chomsky, 1965; Clay, 1991; Ervin, 1964; H. A. Gleason, 1965; Harste, Woodward, & Burke, 1984; W. Miller, 1969; Neuman & Roskos, 1993; Wittgenstein, 1958). As children perceive contrasts, their ability to use language becomes more flexible.

At the same time, expansion of spoken language is not guaranteed in and of itself but depends upon the adult modeler and the child sharing language within a particular situation. When teachers tap the satisfaction that new speakers experience and nurture this naturalness, children should be able to extend and expand their language skills with comfort and satisfaction. The meaning they share provides a deeper structure than the mere order of words in an utterance (N. Chomsky, 1972). Throughout the process of literacy learning, it is more important for young children to use language functionally than to focus merely on being aware of how they are using it.

ORAL LANGUAGE AND LANGUAGE EDUCATION

Significant learning grows out of in-depth conversations (Cazden, 1988). The longer school day offers the time to engage in more involved conversations with children and to model more complex language in active situations.

The focus on oral language is one essential starting point along the path to written representation. Oral language also is rich in structures which serve people as they share important meanings in many societies that do not depend upon written language.

It is instructive to notice that the playfulness of young children is an important factor contributing to the development of creative linguistic possibilities. Babies learn the rules that hold language together. They frequently overregularize these rules logically and creatively, even when they are unconventional. For example, a toddler might say, "I runned home."

As adults and children work and talk together about events, children acquire and strengthen their use of the conventions that form sentences. Teachers can consciously use the expansion, coordination, subordination, or other alterations of sentence pairs in the context of activities. As children hear language in active and physical social settings, they find reasons to use varied sentence forms and their language becomes more efficient. Individual speaking and writing styles are the result of such experiences. Notice that if we expect children to understand words denoting relation and subordination, such as *but, because, which, that, if-then, or, and, of, all, some,* and *any,* they will need to hear them contrasted with other words in sentences. Many of these concepts are essential to an understanding of problem setting and solving in mathematics and other studies, and they deserve our systematic inclusion in situations that make sense to children.

It follows that the process of natural, inductive, early language development could be used to help those children who need additional opportunities to focus and develop their continuing linguistic skills. When modeling of the "rubber band" variety has been used, by informal repetition of sentences that are syntactically equivalent but with varied content, children have been able to induce a more efficient or expanded use of spoken language (Fromberg, 1976; J. B. Gleason, 1981; Yonemura, 1969). That is, when teachers have used concrete, materials-based, playful game situations that are tied to certain contrasting pairs or trios of sentences, children have been exposed to a planned—rather that the usual random—modeling of contrasting sentences. Examples of such "syntax model games" can be found among the works cited. Children with limited English proficiency derive particular benefits from such contextualized physical activities and language accompanied by gestures. Nevertheless, "some children will need a relatively long 'silent period' before they feel comfortable and confident enough to express themselves in the new language" (Hough & Nurss, 1992, p. 142).

In summary, induction in learning syntax (or reading print) includes the following process:

- Repeated models of contrasting patterns of words in sentence pairs (ideally occurring in gamelike situations)

- Imitation by the children as they play the game, followed by acceptance (without expressed evaluation) and expansion by the adult
- Induction of the syntax by the child, evidenced by use in game playing

Within the contexts of daily activities, including games, adults also expect children to be capable of speaking and of learning to speak at their own pace in their own ways (Cambourne, 1988). When children can interchange words more freely, there is much greater flexibility and scope to their speech. Similarly, when children have the sense that they can interchange phonemes more freely, their writing and reading skills gain more flexibility and scope. Thus the inductive social processes within which young children construct their spoken language also function in their development of reading and writing skills, discussed in the next sections. Although presented separately, reading and writing influence one another in a recursive process.

READING

There are entire volumes and courses of study devoted to the abundant variety of reading programs. Rather than a review of the field, this section presents one point of view about integrated literacy instruction in a full-day kindergarten. Keep in mind that you can help children develop their language skills best while they engage in activities that are meaningful to them.

When you provide literature for children to listen to, look through, and read in the kindergarten, the main purpose is to enjoy its meanings and varied forms. Such positive experiences help children to build reasons to want to read. Although the saturation of their school environment with rich and varied language materials—along with a sense of accomplishment in their writing—helps many children to induce for themselves the process of reading, some children need different help. They may need specific, additional focused technical help in using the sound structure of the English language. Phonemic instruction, which deals with the sound structure of language in an inductive way within the context of whole words, is another component in a comprehensive literacy program.

Putting Reading in Its Place

Reading is useful and pleasurable. It is an essential economic and cultural tool, and it also offers aesthetic experiences. When children figure out how to use this tool at an early age, possibilities for independent, vicarious, and extended experiences open up sooner. However, rote decoding without understanding is a meaningless exercise. This is the place, therefore, to talk about how children might learn to read in ways that can support their future, self-directed reading.

Prevailing practices merit review at this time. First, nursery-age children have been able to learn to read. For example, many children have entered kindergarten with independent reading skills already established (Durkin, 1966). Also, most children in our society learn to read before they are 7 years of age, apparently without an increase in ocular problems. Before kindergarten, young children maneuver effectively through a multitude of environmental print, from cereal labels to television channels and computers. However, with recent advances in the diagnosis of perceptual learning disabilities, teachers are finding that about 15% of schoolchildren have displayed such impairments even before they have been expected to read, and the percentage may be higher among children exposed to prenatal substance abuse. A few children who enter kindergarten also need to become more aware of sound itself as a conscious "figure" highlighted against their "background" experiences. For these children, instruction may re-create the earliest kinds of interactions between parent and child, as, for instance, when the parent mentions body parts, labels objects, or sings Mother Goose rhymes or other songs.

It is a constant wonder, in the light of research findings into the great range of capacity within any chronological age group, that adults continue to be concerned with the starting age for reading instruction or school itself. Some school districts or parents, however, expect that progress toward early technical reading is the single criterion for "success" and that it is best to invest in "older" children. Despite contradictory research (Shepard & Smith, 1989), such districts keep raising the age of entry to school, as if all children might behave as one, and some parents "redshirt" their children by keeping them out of school for an extra year. It would be better to regard "readiness" to read as an emerging lifelong state. If you take this view, then your job as teacher boils down to interpreting a child's skill at a given time and providing experiences at the next level of complexity.

Educators speak of "teachable moments" and "sensitive periods" when the time is ripest for learning particular skills (Hunt, 1961; Montessori, 1912/1965). Vygotsky (1962) contends that

> instruction usually precedes development. The child acquires certain habits and skills in a given area before he learns to apply them consciously and deliberatively. . . . Therefore the only good kind of instruction is that which marches ahead of development and leads it; it must be aimed not so much at the ripe as at the ripening function. (pp. 101, 104)

Adults are likely to be more aware of sensitive periods when they have been missed and children develop remediation needs; therefore we would do well to help children in a timely way.

A part of the timing problem in teaching reading during kindergarten is that educators want children to learn as much as they can in ways that make them feel human and competent. At the same time, a program that focuses on the three R's to the exclusion of rich experiences and meaningful content is a program that tries to place disembodied tools into a child's hands. Attempting to develop skills in such a sterile atmosphere is like dosing babies with medication that kills the necessary bacteria along with the unwanted ones. While we might reverse the babies' resulting digestive upsets, we cannot be so certain of reversing as readily the "school game" of feigned attention as a facade for boredom that children learn as a by-product of content-poor early schooling.

The fact remains that learning to read is not an end in itself but a tool skill that can help to capture, support, and extend the range of possible meaning for children. It is particularly unfortunate that the pressure to provide reading instruction for low-income children of color often takes a linear direction, largely excluding inductive methods and meanings that the children can value.

Children's Literature

Although children pick up many concepts about print from their home and community environments, including signs, labels, newspapers, and television advertisements, they need to have considerable exposure to fine-quality literature throughout their lives, beginning as early as infancy. Therefore, before and in conjunction with their earliest writing experiences, throughout the day, children need to be acquainted with books and other forms of print.

Saturating children with relevant print material provides opportunities to create meaning from print and the accompanying illustrations. "Readers, using their background of knowledge and experience, compose meaning from the text; writers, using their background of knowledge and experience, compose meaning into text" (Butler & Turbill, 1984, p. 17). The writer's contribution, however, does not guarantee a particular interpretation. The reader, instead, derives meaning not only from the "verbal context, but also by the context provided by the reader's past experience and present expectations and purpose" (Rosenblatt, 1969, pp. 42–43).

Difficult as it may be to imagine, there are children who enter kindergarten without positive encounters with books. For these children, for others who may have become television addicts by the time they enter kindergarten, as well as for those who have had many positive associations with books or are already reading, it is essential that teachers provide a meaningful, aesthetically varied, cheerful exposure to fine literature.

The reading area, described briefly in Chapter 1, is a place in which you can create a comfortable environment where children can concentrate. It is a setting that you can embellish with "invitations" to expectancy and delight. As you read aloud to the entire group at least once each day, you can extend this atmosphere. Kindergarten children also appreciate sitting close to you in a small group.

In order to extend the pleasures of reading and children's comprehension of books in relation to their own experiences, you can use finger or paper bag puppets to represent story characters, dramatizations, and open-ended and imaginative discussions before and after storytime in order to deepen meanings and positive associations for children. It helps comprehension when children can have some expectations about what you will be reading, so that they can have the pleasure of imagining what is to come and playfully predicting what may be ahead. Before beginning to read, you might ask them to wonder what the book might be about and what questions they might have about it. Depending upon the mood set by the story, you might engage with children in a critical discussion concerning their reactions to the issues raised or actions of the characters portrayed in a story. Children can consider how the story relates to their own experiences and preferences as well as alternative ways in which people behave.

Such "instruction," however, needs to be subsidiary to the focus on children's delight in books. When children hear some poems and stories, the experience itself can be sufficient. The "turned on," totally absorbed atmosphere and the children's very posture tell you when they are aesthetically captivated. It is redundant to ask, "Did you like it?" when their behavior holds the answer. Certainly, if they are fidgeting, looking around, or trying to find stimulation in one another, you have clues that the story or timing is not relevant.

Beyond hearing fine literature read to them, children need to have fine literature to read themselves, as their skills develop. Some teachers provide an opportunity for all children to select reading materials directly following lunch as a matter of course or in response to criticism that most schools offer less than nine minutes each day for meaningful reading (R. C. Anderson, Hiebert, Scott, & Wilkinson, 1985).

Kindergarten children can participate in "book clubs" in which small groups of children share their pleasure in reading about similar topics of interest. They can collaborate by creating posters to advertise the pleasure of particular books as well as share their science or social science studies.

Many kindergarten classes have undertaken author studies, together reading several books by a single author, such as the works of Eric Carle, Ann Jonas, or Ezra Jack Keats. Children have chosen to illustrate their favorite parts of various stories. They have corresponded with living authors and occasionally met and interviewed the authors.

In the following pages we will discuss some examples of fine literature for children. An asterisk (*) will identify sample books that some kindergarten children can read by themselves. These books tend to have cumulative structures, with plenty of repetition, integrated illustrations, brief narrative passages, high predictability, and appealing subject matter. Figure 9.1 outlines criteria with which to select literature for those kindergarten children who are beginning to read.

When we look at books that children find appealing, several forms stand out as distinctly attractive to children. Teachers have the important job of differentiating those that have integrity from those that are gimmicky, fluffy, or "supercute."

Persons in Feathers or Fur. There are many stories about human problems and feelings that are masked by animal forms. The kindergarten child can identify with these animal characters, which serve quite a different purpose than do the violence-prone and violence-immune characters that

FIGURE 9.1: "Great Books": Criteria for Beginning Readers

Criteria for Selection	*Criteria for Rejection*
Characters have integrity, are believable, and can be identified with.	Characters are supercute, mawkish, or contrived.
Characters represent wholesome human relationships.	Characters promote prurience or violence.
Values are integral to the material.	Values are presented as moralizing.
Egalitarian values are present, e.g., gender equality, multiculturalism, etc.	Values include stereotypes or lack of pluralism.
There is a satisfying ending.	There is an anxiety-provoking ending.
There is significant and/or playful content.	Content is trivial, mindless or exploitative.
Language is used beautifully.	Language is stilted or contrived.
There is just one story in each book. Illustrations are integrated with text and are aesthetically appealing.	The book is a series of stories or textbook materials conforming to a pre-established word list.

appear in some other books directed to children. One excellent example of the genre is *Charlotte's Web* (White, 1968), which is laced with life-and-death issues, while involving the listener in an intimate friendship experience with a spider and farm animals. *The Way Mothers Are* (Schlein, 1963) underscores the intimacy of a warm family relationship through animals. *The Noisy Book** (Brown, 1973), filled with repetition that children enjoy participating in, leaves the reader/listener with a sense of empathy for a convalescing dog and provides a satisfying ending.

At their best, these persons in feathers or fur, no less than human story characters in good literature, frequently involve the reader/listener in significant human problems. Issues of growth and achievement; security and dependency; fear, assertion, and power; and life and death are universal themes that can engross a reader. They reflect the kind of dynamic content to which children can commit their attention. The finest children's stories handle these issues with care for children, providing satisfying if not always happy resolutions. They do not titillate children or present suspense and violence as ends in themselves.

Realistic Fiction. Anything that really could happen in a child's experience can be the subject of realistic fiction. Children have opportunities to see how other people, or animals who retain animal characteristics, behave and feel in situations with which the young listener/reader can identify. Sometimes these situations occur at times and places other than the ones in which your children live. These stories can help children to see familiar events in new ways. *Benjie on His Own* (Lexau, 1970), about the securities and insecurities of an urban black child being raised by his grandmother, and *Angus Lost* (Flack, 1932/1989), about curiosity, adventure, and security in familiar things, present believable characters with whom children can identify. Both books transport readers beyond the surface action, touching significant personal realities.

The best authors use mostly direct conversation that focuses the reader on the present time of the story. Often one main idea and character are the focus of these stories. Children are able to validate the possibility of these events and characters. Kindergarten children are satisfied with simple endings. Even if an ending comes as a surprise, it should be within the possibility of a child to imagine it.

A book like *I Saw the Sea Come In* (Tresselt, 1968) stands in contrast to the stories in which character identification is prominent. Tresselt presents a realistic situation but creates an aesthetically powerful mood by the beautiful use of language. Indeed, spoken language is rarely as poetic as this example. Children need to have exposure to a variety of expressive forms, and this variety is most likely to be found in the books that you will read to them.

Folktale Formats. The cumulative form of the folktale, in which each successive event is added to the next and repeated, is frequently found in literature for young children. When the substance is appealing, the cumulative stories are most popular and are easily retold. The repetition helps to make these tales readable. Children also enjoy the repetition since it offers them a sense of mastery due to their being able to predict what is coming, sometimes chanting familiar refrains. Examples of such stories are *Ask Mr. Bear** (Flack, 1958/1968), *If You Give a Mouse a Cookie** (Numeroff, 1985), *The Camel Who Took a Walk* (Tworkov, 1974/1989), *I Went Walking** (S. Williams, 1989), and the folktales *Caps for Sale** (Slobodkina, 1947/1989) and *The Enormous Turnip** (Southgate, 1970). They all have satisfying endings. Folktales themselves also serve children as a window through which to view the perspectives of families and cultures other than their own.

A repetitive form that has symmetry exists in *Blueberries for Sal* (McCloskey, 1948/1968), in which a human child and a bear cub inadvertently switch places. A less plausible fantasy is *The Giant Story** (de Regniers, 1953), in which a boy repeatedly tries out his imaginary power, to the satisfaction of numerous children.

Poetry. Successful authors appeal to children by communicating appreciation for their characters and respect for their audience. There is a kind of sincere "eye contact" made with children's very marrow. A. A. Milne is a master of this craft, as evidenced by his *Winnie-the-Pooh* (1957) and his poetry classics, *Now We Are Six* (1958a) and *When We Were Very Young* (1958b). He manages to touch most concerns and problems of childhood, except for the pain of major deprivation. When adults read "Sand Between the Toes," with coordinated tickles beginning with "sand in the hair," both reader and listener share a rare joy. Using this poem for physical pointing—as well as using pointing with many other books—particularly helps children with limited English proficiency to learn English.

It is worthwhile for children to hear a variety of styles and forms of poetry. Adoff's (1974) poetry anthologies, including the works of Langston Hughes, provide a variety of settings and fine craft. Both children and adults appreciate Nikki Giovanni's (1971) metaphors in *Spin a Soft Black Song*.

Children certainly appreciate poetry that they hear. Narrative poems can serve as a basis for their creative dramatics, right alongside prose stories. Poetry is particularly adaptable to choral speaking, with subgroups taking turns, which helps reticent children or those with limited English proficiency to participate. In addition, when you group together poems that have a perceptual model or metaphor in common, children can experience similar images from various perspectives, a powerful way to learn about different ways of knowing the world.

Your own enjoyment of a poem can be contagious. It is worthwhile to build a stock of familiar, favorite poems that you can integrate incidentally at the "right" moment, even if it is not storytime. Milne's "Happiness" (in Milne, 1958b), Stevenson's (1961) "My Shadow," and Segal's (1952) "Be My Friend" are just right at certain moments. The daily storytime, a planning meeting, or a transition time could include one or two or an entire session of poems for children to hear. Children have favorite poems and ask for their repetition, just as they do with stories.

Nonfiction Trade Books. Many nonfiction trade books are written imaginatively and entertainingly for young children. Illustrations in both fictional and nonfictional works are frequently well integrated with the text and add to the experience of the book for children. In *A House Is a Home for Me** (Hoberman, 1978), for example, the use of metaphor, imagery, rhyme, and detailed illustrations—which are worth exploring with an overhead projector—add a poetic feeling to the acquisition of information. However, as much as these features serve to capture a child's interest, the primary purpose of nonfiction is informational. In addition to information about the world in general, puzzles, riddles, jokes, magic, recipes, and games are found among nonfiction trade books for kindergarten children.

Periodicals. Periodicals for kindergarten children have been published that consist largely of illustrations with just a few labels and captions. Rather than use these as a whole-group, didactic reading activity, provide several copies of newspapers or other appropriate periodicals that children can choose to read in the reading area. Around-the-circle reading is no more acceptable with newsletters for kindergarten children than it is with fine literature or *The New York Times* among adults.

Big Books

By being extralarge, big books provide an opportunity for "shared" reading (Holdaway, 1979; Butler & Turbill, 1984) because a teacher and group of children can share a detailed viewing of the conventions of print and the illustrations together. As they read to the children, for example, teachers point to words and spaces, emphasize sounds and directionality, and welcome children's chanting along.

Publishers of big books (Reading Development Resources; Rigby; Scholastic; Sunshine; Wright Group) also typically provide small copies so that children can reread the stories at other times, sometimes with audiotapes. *Story Box* (Butler, 1984) also suggests that each child use a box in order to collect a few titles that he can reread at his own level of interest and capacity. Many of the stories or poems and songs tend to have a folktale quality, selected because of their repetitive story structures and language. Kindergarten children have their favorites based upon the appeal of empowerment, such as getting filthy in *Mrs. Wishy-Washy* (Cowley, 1980/ 1990) or the sheer nonsense of *The Big Toe* (Melser & Cowley, 1980/1986) and *A Hole in the Bucket* (Hunter-Grundin, 1983).

The enthusiasm of teachers and children for big books, and for the shared reading and language experiences they make possible, has been high. Enthusiasm notwithstanding, the big book titles are not a literature program in themselves. In addition to these titles, children need to hear selections from among the finest of the varied literature that teachers can acquire. With the thousands of new titles that appear each year, along with the classics of varied genres, children should hear and see many fine trade books.

Teachers have embellished the use of big books with such activities as sentence and word strips for matching and sequencing the print in stories as well as comparing sounds within words. In such ways, beyond a focus on meanings, critical discussions, or aesthetic appreciations, they have used big books as exercise material. Louise Rosenblatt (1980) would caution a separation of aesthetic, present-time reading from efferent, technical, future-oriented reading. She reminds us that "although the explicit teaching of skills destroys the aesthetic stance, aesthetic reading may yield much incidental learning or reinforcement of skills" (p. 392). Thus it is useful to reserve as aesthetically oriented events those trade books that are unconnected with a "series" or "reading scheme."

Together with young children or with the help of older children, teachers have created big books that replicate or create variations of smaller favorite books. Children have retold the stories, dramatized events, created murals, and raised related questions in their journals. Children use their knowledge of books to fuel their writing, and writing involves rereading the writing (DeFord, Lyons, & Pinnell, 1991). The next section focuses on writing-into-reading.

WRITING-INTO-READING

The whole point of language-experience activities is to demonstrate to children a written form of their spoken language that communicates meaning. Clearly, children who have opportunities to react, feel trust, and experience delight in school activities have more about which to talk and write, and they also have more background to bring to reading the printed page.

They enjoy using these tool skills to express their views of the world, their place in it, and their relations with other people.

In the language-experience approach to writing and reading, kindergarten teachers write down, in the children's presence, what children dictate to them. They may write on paintings that children have created, on chart paper following a shared experience, and on the labels that name elements in the physical environment of the classroom. After such experiences, children and their teachers often save and revisit their written observations and findings.

In preceding chapters, there are examples of such writing in the content areas. Almost any everyday experience can become an "experience chart." This practice saturates the kindergarten children visually with the medium of writing, in much the same way that they have been saturated with their native spoken language at home and with aural and written forms in community and media environments.

On these occasions, teachers find that it is important to record precisely what children say, so that the written form captures the children's spoken language, even if it is not standard English. In this way, bilingual children, children with limited English proficiency, or children with dialectal differences can feel that their spoken language is acceptable. They also have the repeated experience of seeing their ideas recorded and their experiences saved and retrieved.

With enough modeled repetition, many children begin to sort out the concept of spaces as the limits of words. They need repeated, focused exposure to the left-to-right orientation of the English language. They will observe, however casually, that the teacher always forms each letter from the top to the bottom and from left to right. The teacher might accompany such writing with a running description of what she is doing as she writes, such as calling the letter names, mentioning moving from top to bottom, forming curves and lines, and leaving a space between words. When key words that have unusual configurations appear often, some children sort them out. With many such experiences, some children begin to induce the sound structure of words, while others build a sight vocabulary.

Language-Experience Variations

Large sheets of paper, with or without accompanying pictures, are useful for recording procedures that a group follows, say, in a science activity or in cooking. You can create labels in the classroom for doors and windows. Labels can be pinned on children's clothing that explain their roles in sociodramatic play, such as "doctor," "baby," and "mother" (Mackay,

Thompson, & Schaub, 1978). In addition, leave letters or words on flannel boards and magnet boards with which children can play.

When you feel that a child might like to discuss a drawing or painting, you might ask, "What would you like me to write on your picture?" Be aware that the youngster might not have planned or produced a representational drawing; therefore, it would be inappropriate to ask, "What did you draw?", since that could suggest that realism or a particular standard is required as the only acceptable form.

A group of pictures with brief dictated narratives can be bound into a class book. It can be on a particular topic, such as "Changes Outside the Window," "Friends," "I Hate," or "Motors." The children also might compose a song or write a rhyme about events in a story. Such a book might circulate at the reading area or even overnight at home. Other dictated writing can include menus, diets, tickets, shopping lists, magic spells, plans for parties, notices of special events, schedules of daily activities, special instructions, letters to a sick child, a thank-you note to a toy donor or a senior citizen who visited the class, and invitations for parents to assist on a class trip. A "News-Item Chart," a sort of newspaper broadside, could contain such information as, "Sue has a baby brother," "Ellen has a birthday today," and "Mary's grandmother came to visit last night" (V. D. Anderson, 1968, p. 150). A class message center or working post office, in which each child has a box, can be a place for children to receive mail, such as notices to take home, messages from one another, appointments with the regular teacher or special teachers, or greeting cards.

Occasionally, individual kindergarten children have made "talking compositions" on audiotapes. Some of these have become experience charts, recorded by an older child or an adult. Sometimes individual children retell their stories on the tape, embellishing or varying their material, as close as kindergarten children come to the act of revising or editing. For them the process itself and the satisfaction of the experiences, even though they may be episodic, incomplete, or rambling by adult standards, are more important than the final product.

Most kindergarten children are able to write their own names and recognize the names of other children if they have had repeated opportunities to see them. Motivation to write their own names is high and is a welcome first writing activity. Books about children learning to write their name, such as *The Day of Ahmed's Secret* (Heide & Gilliland, 1990) and *Rosa-Too-Little* (Felt, 1950), can only serve to add inspiration. In the latter book, a preschool city child secretly practices writing her own name in order to obtain a library card. After children can write their own names, teachers can arrange a trip to the local library, where children can receive library cards.

Breakthrough to Literacy Program

Mackay and colleagues (1978) attempt to bypass the need to coordinate handwriting and the recall of word parts in an intriguing way. Their Breakthrough to Literacy program of "sentence makers" has been used with thousands of children. Children use preprinted word cards that capture their thoughts. After children collect their thoughts on the word cards and line them up on a stand similar to those used in "Scrabble," they can copy the resulting statement at their own pace. In this way, the ideas will not be lost during the slow development of the coordination required for handwriting. Moreover, even if a child is not yet able to write or is physically challenged, she can still compose ideas on the stand.

Inasmuch as the child's own ideas and syntax form the material for reading, the Breakthrough to Literacy method is part of the language-experience tradition. Growing out of the New Zealand experience, this format is a precursor of the current "process" writing movement. Although Breakthrough to Literacy accepts children's use of invented spellings, many adherents of "process" writing avoid this approach, because of its heavy reliance on preprinted word cards.

The kindergarten year, or whenever children are beginning to read words, is the ideal time to introduce this "sentence maker." It consists of a three-part oaktag folder, each part 9-by-11 inches. The folder stands up to form a kind of private study carrel and folds flat for easy storage. The interior consists of nine rows of pocket slots in which children can store word cards. The teacher keeps scissors and an oaktag strip at hand, writes a word when a child asks for it, and cuts it off the strip. A child also might ask another child or the teacher to help find a needed word in a word card file or a pouch-pocket storage device that hangs on the wall. The files store cards with commonly used words as well as question-mark and period cards. One child may read her statement to another child or the teacher before or after writing it in a notebook or on a drawing.

The sentence maker contributes to the children's concrete understanding of syntax as they physically set words in the stand. The left-to-right sequence is signaled by a mark at the left side of the stand. When they read back what they have selected, they frequently fill in "grammatical" words and their usual spoken syntax, even though the stand may contain only a few "lexical" words that have "high information content" in random order (Mackay et al., 1978, p. 96). Some researchers note that young children tend to produce simple word inventories (Temple, Nathan, & Burris, 1982). Children also often express themselves with little concern for a possible audience.

The sentence-maker materials serve to situate the activity of writing at the more concrete level of *recognition*, as opposed to *recall*. Even after a child has "graduated" from use of the stand and is writing at the recall level without the stand, teachers will notice that a child may "revert to simple sentence making for a time" (Mackay et al., 1978, p. 156). Later in the year, a few children may begin to play with transforming one word into another, an indication that they are at a recall level. Capital letters, other than in their names, are variables that are added after they have achieved proficiency with the sentence makers. These developmental phases are part of the child's natural rhythm of language development.

The many hundreds of kindergarten children whom I have observed using these materials were enthusiastic. They composed their sentences, recorded them in notebooks, and illustrated their statements. Within these same settings, they also played with a full range of other concrete materials.

Breakthrough to Literacy is a personalized, creative, participatory alternative to workbooks and look–say types of basal readers that depend on rote learning and memory alone. In the context of a rich language environment, the Breakthrough to Literacy materials have also served to satisfy the need that community members and administrators may have to identify concrete reading materials for young readers.

Composing

Carol Chomsky contends that, for the young child, "the natural order is writing first, then reading what you have written" (1971, p. 296). She points out that the child who selects a plastic letter *r* to represent *w* in the word *wet* is reminding adults that this is the way he pronounces his *w*'s. The developmental value of such invented spellings has met with increasing acceptance by people who are concerned with early writing curriculum (Calkins, 1994; Ferreiro, 1991; Newman, 1984; R. Smith, 1983; Sulzby, Teale, & Kamberelis, 1989).

When you ask most young children to read to you, they often respond that they do not know how to read. If you offer these same children writing materials, however, they will demonstrate that they know some things about writing. Although they may not yet be using the alphabet, their written forms resemble the written language of their environment, whether it is Arabic, English, or Hebrew (Harste et al., 1984).

Researchers have described for us a gradient of written representation in which children of kindergarten age and younger increasingly create forms that approximate standard writing (Clay, 1991; Ferreiro & Teberosky, 1982; Harste et al., 1984). At a later date, the children often can read the same messages from these pre-alphabetic written forms. According to Ferreiro and Teberosky (1982), children transform their early forms of writing on the way to alphabetic writing as follows:

1. Curved and/or straight lines
2. "Stable, graphic strings" that include a fixed minimum number of forms
3. A "syllabic hypothesis" in which one letter represents one syllable
4. A conflict between graphic strings and syllabic hypothesis; that is, "conflict between an internal requirement and a reality external to the child" (p. 204)
5. Alphabetic writing that recognizes sound values smaller than syllables

Alphabetic writing usually progresses with children's awareness of beginning sounds, then ending sounds, then medial vowels. Children often begin to write medial vowels when writing their own names (Sowers, 1986a).

Those children who have limited English proficiency or are reticent about writing "may be more able to write when allowed to work through picture-making" (Bridge, 1986, p. 75). This practice focuses on the communication of meanings as the priority in literacy growth.

Children have strong personal motivation for improving their own writing (Clay, 1991; Dyson, 1989; Ferreiro & Teberosky, 1982; Gibson, 1989; Graves & Stuart, 1985). The vagaries of the English language, however, mean that about 15% of the words we frequently use simply do not fit regular patterns (Mazurkiewicz, 1964). Children are more likely to recognize those words if they have seen them written and if they have some background in phonemic associations to guide them. Children who use invented spellings show significant progress in acquiring phonemic associations.

While children learn to write in ways that parallel learning to speak, and by hearing written material read, the written work of beginning writers does have some unique characteristics. For one thing, teachers should expect and value many examples of invented spellings. Since the act of composing, used in the sense of freedom to organize feelings and ideas in a personal way, is the single most important writing task to nurture, you should be a great appreciator of the trust with which young children present their work. Quite simply, you should appreciate the flow, the enthusiasm, and the sense of accomplishment that young children bring to their work.

Rather than ignore early forms or designate these forms as useless scribbles, you should celebrate them as accomplishments that represent progress toward standard writing. Necessarily brief statements should be appreciated, not returned with requests for expansion. Accept creative spelling, handwriting, and punctuation, rather than turning these products into on-the-spot lessons. Technical instruction should take place at times separate from when young children feel the flush of accomplishment.

Indeed, children learn to write much as they learn to talk: by hearing repeated models. They learn the conventions of written language by hearing and seeing the writings of other people. Author Eudora Welty (1984), speaking of her beginnings as a writer, discusses her mother's reading to her repeatedly at many times and places. Her understanding that books are products rather than "natural wonders" developed gradually, from simpler, magical, holistic views to more refined inductions. Thus, as children have contacts with books and other print forms, reading serves to enhance writing; critical reading and critical writing support each other.

In considering the composing process, it may be helpful to think of it as being a set of interwoven, recursive phases: prewriting (experiencing and talking about what children might plan to write about); writing interwoven with sharing with other children and the teacher; and publishing or occasionally preparing a rendition on special paper.

Prewriting

The prewriting phase is a critical time for you to work with children in harnessing and building enthusiasm and motivation for writing. It is a time to develop ideas about which to write. Children have plenty of motivation to represent their experiences in symbolic forms, whether written, artistic, or dramatic. Philosopher Suzanne Langer (1942/1948) has hypothesized that human beings actually have a need to symbolize. Generally, you can focus on simply supporting the flow of composing.

It is particularly helpful to plan some child-centered questions that help children to think about the relation of a story or event to their own experiences, for example, "When did something like that happen to you?" or "What would you have done next with that character if the book could keep going?" or "Who was your favorite character?" or "What might that character have done that did not involve lying?" or "If you could talk to that character, what would you want her to know about your family?" You will find additional ideas for prewriting activities among the discussions of questioning techniques and the uses of analogy in Chapter 2 and the activities connected with the content of Chapters 5, 6, 7, and 8. It is natural that writing and other representational activities are entwined with the range of curriculum. Young children comfortably integrate these activities throughout the day.

WRITING

Prewriting and reading continue throughout the writing process in many areas of the classroom. The sociodramatic area, for example, might include writing tools as props (see Chapter 5). Children might create advertisements for their store (Raines & Canady, 1992). Researchers have found that integrating writing materials with changing sociodramatic play themes generates increased use of literacy skills (Christie, 1991; Morrow, 1990; Schrader, 1989, 1990).

The bulk of kindergarten children's writing products appear and increase after several months of the school year have passed. Sometimes the children's writing involves playing with words and sounds, just as they have done in the course of oral language development. Other products might include labels or captions for pictures that they have drawn in the arts or writing area, one-page stories, or pad book stories of several pages. Some writing could take place as children respond personally in journals to stories that they have heard.

The journal notebook contains an ongoing personal statement in which children can write each day once you feel they are ready to do so. Different children will be ready at different times; you should look for children who are beginning to use the syllabic hypothesis. Journal writing provides an opportunity for you to correspond with the children through their journal.

For example, before the children arrive, a New York City public school kindergarten teacher writes a daily one- or two-sentence letter to each child who has a journal. She might ask about how they like something, or about siblings or other everyday experiences, and the children write their answers in the journal. Often, they will ask a question in return, such as "Dear Ms. Davis, I have 1 sister. She is a baby. How many brothers and sisters do you have? Love, Alex." Sometimes children write in the journal and fold over a page to denote that it is private (Ursula Davis, personal communication, 1985).

With teacher assistance, some kindergarten children compose cinquains about subjects of their choice such as kites, trips, food, Picasso, or books (Biondo, 1992). The example below is by a kindergartner named Bryan:

> Friends
> They're special
> Cheer you up
> They help with problems
> Nice. (in Biondo, 1992, p. 13)

They also enjoy small-group "simile poems," in which children brainstorm: as red as ____, as soft as ____, as loud as ____, as cold as ____, and so forth.

Writing Area. An ongoing commitment to writing as composing can be underscored by creating a kindergarten writing area. The space should be set up away from traffic and labeled as a writing area. It might be part of a larger literacy area that includes children's literature and an audio-tape listening facility. It should contain the following resources:

- Tables, with six to eight chairs facing a wall, room divider, or carrel
- Storage space for journals and writing folders
- Space and procedures for storing work in progress, for example, clip-boards or clothespins on a line of string from which to hang papers
- A place to leave "finished" work for you to see
- Writing implements, reserved exclusively for the writing area (these may change from time to time in order to highlight the area, e.g., when a special magic marker or stunning pencil is provided, one for each seat)
- Paper supplies and teacher-made pad books (four to six sheets of paper stapled together) of varied sizes/shapes
- Stapler, scissors, and Scotch tape
- An optional picture alphabet

Within the writing area, in addition to the physical materials just listed, it makes sense to include the following items:

- A dated schedule of reserved space in the writing center, allowing each child to work consecutively for at least three days at the start of each moderately (as opposed to fully) active work period.[1] As each reserved space is vacated, another child may choose to use the space and add his or her name to the sign-up sheet.
- A dated file of samples of children's completed writing in the form of single sheets or short pad books—some teachers have found it useful to save finished work in a large portfolio, one for each child.
- A personal task card file of your ideas and materials to elicit writing content and energize the writing center.

Writing Conferences. As you appreciate the process of children's writing efforts, you can highlight various aspects of the writing in a conference with an individual child or with several children together. For example, you can reflect back what a child has written and ask the child for confirmation. You might ask what the child perceived to be the most important part of the story or why the child decided to write about this topic. You might ask for additional information about the meanings. You also might ask if the child plans to write about a similar or different topic next time. You might raise some of the questions that were discussed in the section on questioning in Chapter 2, using only those questions for which you really need an answer because the contents grow out of children's insights. Rather than expecting a single "correct" answer, you will find that the best questions may be answered differently by different children. These strategies encourage children to trust you enough to risk sharing honestly and to develop their own critical-thinking skills in relation to stories and events. A teacher whose purpose is to help children to develop independence in writing, reading, and thinking would focus on the structures of meaning: "When you reread that piece, you changed it so that it made sense."

Children can help one another with their writing as they share their work informally, at peer conferences, or in a larger-group sharing time. Other children raise important questions that help the author to clarify meanings. Sharing ideas and written work with others in these many ways helps children build a sense of audience. In these ways, the writing conference as a "thinking conference" serves as a "structured . . . intellectual collaboration" (Newkirk & Atwell, 1986, p. 3).

Beyond adding to their work, a revising or editing phase is usually not relevant for young children. Occasionally a child may add to a piece or see something months after he originally wrote it and marvel at how much more proficient his later work seems. An opportunity for self-directed revision might occur, long after a first flush of creative achievement, if a youngster were preparing some favorite writing on "special" paper for a display or sharing.

PUBLISHING

You can tape a mark on the floor to designate an area for peer sharing. By sitting there, any child is inviting others to share written work. At first, children may read simultaneously to one another. After you have consistently modeled appreciation, the retelling of stories, and clarification questions, children learn to do this for one another; for example, a child who finishes reading to the class in an "author's chair" or on an "author's stump" may fold her arms and ask, "What did I just say?" and then, "What questions do you have to ask about my story?" There are other helpful sources of ideas for teacher and peer writing conferences and publishing (Calkins, 1994; Flemming, 1986; Sowers, 1986b).

Occasionally, you may ask children to select their favorite piece of work so that it can be displayed in or circulated from the classroom reading area. Imagine the excitement of authorship and publication as a child glues a library card holder onto the cover of his own book!

A final product for young children might be a collection of illustrated stories or an exchange of messages into a personal or class book. If children collaborate in creating a book of illustrated stories around a single topic, you can provide a special quality or size of paper on which they can copy a favorite piece of writing. These can be framed in oaktag or colored paper and hung on the walls. More often, kindergarten children and their teachers are likely to be quite satisfied with episodic writing, simple phrases or sentences, and labels. A parade of children holding their products, whether it is a drawing with a child's name or stories of several pages, is a satisfying event.

Yet there should be bulletin board and hallway displays labeled "Kindergarten Writing—[month]" that might include broadsides, an occasional pad book, or labeled drawings arranged in an aesthetically appealing format. There might be photographs of kindergarten children engaged in writing or sharing their writing with others. It is useful to bring to the parents' attention the content of the items listed above.

Parent Involvement

Parents need assistance in understanding those ways of teaching that differ from the ways in which they were taught. It is probably fair to say that most parents experienced a future-oriented technical cast in their education. Because of such a stance, as well as their personal identification with their offspring, parents often focus on their children's products, with only a subsidiary appreciation of the processes that have generated particular achievements. Some parents, for example, may feel aggrieved that their children's "incorrect" spelling is hung on the bulletin board for all to see or wonder whether their children are getting "less" than those who labor in workbooks elsewhere.

It is difficult, but necessary, to persuade parents that their dreams need to be deferred into the near and middle distance; that invented spellings and profusions of artwork, social interaction, and sociodramatic play will nurture attitudes of independent scholarship along with skills. The task of communicating and persuading needs to take place. Here are some suggestions.

To the samples of children's drawn and written work that you have saved, add samples of each child's favorite books. Looking at the progress represented in these materials serves as a focus for parent conferences. As parents see progress and you talk with them about how it took place, they come to trust in the processes. "Like early attempts to walk, talk, and draw, initial attempts to spell do not produce habits to overcome. . . . They are greeted as displays of intelligence and emerging proficiency" (Sowers, 1986a, p. 47).

The use of backpacks is one of the most exciting ways in which parents can learn about the power of a comprehensive, active literacy approach. Once or twice a month, depending on your resources, children take home an actual knapsack for a week's time that includes activities for them to do at home with their parents. Mary Quinn (personal communication, 1991) sends home backpacks that focus on a topic and include the following items:

1. A letter to the parents (see Figure 9.2)
2. A list of projects (see Figure 9.3)
3. Four to six children's books and one or two articles or pamphlets about literacy for parents
4. Some writing or other materials, as seems appropriate for the family
5. A photograph of the contents of the backpack

With those parents who may have limited English proficiency, teachers have asked others to translate the letter and/or work together with a parent in school. (See also Quinn, in press.)

Backpacks usually are funded through Parent–Teacher Associations or school district or teacher association minigrants. If you are interested in developing this form of playful, interactive collaboration with parents, begin with one backpack and add one to your collection every month or two. Before you know it, you may have as many as 10 or 20. I recommend that the topics focus on a committed issue with dynamic possibilities, such as "Friendship and Rejection," "Brave and Frightened," "Competing and Cooperating," "Angry and Happy Feelings," "Saying Goodbye and Moving In," "Wishes and Fears," or "Growing Up and Holding On."

Involving parents in this way, as well as by welcoming them as volunteers in the classroom (with teacher orientation to their roles), helps parents to learn about alternative ways of learning literacy. They can contribute, for example, as game players, small-group readers, language-experience scribes, or oral history interviewees. Inasmuch as parents are pleased to know that you appreciate their child, you also can become a credible model of alternative ways in which to interact with children.

PHONEMIC INSTRUCTION THROUGH INDUCTIVE GAMES

It is worth looking at the most efficient ways of helping children to figure out the phonemic system, while retaining an atmosphere in which rich,

FIGURE 9.2: A Letter to Parents about Backpacks

Dear Parents:

Welcome to the world of Backpack Projects!

Enclosed you will find several books, novelty items, and a poem pertaining to the "Backpack" topic.

You will have a week to linger over and enjoy the books. During the week you are hosting "the backpack" your child, and any members of the household who wish to get involved, will be working on a project.

The backpacks will be signed out on a Thursday and will be returned the following Thursday. If Thursday falls on a school holiday, return the backpack and project the next day school is in session.

Each backpack will contain a journal in which I would like you to write down the process you went through to do your project. You may also wish to write any other comments you or any family members would like to say about your child's efforts. Keep the project enjoyable for both you and your child.

In each Backpack you will find an "adult" reading book or article for your reading pleasure. You may also address any question you have about "adult" reading in the journal.

A pictorial inventory has been taken for each backpack. A copy of this picture will be enclosed in each backpack.

Thank you for your efforts in this matter.

Sincerely,

Mary Quinn

Source: Used with the permission of Mary C. Quinn.

meaningful activity continues to take place. The sooner children reach a level of reading comprehension that approaches their level of interest, the sooner reading can function as a tool. Early success breeds a feeling of competence as well as purposeful, natural use of this tool. As with any skill, coordination and comfort accrue with practice.

For these reasons, when children need help in recognizing the sound structure of printed symbols, many teachers offer focused phonemic instruction, using the same processes that took place in the early development of spoken syntax. Such instruction, however, is only needed for some children and should only form a small part of their exposure to language-enrichment activities.

FIGURE 9.3: Backpack Projects for Children

1. Pretend your teacher runs a bookstore, design a poster to advertise a book, to hang in her bookstore.
2. Make a map or a pictorial time line of one of the books.
3. Model a character from a story in clay.
4. Construct a diorama to represent a scene from a story.
5. Use paper, cardboard, wire, pipe cleaners, to recreate a character from one of the stories.
6. Make a mobile of characters from the books.
7. Create a pie plate movie of scenes from a book: Divide a paper plate into fourths; each part should have a scene; fasten a second plate on top with brass fastener, cut out a section so one fourth is visible; top plate rotates to show scenes.
8. Write a letter to a friend, or family member, telling them about your favorite book.
9. Design a T-shirt advertising a book or character you love.
10. Write a poem to accompany a story.
11. Write a letter to the author of your favorite book.
12. Create a stick puppet character using popsicle sticks or straws; retell the story using your puppets.
13. Record yourself reading one of the stories.
14. Write a "prequel" to one of the books. This means that you will write what you think or imagined happened to the characters before the story began.
15. Create an ad for your favorite book. The ad will be used to entice other children to read your favorite book.
16. Plan a menu for the characters that you have read about in the Backpack. Prepare a shopping list of what they need to buy for that meal.

Source: Used with the permission of Mary C. Quinn

Practice

Varied views of reading include the notion that the reader develops a range of habitual responses to a specific set of contrasting patterns of graphic shapes (Fries, 1963) or learns to exclude those graphic elements that are immaterial to meaning by acquiring a habit of expectancy in relation to symbols (F. Smith, 1978). Since practice strengthens habits, and real habits are self-motivated, your role as integrator and appreciator is to help children look forward to reading. Practice, in and of itself, does not make learning to read take place, but it does provide the time for the inductive processes that do. Children enjoy hearing and seeing the same stories again. This is a form of practice.

The more opportunities children of the same general age have to develop skills, however, the wider the range of abilities among them will become. Therefore any grouping that exists should be for a specific short-range purpose, such as the particular phonemic skill of contrasting *cat* and *can* families of words, or the particular interest in discussing sports books of varied complexity.

When laypeople and many teachers talk about learning to read, they most often refer to the practice of teaching children to sound-out words. The "developmental basal series" marketed by many publishers are built on the method variously referred to as the "whole-word," "look–say," and "sight-word" approach. These words may be found in controlled vocabulary passages that offer children artificial, stilted language structures devoid of committed content. Children, moreover, begin to read by memorizing whole words that may or may not be regularly spelled (i.e., words that have a one-to-one correspondence between each letter and a single sound, such as *fat* or *sun*, are spelled regularly; those that do not fit this description, such as *look, come, said,* and *house*, are irregularly spelled).

When basal reader–oriented teachers begin with the whole-word method, they usually introduce "sounding-out" toward the end of the first year, or after children have achieved a body of "recognition" words. "Phonics," different from phonemics, is the school-based instructional program for sounding-out words. In phonics instruction, children are taught isolated sounds. Vowels are marked phonetically to differentiate *a* as in *fat* from *a* as in *fate*. The children are told the generalizations and are expected to apply them deductively. However, I have contended throughout this book that kindergarten children learn more readily with inductive teaching approaches.

When children begin with irregularly spelled whole words that they are expected to memorize, they usually notice reduced cues, such as the initial letter of the word, the outline of the word's letters that ascend above or descend below the line, the length of the word, or a nearby picture.

The "part," or synthetic, methods vary along a continuum from the traditional "phonics" instruction, with an initial introduction of isolated sounds, to "phonemic" instruction, in which contrasting patterns of sounds are bound within whole words.

My own viewpoint is that children can learn to read without calling letter names first. A great deal of time that involves rote learning has been devoted to calling out alphabet letter names. When teachers spend 26 weeks devoted to studying one letter each week, besides boring Sam during "s week," they provide children with a trivial focus that absorbs the time that should be available for meaningful pursuits and literacy activities. Valuable time is wasted and opportunities are lost to build critical and responsible learning. Although it does not hurt to know the letter names, it is simply not worth belaboring. Functioning rather than labeling is primary. Of course, knowing the alphabet will help children with dictionary skills, but most of them learn the alphabet easily if they have not picked it up before reading. In any case, in this country, knowing the alphabet without meaning, as a jingle, has become part of young children's social knowledge.

Using lowercase letters in language-experience and beginning reading, when possible, helps children to perceive more differentiations than with capital letters. To start out using both capital and lowercase letters is to expect an act of conservation of sound for young children, an added burden.

Although most children will easily infer the regularities in the relationships between sound and print, some will profit from varying degrees of carefully planned instruction. It may be that those children who have not induced the phonemic bases of the English language have had fewer opportunities that highlight the connections between spoken and written representations of ideas or need especially sharpened contrasts between the phonemic "figures" within the "backgrounds" of words. Whether the sources of this discontinuity reside in perceptual focus or unfortunate interactions that lead children, in Jerome Bruner's (1966) terms, to "defend" in order to "cope," a playful approach with contrasting whole words has been helpful with some children. Also bear in mind that, even with plenty of playful phonemic contrasts and story repetition, it is still natural for kindergarten children to make written or visual reversals occasionally. Most of this passes by the time a child reaches 7 years of age.

The Role of the Teacher in Inductive Phonemic Games

Teachers have played phonemic games with children as a way of systematically presenting phonemic contrasts so that those children who need focused help can induce the patterns. Children's motives for playing are the game activity rather than the phonemic learning. These games use concrete materials with controlled phonemic variables within the context of whole words. From two to five children might play together, affording many opportunities for participation. Cooperation rather than competition is stressed. These games are part of a larger experiential setting in which children can become saturated with written as well as spoken language. There are five principles used in these games that replicate some of the strategies by which children have learned to speak, thus also providing particular support to children with limited English proficiency. The principles that follow guide the playing.

Provide Contrasting Patterns. A primary principle is to provide contrasting patterns of phonemes in whole words. The phoneme is the smallest range of sound that can change the meaning of a word. For example, the transformation of the word *mat* to *that* represents a single phonemic substitution. While *th* is written with two graphemes, it is a single sound, or phoneme. When there are too many variables, it is more difficult for children to induce the new phoneme.

To help children be more autonomous, a visible model chart of contrasting pairs of words can be used as a self-checking device. The teacher does not say, "no" or "wrong" or "almost"; nor does the teacher ask another child to "help out" with the "correct" reading. If the child reads inaccurately, the teacher might remodel, pointing to the model chart that is always in sight: "If this is ____ and this is ____, if this is ____ and this is ____, then this is____." If the child cannot decode the word, then the teacher offers the word in a neutral tone and refocuses the child on the action of the game. She takes note of the child's need for additional practice with a less complex contrast at another time.

Use Whole Words. A second principle is that you need to model the new phoneme several times in the functional context of a word. When you avoid "naked consonants" by verbalizing phonemes in a functional whole-word context, subsequent blending problems can be avoided. For example, it is practically impossible to state a consonant sound alone. It comes out as a "*buh*" or "*kuh*" or "*suh.*" When children who are taught to read by using phonics or sounding-out methods meet a new word, the "naked consonants" slow them down so the "suh-tuh-o-puh" for some children becomes distorted as *supper* rather than *stop.*

Control Variables in Sequence. The third principle is that the simpler and more commonly used phonemes should be taught before the more variable and less commonly used phonemes. For example, the common sounds of the vowels, as in *bat, bet, bit, but,* and *lot,* are simpler to learn than the name sounds of the vowels, such as in *bake, beat, be, boat,* or *rule,* which require accompanying patterns. Similarly, consonants such as the *c* in *cat* and *face* or the *g* in *gas* and *gem* are more complex than *m* or *b,* which do not require conservation ability.

Be Flexible. The fourth principle is derived from the third. For example, in case you have planned an activity that is too difficult or too simple for your children, you should be prepared ahead of time to adapt with either a simpler or a more complex alternative. To adapt during an ongoing activity, consider the sequence of phonemic complexity.

You will need to be flexible about the range of abilities in your classroom, too. Many children learn to read without apparent effort by inducing the contrasting patterns of phonemes and are able to become independent readers rather smoothly. However, others require varying amounts of systematic help. The professional teacher's greatest contribution is to give systematic help *only* when children need it. If a child can already decode, then encourage that child to select reading materials from among the fine literature that you have been able to collect.

Build Cooperation. Whenever possible, it is useful to avoid, play down, or minimize competition in these games. It is more helpful to the children when you appreciate their growing skills and focused efforts. If children in kindergarten can perceive their own learning to read in a neutral, straightforward manner, perhaps fewer learning blocks will occur.

You can avoid or reduce competition by creating cards beforehand so that, for example, all the "Bingo" cards finish together because the same words are on them, although in a different order. Kindergarten children insist on playing three or four games with the different cards. With board games, instead of each child moving a marker toward a goal, the entire group might move a single marker toward the goal. A competitive atmosphere may be a signal to you that children's self-confidence is shaky or that they are feeling pressured.

Decoding Activities

It is easiest for children to play decoding games when you model the games by simply doing them, avoiding lengthy preliminary descriptions. Open each session by reading the new words alone first, thereby showing the children a new phonemic variable contrasted several times against known phonemes in words. Then model the game by taking a sample first turn.

Let us say the game involves contrasting patterns of words in which the new variable is the final consonant sound. The original concept is preprinted on oaktag, the model chart, which remains visible to the players throughout the game, for example:

bat : ban
mat : man
fat : fan
pat : pan

A look at specific games will clarify this procedure.

Pairs. The game of "Pairs," or "Concentration," is particularly adaptable to any skill level. It could almost be an entire sequence in and of itself.

In addition, children are highly motivated to focus on the cards that are turned face down, as they try to pick a pair. For this game, it is also possible to set different tasks for children who are playing together.

At the sound level, a set of cards could match pairs of pictures that begin with the same sound as *boy*, *box*, and *ball*, or *milk*, *man*, and *mouse*. The model chart would consist not of words but of rows of other pictures that begin with one or the other sound. Still another game could be pairs of pictures that end with the same sound as *hammer*, *fur*, and *car* or pairs of pictures of words that rhyme. Thus children will be using pictures to discriminate sounds.

First, however, children need to learn to play the "Pairs" game itself. Use the following procedures:

1. Model the action yourself by taking the first turn.
2. The first child takes a turn and turns over two cards, tells what she or he sees, and then replaces them face-down.
3. Be sure that other players see the cards that the player has turned over before they are replaced. Children can see better if they are seated in a row along the same baseline, therefore not seeing the card upside down.
4. As the others take turns, each player tells what he or she turns up.
5. Each player replaces the cards in the same locations if they do not match.

It is an exciting moment when the cards do match, and you can add, "You really are concentrating." The children can then place the matched pair in the group's cooperative storage container, which could be called, say, the "Hungry Hippo." Since children should not have to wait a long time for their turn, from two to five players is a sufficient number.

You can increase the chances for your children to be successful by constructing two identical pairs for each of the new contrasts. The game can build gradually toward ten pairs. The earliest cards may be simply those pictures, shapes, or colors that are the same; or pairs of animals or flowers; or outdoor–indoor picture pairs. When playing with children who have played at matching pairs of pictures, you might add, to an ongoing set of pictures or shapes, a pair of cards with the common sound of *a* pronounced on it, with the total number of cards newly reduced for this occasion. This procedure makes for a smooth transition. When *at* is added, then *mat*, with one set of four cards in each new game, the *a* cards can be retired. Figure 9.4 presents one possible early sequence of words in phonemic games.

Most kindergarten children need such focused activity and are able to handle and enjoy this activity before midyear. By the time that *at* alone has retired and four or five different initial consonants with four cards each

FIGURE 9.4: A Possible Sequence of Words in Phonemic Games

---

a : at

at : mat : sat : pat : fat (etc.)

pat : pan, fan (etc.) or pin, fin (etc.)

pat : pit, sit (etc.) or pit, pin (etc.)

Adding one new variable in each game:

(Game 1)	2 x 4	=	a	a	a	a
			at	at	at	at
(Game 2)	2 x 4	=	at	at	at	at
			mat	mat	mat	mat
(Game 3)	2 x 4	=	mat	mat	mat	mat
			pat	pat	pat	pat
(Game 4)	3 x 4	=	mat	mat	mat	mat
			pat	pat	pat	pat
			rat	rat	rat	rat
(Game 5)	3 x 4	=	pat	pat	pat	pat
			rat	rat	rat	rat
			fat	fat	fat	fat
(Game 6)	2 x 4	=	pat : pan			
			rat : ran			
			fat : fan			
			mat : man			

---

have been added (e.g., *rat* in Game 4 and *fat* in Game 5), the children are ready for the addition of *an* (Game 6). The *an* family can build words with many of the same initial consonants. In this manner, the game of "Pairs" continues to expand through the other simple consonant–vowel–consonant (cvc) word patterns such as *tan, tap, tag,* and so forth, one at a time, over a period of weeks. It is worth noting that younger children find it easier to transform *mat* to *man* than *mat* to *met*. The medial vowel seems to be sequentially more complex.

The ccvc (consonant–consonant–vowel–consonant) patterns, such as the words *flat, slit, stop,* and *plum,* build in a similar way, as well as the cvcc patterns such as *felt, soft,* and *vend.* Words such as *plums* and *send* are natural extensions of these sound patterns. Here we see a progression of common phonemic patterns in which there is a one-to-one correspondence between sound and symbol. This sequence has been loosely adapted with reference to a variety of linguistically based reading works (Bloomfield & Barnhart, 1961; Fries, 1963; Gattegno, 1968).

As children become more proficient, you can add word families gradually and in turn:

Words that end in *ill*, *ick*, and *ack*
Patterns such as *hat:hate*
Patterns in a separate activity, such as *bit:bite*
Commonly used digraphs, such as *shut*, *chip*, *this*, and *think*
Vowel digraphs represented in patterns such as *set:seat* or *got:goat*

For example, well beyond the cvc stage, the following model may comprise one game of "Pairs":

bet : beat
met : meat
net : neat
pet : peat
set : seat

If you try to teach several vowel digraphs together at one time, you impede the natural induction process. Presenting more than one new variable usually depends upon deductive applications of general principles; therefore, it is less accessible for kindergarten children. In this way, children figure out phonemic skills inductively in the functional setting of a game, with one new variable added at a time.

In the course of becoming an independent reader, a child may come to recognize some words as whole entities without really having grasped the underlying phonemic properties. There may be no comprehension problem; however, because a child has acquired the sight-word does not necessarily mean that he can transfer the component patterns in other words. This is one of the diagnostic problems that teachers face.

Children who are independent readers may need to practice with *er*, *ir*, and *ur*, or *scr* and *thr* combinations, within the context of whole words. You can contrast these various phonemic patterns by using the game of "Pairs" as well as other games described in the next section.

Other Card Games. Several card games can be similarly adapted to developing sequential skills. If children have to hold four or more cards in a fan shape, there may be some coordination problems. Consider creating a simple card stand by sawing a lengthwise groove in six-inch lengths of one-by-one wood stock.

An early form of these games uses pictures in order to acquaint children with the game format and to help them focus on similarities and differences in the sounds. For example, in the "Go Fish" game, each player receives four cards from the deck. Then they ask each other for a card that goes with one of the pictures that they are holding. Before the game begins, share common labels for the group to use so that the picture of the mouse is not taken to be a rat, or the dish to be a plate. As each child receives a pair of pictures whose labels rhyme, that pair is set aside. Otherwise, the child "fishes" for an additional card.

Card games serve as an opportunity for you to provide initial instruction through a brief modeling of the game, taking only a minute or two. They give you great flexibility because you can add or remove cards to make the game simpler or more complex. They also provide an opportunity for the children to play later with each other independently, usually for 10 to 15 minutes or so. In this way, the children are practicing a particular skill in a playful way.

Lotto board games are helpful because the cards are open for all participants to see. These games capitalize on the fact that children can match word forms before they can read them. A useful lotto sequence includes (1) picture-and-word : picture-and-word; (2) picture-and-word : word; and (3) word : word. You can provide a model for the contrasting phonemes in these games, as you did for the "Pairs" game, using a preprinted model chart.

Board Games. Board games represent still another form in which phonemic instruction can take place. You can adapt games that use:

Dice or a die made of a wooden cube
A set of cards
A spinner card
Tokens

These games can be adjusted to the various reading levels that have been mentioned previously. Dice or spinners direct players to move a token along a path that is marked on the board. When the commercial "Twister" game is adapted, for example, the markings on the spinner card and the playing "board" represent phonemic patterns that the children are ready to use. You can construct your own "Twister" boards by attaching together four large paper bags from the supermarket with masking tape.

In other games, 1-inch wooden cubes can serve as substitute dice, with words taped onto the cubes. You can prepare a set of cards that direct the movement of pieces to sections of the board marked for particular words. When cards or cubes are marked for directions, you can change the game more easily by changing the cards or cubes rather than an entire board.

There is also a flexible aspect to using cards with a spinner device that points to where a player will go. Each of several concentric circles can be designated for each of the players. In this way, you can individualize the game.

There are many imaginative, colorful themes and arrangements that you can use when you custom-design board games for the children with whom you work. Among popular topics for board games are "Snoopy Goes Home," "Rainbow with a Pot of Gold," "Baseball," "Haunted House," and television characters. Since it is time-consuming to develop these games, it is worthwhile to use sturdy materials, to cover them with clear plastic, and to create "universal" boards on which you can change cards, spinners, and dice. Plan the board so that the markers move from top to bottom and left to right, without reverse-movement penalties. These materials become part of your collected stock of other activities that children can find so stimulating.

Games with Objects. You will need games with objects, particularly for those children who need help with visual and auditory discrimination in their daily activities and for children who have limited English proficiency. Children can sort objects that begin with the same sound as *house* and *hat* into the brightly colored "horse" box while they place objects that begin with the same sound as *feather* and *fig* into the "fruit" box. Also, they can sort objects that rhyme. Notice how the use of whole-word models that contrast sounds, rather than the isolated sound or letter name, make it possible for children to grasp inductively how the sorting works.

Another sorting device that has prestige appeal in the child's culture is a cabinet of small transparent plastic drawers of the sort usually found in carpentry shops. You can tape a word beginning with a different sound on each drawer. Inside the drawer are miniature objects that begin with the same sound, such as *doll* and *dog*; or that rhyme, such as *bee* and *tree*. Children can empty a few drawers onto a cloth and sort the objects into the drawers, or remove objects from a drawstring bag and sort them into the drawers. You can find choices of miniature objects in arts and crafts shops.

Educators engage in considerable debate concerning the place of phonics instruction within the whole language philosophy, because phonics practice isolates sounds from whole words and meaningful contexts. The inductive phonemic games described above, however, use only whole words in contrasting patterns within a playful game format. The game format supports children's sense of competence because teachers invite only some children to engage in those custom-made games that are relevant. In this way, professional teachers adapt approaches and activities to different children.

REFLECTIONS

You can see children make significant progress in the components of a kindergarten literacy program when you have a longer day that focuses on meanings. They simply have more time and opportunity to explore and play with language. While you have provided a reading area, a writing area, and a teacher's instructional area, literacy activities go on in many other areas of the classroom as well.

Literacy and reading instruction in the full-day kindergarten is largely auditory and social. Many legitimate opportunities exist for children to talk to one another and to the teacher in small groups and one to one. For example, children can choose to be members of a writing or book discussion group because they share in common an interest such as animals or motors, although they may be more or less independent readers. This kind of format adds to inclusionary practices.

As you work with kindergarten children in language instruction it is important to remember not to expect instant results and to help parents, as well as the teacher next year, to appreciate small benchmarks. The impact of whatever you have done to expose children to activities for which they appear receptive may become apparent to you days or weeks later. Since children develop so quickly, your wait is limited. You can feel successful when you have helped children to feel successful and competent by appreciating what they have tried to do as well as what they have accomplished.

PART III

Conclusion

10

Establishing a
Full-Day Kindergarten

ONGOING ARGUMENTS ABOUT FULL-DAY KINDERGARTEN

Impact on First Grade

If you could be a fly on the wall of the teachers' room and hear the first-grade teachers talking about the new graduates of the full-day kindergarten program, you might hear their concerns that (1) although the children who enter first grade appear to have had varied literacy experiences, they also come with more variable needs for instruction and (2) the children appear to implement the teacher's instructions in more diverse, independent ways, although their achievements do appear to be satisfactory. Those teachers who are prepared and willing to engage in multiple approaches and organize instruction for small groups and individuals have found that their children's adjustment is smoother.

If only kindergarten teachers, informed principals, and first-grade teachers could communicate better, it might just be possible to focus on the children's accomplishments: accrued skill development and independent, diverse ways of working. Perhaps better continuity between the full-day kindergarten and first grade could take place if there were an adjustment period and staff development that included first-grade teachers, such as

- Visits to the kindergarten by first-grade teachers
- Videotapes that emphasize how successful kindergarten teachers manage varied teaching with small groups
- Sharing of techniques and activities that kindergarten teachers use to stimulate children's independence and responsibility, with collaborative efforts made to adapt these for first-grade use

Related arguments for and against the full-day kindergarten surface in community attitudes toward the education of young children. Kindergarten teachers must deal with the inevitable disparagement of their function as "babysitting" or "only playing," countering it with explanations of what children are doing that is meaningful and valuable to their learning and overall development, including their transition to first grade.

Affluence and Achievement

A significant issue has been the impact of the longer day on children from different socioecomonic backgrounds. There is a growing body of evidence, based on standardized testing, suggesting that the greatest comparative benefit of the longer day seems to take place for children who are less affluent (Lawrence Public Schools, 1983, 1984). This does not negate the benefit, albeit comparatively smaller, that children from more affluent homes might experience.

The impact on all children should not be measured and compared only by means of test scores. There needs to be a reasoned consideration of how children, even affluent children, would be spending their time otherwise. There would likely be more time for television and less time for social interaction and collaborative work with other children. The myth of a doting parent or other adult playing games and having significant, in-depth conversations with children at home needs to be exposed. That is usually not what happens. When both parents are wage earners, when families move often, when we live in a society that includes single-parent households, few siblings, increased isolation in expanded suburbia, and less contact with grandparents and other extended family, we need to rethink the myth of what children find when they come home. At the same time, we need to assure that children's time in school is used in worthwhile ways in order to help them become increasingly human, civilized, and successful.

ADMINISTRATIVE CONDITIONS

Taking all this into consideration, it is reasonable to suggest that a full-day kindergarten can be a positive force for development. While it will not hurt children to continue in a sensitive half-day program, it is my contention that children can benefit by participating in an experiential full-day kindergarten that is organized around the meanings in perceptual models. Having said this, there are some qualifying administrative conditions that characterize successful full-day programs.

Adjustment to School. The first month of the school year would begin with a gradual introduction to kindergarten, starting with part of a morning and then half a day for a few weeks, before adding the full-day schedule. In some districts, teachers make home visits, meeting parents and children.

Parent Options. Parents can choose a half day. Since states do not mandate compulsory full-day kindergarten, this is not a legal issue. In practice, a handful of parents have initially taken this option. In the Hewlett and Lawrence, New York, school districts it was found that 3% of eligible families chose the half-day program in the first year that the full day was offered (Joyce McGinn, personal communication, 1984; Sheila Terens, personal communication, 1984). One or two parents declined the full day in subsequent years.

School District Options. The school district professionals should reserve the right to decide if an individual child may need a different schedule. For example, when most kindergarten children in the full-day program have made an initial adjustment, a staff team may decide on a modified individual schedule for some. Individual children may be invited to attend the full day after a few months of half-day and extended-day participation. Sometimes an individual child will attend half a day on Mondays only and then full days during the rest of the week. In other cases, a family crisis may suggest to adults that an individual child needs to have a shorter schedule for a few weeks midyear.

Parent Involvement. Teachers and parents should confer often. They can plan for cultural activities and be involved in curriculum activities. Parents generally can serve as resources to the principal and teachers. The school district can also offer discussion groups and parent/toddler programs.

Staff Development and Planning. Returning kindergarten teachers and newly hired ones should be involved together in planning the opening of school and the kindergarten program. There should also be a provision for ongoing dialogue concerning the program, particularly during the first two years of a new program. This requires additional "preparation" time for teachers, in order to engage in dialogue and to make individual preparations. After the program has been installed, there should be dialogue with the first-grade teachers who will be inheriting the kindergarten classes.

Class Size and Budget. Class size in the full-day kindergarten should not be larger than in the half-day kindergarten.

The budget should reflect some of the following start-up considerations:

- *Additional classroom space.* Furnishing a new kindergarten classroom may cost between $5,000 and $10,000.
- *Additional salaries.* Allocations must be made to cover kindergarten teacher and lunchroom aide salaries and fringe benefits.
- *Additional expendable materials.* The arts and writing consumables double in cost for each classroom.
- *Other facilities.* Lunchroom services may need to be increased.
- *Transportation.* The midday bus service budget will be smaller for a full-day program. Additional bus service will be needed at the start and end of the kindergarten day.
- *State aid.* It may be possible to gain an increase in state aid.

HIGHLIGHTS OF THE FULL-DAY KINDERGARTEN CURRICULUM

Once all the emotional and political dust has settled, an ongoing argument regarding the longer day involves the need to outline how the additional time should be used and what the curriculum for the full kindergarten day should be. How much content and skill work should full-day kindergarten children do? This book has been an attempt to respond to this question, so in this section I will review the main components of the full-day kindergarten curriculum that has been presented.

The full-day kindergarten curriculum design in this book focuses on four interconnected features: (1) skills and attitudes, (2) child development, (3) extradisciplinary activity in the form of perceptual models/dynamic themes, and (4) interdisciplinary, multiple ways of knowing.

Skills and Attitudes. The additional time in the full-day kindergarten is an opportunity for children to have more extended instruction and develop a broad range of skills. Children learn these skills in integrated, playful ways as they use many materials and have rich, meaningful activities.

Through the use of manipulative materials and social transactions, kindergarten children acquire mathematics concepts as they set and solve problems and learn about mathematical relationships that develop out of their active experience. Cooperatively developed mathematical ideas derive their meanings from exploring and playing with the three-dimensional world.

Language and reading development take place inductively as children develop self-directed motives for learning and using these skills. The four components of a full-day kindergarten reading and language program include (1) a variety of oral language experiences, (2) a frequent, exciting exposure to fine-quality literature, (3) writing-into-reading, and (4) an inductive, playful approach to phonemic games.

Problem solving and connection making take place as children encounter cognitive dissonance and their teacher uses analogies systematically in teaching. Children become increasingly comfortable with ambiguity and differences of viewpoint, since they are setting problems as well as seeking solutions to questions that have more than only one possible answer. In turn, they become more able to question, transform their ways of thinking, and engage in critical thinking.

Social learning skills and attitudes develop through legitimate social activity; therefore, exemplary teachers plan cooperative learning activities, some of which might involve only children in the kindergarten and others incorporating other children as well.

Child Development. Children learn best when seven conditions are integrated: inductive experiences, cognitive dissonance, social interaction, physical experiences, play, revisiting phenomena, and a feeling of competence. Teachers who create such conditions are not "metacognitive nudgers." Rather, they respect children as human beings who learn by actively constructing their own thinking. Teachers create an environment where such learning can take place.

Extradisciplinary Activity. Teachers plan activities with children that offer the potential for children to make connections and to network their knowledge in natural ways that may be reflected in the various surface forms of underlying perceptual models/dynamic themes. Teachers explore together many forms for representing meanings as they adjust to children's concerns and needs. Exemplary teachers engage in re-forming an intellectual kindergarten education that takes on its own unique and emerging contours, rich in variety and substance.

Interdisciplinary Conceptions. Children engage in activities that employ multiple, dynamic ways of knowing drawn from disciplines. These activities provide the content and motives for children to integrate their practice of skills. Effective teachers plan such worthwhile activities at a pace that keeps content fresh and helps children to improve and expand their skills in ways that enable them to feel successful.

REFLECTIONS

The full-day kindergarten is not a stepping-stone to first grade. It is not a traditional first grade begun one year earlier, nor is it an extended nursery school. Ideally, it is a unique time with its own distinct knowledge bases and practices that adjust to children's diverse personal cultures.

If you begin to plan for a full-day kindergarten and you already have an integrated half-day kindergarten, you are likely to extend this integrated outlook to the full day. If, on the other hand, you have already been using largely whole-group, teacher-directed activities and sedentary tasks, you are likely to extend this segmented outlook to the full day.

The time is ripe for reexamining such basic attitudes. You have an opportunity in either a full- or half-day kindergarten to re-form kindergarten education so that it takes on its own unique forms. Beyond institutionalizing novelty and surprise in your own classroom, you also might consider advocating for qualitative change by lobbying for the release of textbook funds for fine-quality trade book literature and manipulative materials. This book has looked at the full-day kindergarten in terms of the quality of time and the real educational time that children and teachers experience.

There are so many activities to choose from that your only problem will be an economic one—limited time and seemingly unlimited choices. The perceptual-models conception, based on children's capacity for isomorphic imagery, can offer a dynamic basis for planning together with children. With children's emerging changes, this approach can "bend with the twig" at the same time that it supports growth toward serendipitous "light."

Your responsibility remains one of trying to make the kindergarten year the best you can for your group. Since young children naturally construct meanings in their own ways, it bears reiterating one more time that different children doing different things at different times can have equivalent experiences. The form that experiences take is relative to the capacity of the learners and the varying paces at which they can proceed. Also, you can expect, and you will find the need to adjust to the reality, that children will become more different from one another as they grow. Each group's increasing diversity becomes a strength upon which you can build when you welcome a decentralized organization that supports small-group and individual efforts. Your task is to choose the most relevant activities from among those that are most reasonable.

You can take this opportunity to create a place and time in which young children can feel successful, can take responsibility for many activities, and can legitimately learn collaboratively with other children and with you, their teacher. If you take this option, then your children may well have an opportunity to look forward to great expectations in their lives.

Notes

CHAPTER 1

1. The books referred to here—Rey's *Curious George* (1973), Slobodkina's *Caps for Sale* (1947/1989), Sendak's *Where the Wild Things Are* (1963), Rockwell's *Cars* (1984), and Jonas' *The Trek* (1985)—and all other children's titles mentioned in the text are included in the References to Children's Literature section that follows the References at the end of this book.

CHAPTER 2

1. It is worth noting that a review of research on retention, which includes variations of "junior" or "transition" kindergarten or first grade, concludes that "retained students are negatively affected academically, socially, and emotionally. As a strategy, retention fails" (Haberman & Dill, 1993, p. 355).

CHAPTER 3

1. Transformational theorists in various disciplines include N. Chomsky, 1972 (linguistics); Jung, 1970 (psychology); Levi-Strauss, 1949/1969a, 1964/1969b (anthropology); McLuhan, 1963 (communications theory); Minsky, 1967 (computer technology); Moore & Anderson, 1968 (game theory); Nelson et al., 1986, and Schank & Abelson, 1977 (script theory); Pfeiffer, 1962 (genetic research); and Steiner, 1970 (topology). The idea of the interdisciplinary confluences between visual art, music, and mathematics, presented by Hofstadter (1980) as "recursive loops," is a compatible theory, as are the general domains of "chaos" theory (Gleick, 1987) and "complexity" theory (Waldrop, 1992).

2. The use of "binary opposites" in a metaphoric approach to teaching through storytelling offers a similar "rhythm of expectation" (Egan, 1986, p. 25).

CHAPTER 5

1. Adapted from a dialogue with Sunitee Dutt of the University of Dehli, after she visited Gertrude Luttgen and a kindergarten group in Minneapolis in 1961.

Chapter 6

1. Note that air pressure or magnetism at this level might be part of chemistry. When considering "conceptual literacy" or perceptual models for kindergarten children, however, there is an emphasis on helping children to become exposed to the underlying pattern.

2. In the dialogues presented in this chapter, "Child 1" refers to the first child to speak in each dialogue. Thus a given number will represent different children in the different episodes that are reported; within each episode, however, the same child's contribution is indicated by the same number.

3. The issue of context in science is particularly relevant in order to overcome the tendency to become complacent with "truths." The history of science is replete with examples of creative thinkers who shattered the myths of objectivity and neutrality in science. In effect, scientists often are able to see mainly what is politically possible within a particular scientific time and context. While Galileo's work is one well-known example of a society's exercise-with-blinders, it may be that some of today's so-called "alternative" medicines are among contemporary blind-sided phenomena.

4. For example, Connecticut Valley Biological, 82 Valley Rd., PO Box 325, Southampton, MA 01073.

5. Note that the dialectical reversibility of evaporation and condensation is similar to simple square dances in which children divide, regroup, and then reconstitute original patterns.

Chapter 7

1. Pages that are most useful for the kindergarten, arranged here in the sequence I recommend, are 55, 61, 63, 69, 75, 83, 91, 87, 95, 115, 121, 123, and 147.

Chapter 8

1. Some teachers have used role playing in this and similar folk tales as a way to help children practice saying no in situations involving child abuse or drugs (Lynn, McGinn & Wohlstadter, 1991). "Scared and Hurt" (Kuhmerker, 1984) briefly summarizes many of the issues in child abuse, which you might adapt to role playing.

Chapter 9

1. A moderately active work period might exclude woodworking or other pastime that requires the teacher's continuous supervision.

References

Adcock, E. P., et al. (1980). *A comparison of half-day and full-day kindergarten classes on academic achievement.* Baltimore: Maryland State Department of Education.

Aiken, S. H., Anderson, K., Dinnerstein, M., Lensink, J. N., & MacCorquodale, P. (1988). Changing our minds: The problematics of curriculum integration. In S. H. Aiken, K. Anderson, M. Dinnerstein, J. N. Lensink, & P. MacCorquodale (Eds.), *Changing our minds: Feminist transformations of knowledge* (pp. 134–163). Albany, NY: State University of New York Press.

Althouse, R. (1988). *Investigating science with young children.* New York: Teachers College Press.

Anderson, R. C., Hiebert, E. H., Scott, J. A., & Wilkinson, I. A. G. (1985). *Becoming a nation of readers.* Champaign: University of Illinois Press.

Anderson, V. D. (1968). *Reading and young children.* New York: Macmillan.

Anonymous. (1978). Untitled. In H. Brown, P. Lopate, D. Sklarew, & T. Vorsanger (Eds.), *The memories of kindergartners* (p. 16). New York: Teachers and Writers Collaborative.

Atkinson, S. (Ed.). (1992). *Mathematics with reason: The emergent approach to primary maths.* Portsmouth, NH: Heinemann.

Ayers, S. W. (1993, January). *Bridging into numbers and calculations—Estimations, probabilities, and fractals.* Paper presented at the Hofstra University Kindergarten-First Grade Conference, Hempstead, NY.

Banks, J. A. (1993). Multicultural education for young children: Racial and ethnic attitudes and their modification. In B. Spodek (Ed.), *Handbook of research on the education of young children* (pp. 236–250). New York: Macmillan.

Baratta-Lorton, M. (1976). *Mathematics their way.* Menlo Park, CA: Addison-Wesley.

Barnes, R. (1987). *Teaching art to young children 4–9.* New York: Routledge.

Barnes, S., & Edwards, S. (1984, April). *More effective and less effective student teaching experiences: Qualitative comparison of extreme groups.* Paper presented at the annual meeting of the American Educational Research Association, New Orleans, LA.

Baroody, A. J., & Standifer, D. J. (1993). Addition and subtraction in the primary grades. In R. J. Jensen (Ed.), *Research ideas for the classroom: Early childhood mathematics* (pp. 72–102). New York: Macmillan.

247

Barson, A. (n.d.). *Geoboard activity cards: Primary.* Ft. Collins, CO: Scott Resources.

Bertalanffy, L. von. (1960). *Problems of life.* New York: Harper Torchbooks.

Berti, A. E., & Bombi, A. S. (1988). *The child's construction of economics* (G. Duveen, Trans.). New York: Cambridge University Press.

Biggs, E. (1971). *Mathematics for young children.* New York: Citation.

Biondo, C. (Ed.) (1992, Summer). *Franklin Early Childhood Center PTA Newsletter.* Hewlett, NY: Hewlett-Woodmere Public Schools.

Bird, J. (1978). *Science from water play.* Milwaukee: Macdonald-Raintree.

Bloomfield, L., & Barnhart, C. L. (1961). *Let's read.* Detroit: Wayne State University Press.

Bridge, S. (1986). Squeezing from the middle of the tube. In T. Newkirk & N. Atwell (Eds.), *Understanding writing* (pp. 68–75). Portsmouth, NH: Heinemann.

Briscoe, J. S. (1984, November 1). Tides, solutions and nutrients. *Nature*, p. 15.

Brown, R., & Bellugi, U. (1964). Three processes in the child's acquisition of syntax. In E. H. Lenneberg (Ed.), *New directions in the study of language* (pp. 131–161). Cambridge, MA: MIT Press.

Bruner, J. S. (1961). *The process of education.* Cambridge, MA: Harvard University Press.

Bruner, J. S. (1966). *Toward a theory of instruction.* Cambridge, MA: Harvard University Press.

Buber, M. (1958). *I and thou* (2nd ed.; T. G. Smith, Trans.). New York: Charles Scribner's Sons. (Original work published 1923)

Burg, K. (1984, March). The microcomputer in the kindergarten. *Young Children*, pp. 28–33.

Burk, D., Snider, A., & Symonds, P. (1988). *Box it and bag it mathematics: Teacher's resource guide, kindergarten.* Salem, OR: MLC Publications.

Burk, D., Snider, A., & Symonds, P. (1992). *Math excursions K: Project-based math for kindergartners.* Portsmouth, NH: Heinemann.

Burton, G., Coburn, T., Del Grande, J., Lindquist, M. M., Morrow, L., with Clements, D., Firkins, J., & Joyner, J. (1991). *Curriculum and evaluation standards for school mathematics: Kindergarten book.* Reston, VA: National Council of Teachers of Mathematics.

Butler, A. (1984). *Story box: Teacher's guide.* San Diego, CA: Wright Group.

Butler, A., & Turbill, J. (1984). *Towards a reading–writing curriculum.* Portsmouth, NH: Heinemann.

Calkins, L. M. (1994). *The art of teaching writing* (2nd ed.). Portsmouth, NH: Heinemann.

Cambourne, B. (1988). *The whole story: Natural learning and the acquisition of literacy in the classroom.* New York: Ashton Scholastic.

Capra, F. (1982). *The turning point: Science, society, and the rising culture.* New York: Simon & Schuster.

Cazden, C. B. (1971). Language programs for young children: Notes from England and Wales. In C. S. Lavatelli (Ed.), *Language training in early childhood education* (pp. 119–153). Urbana, IL: ERIC.

Cazden, C. B. (1972). *Child language and education.* New York: Holt, Rinehart & Winston.

Cazden, C. B. (Ed.). (1981). *Language in early childhood education* (rev. ed.). Washington, DC: National Association for the Education of Young Children.

Cazden, C. B. (1988). *Classroom discourse*. Portsmouth, NH: Heinemann.

Charlesworth, R., & Lind, K. K. (1990). *Mathematics and science for young children*. New York: Delmar.

Cherryholmes, C. (1988). *Power and criticism: Poststructural investigations in education*. New York: Teachers College Press.

Children's Defense Fund. (1992). *The state of America's children 1992*. Washington, DC: Author.

Chomsky, C. (1971). Write now, read later. *Childhood Education, 47*, 296–299.

Chomsky, N. (1965). *Aspects of a theory of syntax*. Cambridge, MA: MIT Press.

Chomsky, N. (1972). *Language and mind* (enlarged ed.). New York: Harcourt Brace Jovanovich.

Christie, J. (Ed). (1991). *Play and early literacy development*. Albany, NY: State University of New York Press.

Clark, K., & Clark, M. (1939). The development of consciousness of self and the emergence of racial identity in Negro preschool children. *Journal of Social Psychology, 10*, 591–599.

Clay, M. M. (1991). *Becoming literate*. Exeter, NH: Heinemann

Clements, D. H., & Nastasi, B. K. (1993). Electronic media in early childhood education. In B. Spodek (Ed.), *Handbook of research on the education of young children* (pp. 251–275). New York: Macmillan.

Commission for Teaching Standards for School Mathematics. (1991). *Professional standards for teaching mathematics*. Reston, VA: National Council of Teachers of Mathematics.

Copeland, R. W. (1984). *How children learn mathematics* (4th ed.). New York: Macmillan.

Craig, G. S. (1958). *Science for the elementary school teacher*. New York: Ginn.

Cratty, B. J. (n. d.). *Learning and playing*. Freeport, NY: Educational Activities.

Cruikshank, D. E., Fitzgerald, D. L., & Jensen, L. R. (1980). *Young children learning mathematics*. Boston: Allyn & Bacon.

Cryan, J. R., Sheehan, R., Wiechel, J., & Bandy-Hedden, I. G. (1992). Success outcomes of full-day kindergarten: More positive behavior and increased achievement in the years after. *Early Childhood Research Quarterly, 7* (2), 187–203.

Csikszentmihalyi, M., & Csikszentmihalyi, I. S. (Eds.). (1988). *Optimal experience: Psychological studies in flow consciousness*. New York: Cambridge University Press.

Cullinan, B., & Galda, L. (1994). *Literature and the child* (3rd ed.). New York: Harcourt Brace Jovanovich.

Davidson, J. I. (1989). *Children and computers together in the early childhood classroom*. New York: Delmar.

Davidson, P. S. (1977). *Idea book for Cuisenaire rods at the primary level*. New Rochelle, NY: Cuisenaire Co. of America.

Davis, A., & Dollard, J. (1940). *Children of bondage*. Washington, DC: American Council on Education.

DeFord, D. E., Lyons, C. A., & Pinnell, G. S. (Eds.). (1991). *Bridges to literacy: Learning from Reading Recovery.* Portsmouth, NH: Heinemann.

Department of Education & Science. (1989). *Aspects of primary education: Teaching and learning of science.* London: Her Majesty's Stationery Office.

Department of Education & Science. (1991). *Aspects of primary education: The teaching and learning of design and technology.* London: Her Majesty's Stationery Office.

Derman-Sparks, L. (1992). "It isn't fair!" Antibias curriculum for young children. In B. Neugebeuer (Ed.), *Alike and different: Exploring our humanity with young children* (rev. ed.; pp. 2–10). Washington, DC: National Association for the Education of Young Children.

Derman-Sparks, L., and the ABC Task Force. (1989). *The Anti-Bias Curriculum.* Washington, DC: National Association for the Education of Young Children.

Developmental Learning Materials Teaching Resources. (1985). *Pattern cards.* Allen, TX: Author.

DeVries R., & Zan, B. (1994). *Moral classrooms, moral children: Creating a constructivist atmosphere in early education.* New York: Teachers College Press.

Dewey, J. (1933). *How we think.* Boston: D. C. Heath.

Dewey, J. (1958). *Art as experience.* New York: Capricorn. (Original work published 1934)

Dienes, Z. (1969). *Building up mathematics.* London: Hutchinson Educational.

Dienes, Z. (1973). *Mathematics through the senses.* Boston: Fernhill.

Dinkmeyer, D., & Dinkmeyer, D., Jr. (1982). *Developing understanding of self and others* (rev. ed.). Circle Pines, MN: American Guidance Service.

Dodge, D. T., & Colker, L. J., with Goldhammer, M., Jablon, J., & Copple, C. (1992). *The creative curriculum for early childhood* (3rd ed.). Mt. Rainier, MD: Gryphon House.

Donaldson, M. (1978). *Children's minds.* New York: Norton.

Downie, D., Slesnick, T., & Stenmark, J. K. (1981). *Math for girls and other problem solvers.* Berkeley: Lawrence Hall of Science, University of California.

Durkin, D. (1966). *Children who read early.* New York: Teachers College Press.

Dyson, A. H. (1989). *Multiple worlds of child writers.* New York: Teachers College Press.

Educational Teaching Aids. (1985). *Mathematics catalog.* Chicago: Author.

Edwards, C. P., Gandini, L., & Forman, G. (1993). *The hundred languages of children.* Norwood, NJ: Ablex.

Egan, K. (1986). *Teaching as storytelling.* Ontario: Althouse.

Egan, K. (1988). The origins of imagination and the curriculum. In K. Egan & D. Nadaner (Eds.), *Imagination and education* (pp. 91–127). New York: Teachers College Press.

Eisner, E. (Ed.). (1985). *Learning and teaching the ways of knowing: Part II* (Eighty-fourth yearbook of the National Society for the Study of Education). Chicago: Chicago University Press.

Elementary Science Study Teachers' Guides. (1970a). *Animals in the classroom.* New York: McGraw-Hill.

Elementary Science Study Teachers' Guides. (1970b). *Pattern blocks*. New York: McGraw-Hill.

Elementary Science Study Teachers' Guides. (1971a). *Drops, streams, and containers*. New York: McGraw-Hill.

Elementary Science Study Teachers' Guides. (1971b). *Match and measure*. New York: McGraw-Hill.

Elementary Science Study Teachers' Guides. (1974a). *Attribute games and problems*. New York: McGraw-Hill.

Elementary Science Study Teachers' Guides. (1974b). *Eggs and tadpoles*. New York: McGraw-Hill.

Elementary Science Study Teachers' Guides. (1974c). *Growing seeds*. New York: McGraw-Hill.

Elementary Science Study Teachers' Guides. (1976a). *Primary balancing*. New York: McGraw-Hill.

Elementary Science Study Teachers' Guides. (1976b). *Tangrams*. New York: McGraw-Hill.

Elementary Science Study Teachers' Guides. (1976c). *Changes*. New York: McGraw-Hill.

Elliott, J. (Ed.). (1993). *Restructuring teacher education*. Washington, DC: Falmer.

Erickson, F., & Mohatt, G. (1982). Cultural organization or participation structures in two classrooms of Indian students. In G. Spindler (Ed.), *Doing the ethnography of schooling: Educational anthropology in action* (pp. 132–174). New York: Holt, Rinehart & Winston.

Ervin, S. M. (1964). Imitation and structural change in children's language. In E. H. Lenneberg (Ed.), *New directions in the study of language* (pp. 163–189). Cambridge, MA: MIT Press

Fagot, B. I. (1975, April). *Teacher reinforcement of feminine-preferred behavior revisited*. Paper presented at the biennial meeting of the Society for Research in Child Development, Denver, CO.

Ferreiro, E. (1991). Literacy acquisition and the representation of language. In C. Kamii, M. Manning, & G. Manning (Eds.), *Early literacy: A constructivist foundation for whole language* (pp. 31–56). Washington, DC: National Education Association.

Ferreiro, E., & Teberosky, A. (1982). *Literacy before schooling* (K. G. Castro, Trans.). Exeter, NH: Heinemann.

Festinger, L. (1957). *A theory of cognitive dissonance*. New York: Harper & Row.

Flemming, P. (1986). Writing and reading: The write way to read. In T. Newkirk & N. Atwell (Eds.), *Understanding writing* (pp. 93–100). Portsmouth, NH: Heinemann.

Fleuegelman, A. (1976). *The new games book*. Garden City, NY: Doubleday.

Foote, M., Stafford, P., & Cuffaro, H. K. (1992). Linking curriculum and assessment in preschool and kindergarten. In C. Genishi (Ed.), *Ways of assessing children and curriculum* (pp. 58–93). New York: Teachers College Press.

Forman, G. (1992a). Television issues. In L. R. Williams & D. P. Fromberg (Eds.), *The encyclopedia of early childhood education* (p. 374). New York: Garland.

Forman, G. (1992b). Video, robots, and other technologies. In L. R. Williams & D. P. Fromberg (Eds.), *The encyclopedia of early childhood education* (pp. 372–374). New York: Garland.

Forman, G., & Landry, D. (1992). Research on early science education. In C. Seefeldt (Ed.), *The early childhood curriculum: A review of current research* (2nd ed.; pp. 175–192). New York: Teachers College Press.

Foucault, M. (1982). Afterword: The subject and power. In H. L. Dreyfus & P. Rabinow, *Michel Foucault: Beyond structuralism and hermeneutics* (pp. 208–226). Chicago: University of Chicago Press.

Fox, G. T., Jr., Anglin, L., Fromberg, D., & Grady, M. (1986). *Collaboration: Lessons learned from experience.* Washington, DC: American Association of Colleges for Teacher Education.

Fries, C. C. (1963). *Linguistics and reading.* New York: Holt, Rinehart & Winston.

Fromberg, D. P. (1965). *The reactions of kindergarten children to intellectual challenges.* Unpublished doctoral dissertation, Teachers College, Columbia University, New York.

Fromberg, D. P. (1976). Syntax model games and language in early education. *Journal of Psycholinguistics Research, 5* (3), 245–260.

Fromberg, D. P. (1977). *Early childhood education: A perceptual models curriculum.* New York: Wiley.

Fromberg, D. P. (1992). A review of research on play. In C. Seefeldt (Ed.), *The early childhood curriculum: A review of current research* (2nd ed.; pp. 42–84). New York: Teachers College Press.

Fromberg, D. P. (1993). The content of integrated early childhood education. In Kraus International (Ed.), *Early childhood education: A curriculum resource book* (pp. 66–79). Millwood, NY: Kraus International.

Frost, J. L. (1986). Children in a changing society. *Childhood Education, 4,* 242–249.

Gardner, H. (1980). *Artful scribbles.* New York: Basic Books.

Gardner, H. (1983). *Frames of mind.* New York: Basic Books.

Gattegno, C. (1968). *Teaching reading with words in color.* New York: Educational Solutions.

Genishi, C. (Ed.). (1992). *Ways of assessing children and curriculum.* New York: Teachers College Press.

Genovese, E. P. (1974). *Roll, Jordan, roll: The world the slaves made.* New York: Pantheon.

Gibson, L. (1989). *Literacy learning in the early years.* New York: Teachers College Press.

Gilligan, C. (1982). *In a different voice.* Cambridge, MA: Harvard University Press.

Ginsburg, H., & Baron, J. (1993). Cognition: Young children's construction of mathematics. In R. J. Jensen (Ed.), *Research ideas for the classroom: Early childhood mathematics* (pp. 3–21). New York: Macmillan.

Gleason, H. A., Jr. (1965). *Linguistics and English grammar.* Holt, Rinehart & Winston.

Gleason, J. B. (1981). An experimental approach to improving children's communicative ability. In C. Cazden (Ed.), *Language in early childhood education* (rev. ed.; pp. 77–82). Washington, DC: National Association for the Education of Young Children.

Gleick, J. (1987). *Chaos.* New York: Viking.

Gombrich, E. H. (1957). *The story of art.* New York: Phaidon.

Goodman, M. E. (1964). *Race awareness in young children.* New York: Collier.

Gordon, W. J. J. (1961). *Synectics.* New York: Collier.

Gordon, W. J. J., & Poze, T. (1968). *Making it strange.* New York: Harper & Row.

Gordon, W. J. J., & Poze, T. (1972). *Strange and familiar.* Cambridge, MA: Porpoise Books.

Gordon, W. J. J., & Poze, T. (1980). *The art of the possible.* Cambridge, MA: Porpoise Books.

Grant, G. S. (Ed.). (1977). *In praise of diversity: Multicultural classroom applications.* Omaha: Teachers Corps, Center for Urban Education, The University of Nebraska.

Graves, D., & Stuart, V. (1985). *Write from the start.* New York: E. P. Dutton.

Guillen, M. (1983). *Bridges to infinity: The human side of mathematics.* Boston: Houghton Mifflin.

Gullo, D. F. (1994). *Understanding assessment and evaluation in early childhood.* New York: Teachers College Press.

Guthrie, W. (1963). Put your finger in the air. In P. Seeger (Ed.), *Woody Guthrie folk songs* (p. 60). New York: Ludlow.

Guttentag, M. (1978). The social psychology of sex-role intervention. In B. Sprung (Ed.), *Perspectives on nonsexist early childhood education* (pp. 71–78). New York: Teachers College Press.

Haberman, M. (1991). The pedagogy of poverty versus good teaching. *Phi Delta Kappan, 73* (4), 290–294.

Haberman, M., & Dill, V. (1993). The knowledge base on retention vs. teacher ideology: Implications for teacher preparation. *Journal of Teacher Education, 44* (5), 352–360.

Halford, G. S. (1993). *Children's understanding: The development of mental models.* Hillsdale, NJ: Lawrence Erlbaum.

Harste, J. C., Woodward, V. A., & Burke, C. L. (1984). *Language stories and literacy lessons.* Portsmouth, NH: Heinemann.

Haskell, L. L. (1984). *Art in the early childhood years.* Columbus, OH: Charles E. Merrill.

Hawking, S. (1988). *A brief history of time: From the big bang to black holes.* New York: Bantam.

Heath, S. B. (1983). *Ways with words: Language, life, and work in communities and classrooms.* New York: Cambridge University Press.

Hembree, R., & Marsh, H. (1993). Problem solving in early childhood: Building foundations. In R. J. Jensen (Ed.), *Research ideas for the classroom: Early childhood mathematics* (pp. 151–170). New York: Macmillan.

Hess, R. D. (1968). Political socialization in the schools. *Harvard Educational Review, 38,* 528–536.

Hess, R. D., & Torney, J. V. (1967). *The development of political attitudes in children.* Chicago: Aldine.

Hill, S. (1985). Beware of commercials: Young children may not need microcomputers. *Australian Journal of Early Childhood, 10* (3), 16–21.

Hofstadter, D. R. (1980). *Gödel, Escher, Bach: An eternal golden braid.* New York: Viking.

Hofstadter, D. R. (1985). *Metamagical themas: Questing for the essence: Mind and pattern.* New York: Basic Books.

Holdaway, D. (1979). *The foundations of literacy.* New York: Ashton Scholastic.

Honig, A. S. (1983). Television and kindergarten children. *Young Children, 38,* 63–76.

Hoot, J. L., & Silvern, S. B. (1988). *Writing with computers in the early grades.* New York: Teachers College Press.

Horney, K. (1939). *New ways in psychoanalysis.* New York: W. W. Norton.

Hough, R. A., & Nurss, J. R. (1992). Language and literacy for the Limited English Proficient child. In L. O. Ollila & M. I. Mayfield (Eds.), *Emerging literacy* (pp. 137–165). Boston: Allyn & Bacon.

Humphreys, J. W. (1983). *A longitudinal study of the effectiveness of full day kindergarten.* Evansville, IN: Evansville-Vanderburgh School Corp.

Hunt, J. McV. (1961). *Intelligence and experience.* New York: Ronald Press.

Hutt, C. (1976). Exploration and play in children. In J. S. Bruner, A. Jolly, & K. Sylva (Eds.), *Play—Its role in development and evolution* (pp. 202–215). New York: Basic Books.

Imhoff, M. M. (1959). *Early elementary education.* New York: Appleton-Century-Crofts.

Jensen, R. J. (Ed.). (1993). *Research ideas for the classroom: Early childhood mathematics.* New York: Macmillan.

Johnson, D. W., Johnson, R. T., Holubec, E. J., & Roy, P. (1984). *Circles of learning.* Washington, DC: Association for Supervision and Curriculum Development.

Jung, C. G. (1970). *Analytical psychology.* New York: Vintage. (Original work published 1968)

Kamii, C. K., & DeClark, G. (1984). *Young children reinvent arithmetic.* New York: Teachers College Press.

Kamii, C., & DeVries, R. (1980). *Group games in early education.* Washington, DC: National Association for the Education of Young Children.

Kamii, C., & DeVries, R. (1993). *Physical knowledge in the preschool education.* New York: Teachers College Press. (Original work published 1978)

Karp, K. (1988). *The teaching of elementary school mathematics: The relationship between how math is taught and teachers' attitudes.* Unpublished Ed.D. dissertation, Hofstra University.

Karplus, R., & Thier, H. D. (1967). *A new look at elementary school science: Science curriculum improvement study.* Chicago: Rand McNally.

Koblinsky, S., & Behana, N. (1984, September). Child sexual abuse: The educator's role in prevention, detection, and intervention. *Young Children, 39,* 3–15.

Kohl, M. A. F. (1985). *Scribble cookies* (J. McCoy, Illus.). Bellingham, WA: Bright Ring.

Kranowitz, C. S. (1992). Obstacle courses are for every body. In B. Neugebauer (Ed.), *Alike and different: Exploring our humanity with young children* (rev. ed.; pp. 20– 30). Washington, DC: National Association for the Education of Young Children.

Kreinberg, N., Alper, L., & Joseph, H. (1985, March). Computers and children: Where are the girls? *PTA Today*, pp. 13–15.

Kuhmerker, L. (1984). Scared and hurt. *Ms. Magazine, 12,* 69.

Landeck, B. (1950). *Songs to grow on.* New York: William Sloane Associates.

Langer, S. (1948). *Philosophy in a new key.* New York: Mentor. (Original work published 1942)

Langer, S. (1953). *Feeling and form.* New York: Charles Scribner's Sons.

Langer, S. (1957). *Problems of art.* New York: Charles Scribner's Sons.

Lasswell, H. D. (1958). *Politics: Who gets what, when, and how.* New York: Meridian.

Lather, P. (1991). *Getting smart: Feminist research and pedagogy with/in the postmodern.* New York: Routledge.

Lavatelli, C. S. (1970). *Piaget's theory applied to an early childhood curriculum.* Cambridge, MA: American Science and Engineering.

Lawrence Public Schools (Number Four School). (1983). *Full day kindergarten program evaluation.* Lawrence, NY: Author.

Lawrence Public Schools (Number Four School). (1984). *Full day kindergarten program evaluation.* Lawrence, NY: Author.

Lazar, I., Darlington, R., Murray, H., Royce, J., & Snipper, A. (1982). Lasting effects of early childhood education: A report from the Consortium for Longitudinal Studies. *Monographs of the Society for Research on Child Development, 47* (2–3), 1–151.

Lee, P. C. (1989). Is the young child egocentric or sociocentric? *Teachers College Record, 90* (3), 375–391.

Leipzig, J. (1992). Helping whole children grow: Nonsexist childrearing for infants and toddlers. In B. Neugebauer (Ed.), *Alike and different: Exploring our humanity with young children* (rev. ed.; pp. 32–41). Washington, DC: National Association for the Education of Young Children.

Levi-Strauss, C. (1969a). *The elementary structures of kinship* (J. H. Bell & J. R. von Sturmer, Trans.; R. Needham, Ed.). Boston: Beacon Press. (Original work published 1949)

Levi-Strauss, C. (1969b). *The raw and the cooked* (J. & D. Weightman, Trans.). New York: Harper Torchbooks. (Original work published 1964)

Lieberman, J. N. (1977). *Playfulness.* New York: Academic Press.

Little Soldier. (1992). Working with Native American children. *Young Children, 47* (6), 15–21.

Locke, P. (1978). An ideal school system for American Indians—A theoretical construct. In T. Thompson (Ed.), *The schooling of Native America* (pp. 119–137). Washington, DC: American Association of Colleges for Teacher Education and Teacher Corps.

Luria, A. R. (1968). *The mind of a mnemonist*. (L. Solotaroff, Trans.). New York: Basic Books.

Lynn, F., McGinn, J., & Wohlstadter, K. (1991). *SEE: Self-esteem enhancement drug prevention program*. Hewlett, NY: Hewlett Woodmere Public Schools.

Maccoby, E. E., & Jacklin, C. N. (1974). *The psychology of sex differences*. Stanford, CA: Stanford University Press.

Mackay, D., Thompson, B., & Schaub, P. (1978). *Breakthrough to literacy*. New York: Longman.

May, R. (1972). *Power and innocence*. New York: W. W. Norton.

Mazurkiewicz, A. J. (1964). *New perspectives in reading instruction*. New York: Pitman.

McCaslin, N. (1980). *Creative drama in the classroom* (3rd ed.). New York: Longman.

McDermott, J. (1983). Geometrical forms known as fractals find sense in chaos. *Smithsonian, 14* (9), 110–117.

McLuhan, M. (1963). We need a new picture of knowledge. In A. Frazier (Ed.), *New insights and the curriculum* (pp. 57–70). Washington, DC: Association for Supervision & Curriculum Development.

McNeil, D. (1970). *The acquisition of language*. New York: Harper & Row.

McNeil, J. D. (1984). *Reading comprehension*. Glenview, IL: Scott, Foresman.

Merleau-Ponty, M. (1964). *The primacy of perception* (J. M. Edie, Ed.). Evanston, IL: Northwestern University Press.

Meyerhoff, H. (Ed.). (1959). *The philosophy of history in our time*. Garden City, NY: Doubleday Anchor.

Miller, E. (1994). Letting talent flow: How schools can promote learning for the sheer love of it. *Harvard Education Letter, 10* (2), 1–3, 8.

Miller, W. R. (1969). Language acquisition and reading. In J. Walden (Ed.), *Oral language and reading* (pp. 31–47). Champaign, IL: National Council of Teachers of English.

Mini VeriTech. (1977a). *Early childhood series for: Perception, visual discrimination, concept formation*. Montreal: Brault & Bouthillier.

Mini VeriTech. (1977b). *Figures and forms*. Montreal: Brault & Bouthillier.

Minsky, M. (1967). *Computation: Finite and infinite machines*. Englewood Cliffs, NJ: Prentice-Hall.

Mitchell, L. S. (1921). *Here and now story books*. New York: E. P. Dutton.

Mitchell, L. S. (1934). *Young geographers*. New York: John Day.

Montessori, M. (1965). *The Montessori method*. (A. E. George, Trans.). New York: Schocken. (Original work published 1912)

Moore, O. K., & Anderson, A. R. (1968). The responsive environment project. In R. D. Hess & R. M. Bear (Eds.), *Early education* (pp. 171–189). Chicago: Aldine.

Morgan, R. (1982). *The anatomy of freedom: Feminism, physics, and global politics*. New York: Anchor.

Morris, J. B. (1983). Classroom methods and materials. In O. N. Saracho & B. Spodek (Eds.), *Understanding the multicultural experience in early childhood education* (pp. 77–90). Washington, DC: National Association for the Education of Young Children.

Morrow, L. M. (1990). Preparing the classroom environment to promote literacy during play. *Early Childhood Research Quarterly, 5* (4), 537–554.

Muessig, R. H., & Rogers, V. R. (1965). Suggested methods for teachers. In P. J. Pelto (Ed.), *The study of anthropology* (pp. 81–116). Columbus, OH: Merrill.

Naisbitt, J. (1982). *Megatrends: Ten new directions transforming our lives.* New York: Warner.

Nalim. (1978). Untitled. In H. Brown, P. Lopate, D. Sklarew, & T. Vorsanger (Eds.), *The memories of kindergartners* (p. 20). New York: Teachers and Writers Collaborative.

Nelson, K., et al. (1986). *Event knowledge: Structure and function in development.* Hillsdale, NJ: Lawrence Erlbaum.

Neuman, S. B., & Roskos, K. A. (1993). *Language and literacy learning in the early years.* New York: Harcourt Brace Jovanovich.

Newkirk, T., & Atwell, N. (1986). Introduction. In T. Newkirk & N. Atwell (Eds.), *Understanding writing* (pp. 1–5). Portsmouth, NH: Heinemann.

Newman, J. (1984). *The craft of children's writing.* Portsmouth, NH: Heinemann.

Nichols, W., & Nichols, K. (1990). *Wonderscience.* Albuquerque, NM: Learning Expo.

Nieman, R. H., & Gastright, J. F. (1975, April). *Preschool plus all-day kindergarten: The cumulative effects of early childhood programs on the cognitive growth of four and five year old children.* Paper presented at the annual meeting of the American Educational Research Association, Washington, DC.

Nuffield Mathematics Project. (1967). *Beginnings.* New York: John Wiley.

Nuffield Mathematics Project. (1970). *Mathematics—The first three years.* New York: John Wiley.

Orlick, T. (1978). *The cooperative sports and games book: Challenge and competition.* New York: Pantheon.

Paley, V. G. (1984). *Boys and girls: Superheroes in the doll corner.* Chicago: University of Chicago Press.

Pellegrini, A. T., & Galda, L. (1982). The effects of thematic-fantasy play training on the development of children's story comprehension. *American Educational Research Journal, 19,* 443–452.

Perner, J. (1991). *Understanding and the representational world.* Cambridge, MA: MIT Press.

Peters, R. S. (1967). *Ethics and education.* Glenview, IL: Scott, Foresman.

Pfeiffer, J. (1962). *The thinking machine.* Philadelphia: J. B. Lippincott.

Phenix, P. (1964). *Realms of meaning.* New York: McGraw-Hill.

Piaget, J. (1950). *The psychology of intelligence* (M. Piercy & D. E. Berlyne, Trans.). London: Routledge & Kegan Paul. (Original work published 1947)

Piaget, J. (1962). *Play, dreams, and imitation in childhood* (C. Gattegno & F. M. Hodgson, Trans.). New York: W. W. Norton. (Original work published 1951)

Piaget, J. (1976). *The grasp of consciousness.* Cambridge, MA: Harvard University Press.

Piaget, J., et al. (1965). *The moral judgment of the child* (M. Gabain, Trans.). New York: Free Press.

Piaget, J., & Inhelder, B. (1963). *The child's conception of space* (F. J. Langdon & J. L. Lunzer, Trans.). London: Routledge & Kegan Paul. (Original work published 1956)

Piaget, J., & Inhelder, B. (1964). *The early growth of logic in the child* (E. A. Lunzer & D. Papert, Trans.). New York: Harper & Row.

Piaget, J., & Inhelder, B. (1973). *Memory and intelligence.* New York: Basic Books.

Polanyi, M. (1963). *The study of man.* Chicago: University of Chicago Press.

Porter, J. D. R. (1971). *Black child, white child.* Cambridge, MA: Harvard University Press.

Provenzo, E. F., Jr., & Brett, A. (1983). *The complete block book* (M. Carleback, Photos.). Syracuse, NY: Syracuse University Press.

Purves, A. C. (1990). *The scribal society.* New York: Longman.

Quinn, M. C. (Spring, 1992). What a wonderful world: A response to music. *Hofstra School of Education Report, 4* (2), 13,18.

Quinn, M. C. (In press). *Take home literacy backpacks.* New York: Scholastic.

Raines, S. C., & Canady, R. J. (1992). *Story s-t-r-e-t-c-h-e-r-s for the primary grades.* Mt. Rainier, MD: Gryphon House.

Ramsey, P. G. (1987). *Teaching and learning in a diverse world: Multicultural education for young children.* New York: Teachers College Press.

Raywid, M. A., & Shaheen, J. A. (1983, October). Diversity: Surviving and thriving. *Early Years,* pp. 28–31.

Reifel, S. (1984, November). Block construction. *Young Children, 40,* 61–67.

Richards, R., et al. (1976a). *Early experiences.* Milwaukee: Raintree-Macdonald.

Richards, R., et al. (1976b). *Ourselves.* Milwaukee: Raintree-Macdonald.

Robison, H. F., & Spodek, B. (1965). *New directions in the kindergarten.* New York: Teachers College Press.

Roldão, M., & Egan, K. (n. d.). *The social studies curriculum: The case for its abolition.* Unpublished manuscript.

Rosenblatt, L. (1969). Towards a transactional theory of reading. *Journal of Reading Behavior, 10* (1), 31–43.

Rosenblatt, L. M. (1978). *The reader, the text, the poem.* Carbondale: Southern Illinois University Press.

Rosenblatt, L. (1980). What facts does this poem teach you? *Language Arts, 57* (4), 386–394.

Russell, H. R. (1990). *Ten-minute field trips: Using the school grounds for environmental studies* (2nd ed.; K. Winckelmann, Illus.). Washington, DC: National Science Teachers Association.

Sauvy, J., & Sauvy, S. (1974). *The child's discovery of space* (P. Wells, Trans.). Baltimore: Penguin.

Schank, R., & Abelson, R. (1977). *Scripts, plans, goals and understanding: An inquiry into human knowledge.* Hillsdale, NJ: Erlbaum.

Schirrmacher, R. (1988). *Art and creative development for young children.* Albany, NY: Delmar.

Schrader, C. T. (1989). Written language use within the context of young children's symbolic play. *Early Childhood Research Quarterly, 4* (2), 225–244.

Schrader, C. T. (1990). Symbolic play as a curricular tool for early literacy development. *Early Childhood Research Quarterly, 5* (1), 79–103.

Schweinhart, L. J., Weikart, D. P., & Larner, M. B. (1986). Consequences of three preschool models through age 15. *Early Childhood Research Quarterly, 1* (1), 15–45.

Seefeldt, C. (1993). *Social studies for the preschool-primary child* (4th ed.). New York: Merrill.

Serbin, L. A. (1978). Teachers, peers, and play preferences: An environmental approach to sex typing in the preschool. In B. Sprung (Ed.), *Perspectives on nonsexist early childhood education* (pp. 79–93). New York: Teachers College Press.

Shaftel, F. R., & Shaftel, G. (1983). *Role-playing for social values* (2nd ed.). Englewood Cliffs, NJ: Prentice-Hall.

Sheehy, E. D. (1954). *The fives and sixes go to school.* New York: Holt.

Shepard, L. A., & Smith, M. L. (Eds.). (1989). *Flunking grades: Research and policies on retention.* Washington, DC: Falmer.

Sherwood, E. A., Williams, R. A., & Rockwell, R. D. (1990). *More mudpies to magnets* (L. J. Sweetman, Illus.). Mt. Rainier, MD: Gryphon.

Siks, G. B. (1958). *Creative dramatics.* New York: Harper & Row.

Singer, D. G., & Singer, J. L. (1992). Television, influences. In L. R. Williams & D. P. Fromberg (Eds.), *The encyclopedia of early childhood education* (pp. 374–376). New York: Garland.

Skeen, P., Garner, A. P., & Cartwright, S. (1984). *Woodworking for young children.* Washington, DC: National Association for the Education of Young Children.

Skinner, P. (1990). *What's your problem?* Portsmouth, NH: Heinemann.

Slavin, R. E. (1992). Grouping. In L. R. Williams & D. P. Fromberg (Eds.), *The encyclopedia of early childhood education* (pp. 394–396). New York: Garland.

Sleeter, C. E., & Grant, C. A. (1987). An analysis of multicultural education in the United States. *Harvard Educational Review, 57* (4), 421–444.

Smilansky, S. (1968). *The effects of sociodramatic play on disadvantaged preschool children.* New York: Wiley.

Smilansky, S., Hagan, J., & Lewis, H. (1988). *Clay in the classroom.* New York: Teachers College Press.

Smilansky, S., & Shefatya, L. (1990). *Facilitating play.* Gaithersburg, MD: Psychosocial & Educational Publications.

Smith, F. (1978). *Understanding reading* (2nd ed.). New York: Holt, Rinehart & Winston.

Smith, R. (1983). *Essays in literacy.* Exeter, NH: Heinemann.

Sorauf, F. J. (1965). *Political science.* Columbus, OH: Charles E. Merrill.

Sowers, S. (1986a). Six questions teachers ask about invented spelling. In T. Newkirk & N. Atwell (Eds.), *Understanding writing* (pp. 47–54). Portsmouth, NH: Heinemann.

Sowers, S. (1986b). Reflect, expand, select: Three responses in the writing conference. In T. Newkirk & N. Atwell (Eds.), *Understanding writing* (pp. 76–90). Portsmouth, NH: Heinemann.

Spiegelman, J. (1966). *UNICEF's festival book* (A. Pressler, Illus.). New York: US Committee for UNICEF, United Nations.

Spodek, B. (1962). *Developing social studies concepts in the kindergarten.* Unpublished doctoral dissertation, Teachers College, Columbia University, New York.

Sprung, B., Froschl, M., & Campbell, P. B. (1985). *What will happen if . . . ?* New York: Educational Equity Concepts.

Steiner, G. (1970). *Language and silence.* New York: Atheneum.

Stenhouse, L. (Ed.). (1980). *Curriculum research and development in action.* London: Heinemann.

Stoessinger, R., & Edmunds, J. (1992). *Natural learning and mathematics.* Portsmouth, NH: Heinemann.

Sullivan, W. (1972, March 28). The Einstein papers: A flash of insight came after long reflection on relativity. *The New York Times,* pp. 1ff.

Sullivan, W. (1974, July 14). A hole in the sky. *The New York Times,* pp. 11ff.

Sullivan, W. (1985, January 8). Strange, scroll-like wave is linked to biological processes. *The New York Times,* p. C3.

Sulzby, E., Teale, W. H., & Kamberelis, G. (1989). Emergent writing in the classroom. In D. S. Strickland & L. M. Morrow (Eds.), *Emergent Literacy: Young children learn to read and write* (pp. 63–79). Newark, DE: International Reading Association.

Swett, S. (1984, April). Get good mileage out of Big Trak. *Teaching and Computers,* pp. 26–28.

Teacher Corps (n. d.). *Navajo etiquette for anglos.* Washington, DC: Author.

Temple, C. A., Nathan, R. G., & Burris, N. A. (1982). *The beginnings of writing.* Boston: Allyn & Bacon.

Toulmin, S. (1960). *The philosophy of science.* New York: Harper & Row. (Original work published 1953)

Vygotsky, L. S. (1962). *Thought and language* (E. Hanfmann & G. Vakar, Trans.). New York: Wiley.

Vygotsky, L. S. (1978). *Mind in society* (M. Cole, V. John-Steiner, S. Scribner, & E. Souberman, Eds.). Cambridge, MA: Harvard University Press.

Waldrop, M. M. (1992). *Complexity: The emerging science at the edge of order and chaos.* New York: Simon & Schuster.

Ward, W. (1960). *Drama with and for children.* Washington, DC: U.S. Government Printing Office.

Waters, B. (1973). *Science can be elementary.* New York: Citation.

Weininger, O. (1990). From the fast track to the fast lane—To what? *International Journal of Early Childhood, 22* (1), 43–58.

Welty, E. (1984). *One writer's beginnings.* Cambridge, MA: Harvard University Press.

White, R. W. (1959). Motivation reconsidered: The concept of competence. *Psychological Review, 65,* 297–333.

Whitehead, A. N. (1929). *The aims of education.* New York: Mentor.

Whitehead, A. N. (1958). *An introduction to mathematics.* New York: Oxford University Press. (Original work published 1911)

Williams, L., De Gaetano, Y., Harrington, C. C., & Sutherland, I. (1985). *ALERTA: A multicultural approach to teaching young children.* Menlo Park, CA: Addison-Wesley.

Wilmes, L., & Wilmes, D. (1991). *Learning centers for open-ended activities.* Mt. Rainier, MD: Gryphon House.

Wilson, P. S., & Rowland, R. (1993). Teaching measurement. In R. J. Jensen (Ed.), *Research ideas for the classroom: Early childhood mathematics* (pp. 171–194). New York: Macmillan.

Winn, M. (1977). *The plug-in drug.* New York: Viking.

Winter, M., & Klein, A. E. (1970). *Extending the kindergarten day: Does it make a difference in the achievement of educationally advantaged and disadvantaged pupils?* Washington, DC: Bureau of Elementary & Secondary Education.

Wittgenstein, L. von. (1958). *Philosophical investigations* (G. E. M. Anscombe, Trans.). New York: Macmillan.

Yonemura, M. (1969). *Developing language programs for young disadvantaged children.* New York: Teachers College Press.

Zaslavsky, C. (1973). *Africa counts.* Boston: Prindle, Weber & Schmidt.

Zukav, G. (1980). *The dancing wu li masters: An overview of the new physics.* New York: Bantam.

References to Children's Literature

Book entries that kindergarten children might read themselves, after having heard an adult reading, are identified with an asterisk (*).

Aardema, V. (1991). *Borreguita and the coyote*. New York: Knopf.

Adoff, A. (Ed.). (1974). *My black me* [Poetry]. New York: E. P. Dutton.

Anderson, L. (1976). *Mary McLeod Bethune* (W. Hutchinson, Illus.). Champaign, IL: Garrard.

Brown, M. W. (1973). *The noisy book* (R. Thomson, Illus.). New York: Scroll Press.*

Bruchac, J., & London, J. (1992). *Thirteen moons on turtle's back* (T. Locker, Illus.). New York: Philomel.

Burton, V. L. (1988). *The little house*. Boston: Houghton Mifflin. (Original work published 1942)

Carle, E. (1970). *The very hungry caterpillar*. New York: G. P. Putnam's Sons.

Clark, A. N. (1962). *The desert people* (J. Lasker, Illus.). New York: Viking.

Cleary, B. (1968). *Ramona the pest* (L. Darling, Illus.). New York: Morrow.

Cohen, M. (1967). *Will I have a friend?* (L. Hoban, Illus.). New York: Macmillan.

Cowcher, H. (1988). *Rain forest*. New York: Farrar, Strauss & Giroux.

Cowley, J. (1990). *Mrs. Wishy-Washy*. San Diego, CA: Wright Group. *(Original work published 1980)

Credle, E. (1934). *Down down the mountain* (E. Credle, Illus.). Nashville, TN: Thomas Nelson.

dePaola, T. (1975). *Strega Nona*. Englewood Cliffs, NJ: Prentice-Hall.

dePaola, T. (1989). *The art lesson*. New York: G. P. Putnam's Sons.

de Regniers, B. S. (1953). *The giant story* (M. Sendak, Illus.). New York: Harper & Row.*

Feelings, M. (1971). *Moja means one: Swahili counting book* (T. Feelings, Illus.). New York: Dial.

Felt, S. (1950). *Rosa-too-little*. Garden City, NY: Doubleday.

Flack, M. (1989). *Angus lost*. Garden City, NY: Doubleday. (Original work published 1932)

Flack, M. (1968). *Ask Mr. Bear*. New York: Macmillan.*(Original work published 1958)

Frasier, D. (1991). *On the day you were born*. New York: Harcourt, Brace Jovanovich.

Giovanni, N. (1971). *Spin a soft black song: Poems for children* (C. Bible, Illus.). New York: Hill & Wang.

Greenfield, E. (1980). *Grandma's joy* (C. Bayard, Illus.). New York: Philomel.

Greenfield, M. M. (1977). *Mary McLeod Bethune* (J. Pinkner, Illus.). New York: Thomas Y. Crowell.

Haskins, J. (1987). *Count your way through Japan* (M. Skoro, Illus.). Minneapolis: Carolrhoda Books.

Havill, J. (1989). *Jamaica-tag-along* (A. S. O'Brien, Illus.). Boston: Houghton Mifflin.

Heide, F. P., & Gilliland, J. H. (1990). *The day of Ahmed's secret* (T. Lewis, Illus.). New York: Lothrop, Lee & Shepard.

Hoberman, M. A. (1978). *A house is a home for me* (B. Fraser, Illus.). New York: Viking.*

Hunter-Grundin, E. (1983). *A hole in the bucket*. Louisville, KY: Reading Development Resources.*

Hutchins, P. (1968). *Rosie's walk*. New York: Greenwillow.*

Jacobs, J. (Ed.) (1968). *Pied piper and other fairy tales* (J. Hill, Illus.). New York: Macmillan.

Jonas, A. (1982). *When you were a baby*. New York: Greenwillow.*

Jonas, A. (1983). *Round trip*. New York: Greenwillow.

Jonas, A. (1984). *The quilt*. New York: Greenwillow.

Jonas, A. (1985). *The trek*. New York: Greenwillow.

Krauss, R. (1947). *The growing story* (P. Rowand, Illus.). New York: Harper & Row.

Lamorisse, A. (1956). *The red balloon*. Garden City, NY: Doubleday.

Lent, B. (1987). *Bayberry bluff*. Boston: Houghton Mifflin.

Lexau, J. (1970). *Benjie on his own* (D. Bolognese, Illus.). New York: Dial.

Lipkind, W., & Mordvinoff, N. (1962). *Russet and the two reds*. New York: Harcourt Brace & World.

MacDonald, G. [pseud.]. (1971). *The little island* (L. Weisgard, Illus.). Garden City, NY: Doubleday.

McCloskey, R. (1968). *Blueberries for Sal*. New York: Viking. (Original work published 1948)

McCloskey, R. (1952). *One morning in Maine*. New York: Viking.

Melser, J., & Cowley, J. (1986). *The big toe* (M. Bailey, Illus.). San Diego, CA: Wright Group. (Original work published 1980)*

Merriam, E. (1989). *Mommies at work* (B. Montresor, Illus.). New York: Simon & Schuster. (Original work published 1961)

Miles, M. (1971). *Annie and the old one*. Boston: Little Brown.

Milne, A. A. (1957). *Winnie-the-Pooh* (E. H. Shepard, Illus.). New York: Dutton.

Milne, A. A. (1958a). *Now we are six* [Poetry] (E. H. Shepard, Illus.). New York: Dutton.

Milne, A. A. (1958b). *When we were very young* [Poetry] (E. H. Shepard, Illus.). New York: Dutton.

Numeroff, L. J. (1985). *If you give a mouse a cookie*. New York: Scholastic.*

Polacco, P. (1992). *Chicken Sunday*. New York: Philomel.

Rey, A. H. (1973). *Curious George*. Boston: Houghton Mifflin.

Rockwell, A. (1984). *Cars*. New York: Dutton.

Rosenberg, M. B. (1986). *Living in two worlds* (G. Ancona, Photo.). New York: Lothrop, Lee & Shepard.

Schlein, M. (1963). *The way mothers are* (J. Lasker, Illus.). Chicago: Albert Whitman.

Schneider, H., & Schneider, N. (1952). *Follow the sunset* (L. Corcos, Illus.). Garden City, NY: Doubleday.

Segal, E. (1952). *Be my friend* [Poetry]. New York: Citadel.

Sendak M. (1963). *Where the wild things are*. New York: Harper & Row.

Simon, N. (1976). *All kinds of families* (J. Lasker, Illus.). Morton Grove, IL: Whitman.

Slobodkina, E. (1989). *Caps for sale*. New York: Scholastic. (Original work published 1947)*

Southgate, V. (Retold). (1970). *The enormous turnip*. Loughborough, Eng: Wills & Hepworth.*

Stevenson, R. L. (1961). My shadow. In *The child's garden of verses* [Poetry]. New York: Platt & Munk. (Original work published 1885)

Thornhill, J. (1992). *A tree in a forest*. New York: Simon & Schuster.

Tresselt, A. (1968). *I saw the sea come in* (R. Duvoisin, Illus.). New York: Lothrop, Lee & Shepard.

Tworkov, J. (1989). *The camel who took a walk* (R. Duvoisin, Illus.). New York: Dutton. (Original work published 1974)

White, E. B. (1968). *Charlotte's web* (G. Williams, Illus.). New York: Dell.

Williams, S. (1989). *I went walking* (J. Vivas, Illus.). New York: Gulliver Books.*

Williams, V. B. (1982). *A chair for my mother*. New York: Greenwood.

Yashima, T. (1970). *The umbrella*. New York: Viking.

Yenawine, P. (1991). *Lines*. New York: Delacorte.

Zolotow, C. (1972). *William's doll* (W. P. DuBois, Illus.). New York: Harper & Row.

Index

About the Author

Doris Pronin Fromberg is Professor of Education and Director of Early Childhood Teacher Education at Hofstra University. She has served as president of the National Association of Early Childhood Teacher Educators and is an advocate for high quality early childhood teacher and administrator education. She has been a teacher and administrator in public and private schools, as well as a field-based curriculum and administration consultant to school districts. She also has served as a Teacher Corps director. Her special interests are early childhood curriculum, teacher education, school climate, and classroom organization. Among her publications are *The Encyclopedia of Early Childhood Education* (New York: Garland Press, 1992), co-edited with Leslie Williams, and *The Successful Classroom: Management Strategies for Regular Elementary and Special Education Teachers* (New York: Teachers College Press, 1985), with Maryann Driscoll. She currently is working on a book, *Contexts, Perspectives, and Meanings of Play in Childhood* (New York: Garland Press, forthcoming), co-edited with Doris Bergen.